BICULTURAL PARENT ENGAGEMENT

BICULTURAL PARENT ENGAGEMENT

Advocacy and Empowerment

Edited by

Edward M. Olivos
Oscar Jiménez-Castellanos
Alberto M. Ochoa

Teachers College
Columbia University
New York and London

Published by Teachers College Press, 1234 Amsterdam Avenue, New York, NY 10027

Library of Congress Cataloging-in-Publication Data

Bicultural parent engagement : advocacy and empowerment / edited by Edward M. Olivos, Oscar Jiménez-Castellanos, Alberto M. Ochoa.
    p. cm.
  Includes bibliographical references and index.
    ISBN 978-0-8077-5264-7 (pbk. : alk. paper) — ISBN 978-0-8077-5265-4 (hardcover : alk. paper)
    1. Education—Parent participation—United States. 2. Hispanic American children—Education. 3. Bilingual education—United States. 4. Biculturalism—United States. I. Olivos, Edward M., 1967– II. Jiménez-Castellanos, Oscar. III. Monroy Ochoa, Alberto. LB1048.5.B53 2011
370.117'50973—dc23

                                                                        2011033895

ISBN 978-0-8077-5264-7 (paperback)
ISBN 978-0-8077-5265-4 (hardcover)

Printed on acid-free paper

Manufactured in the United States of America

18 17 16 15 14 13 12 11   8 7 6 5 4 3 2 1

Dedicated to René Núñez, Ph.D. (1936–2006).
Teacher, Scholar, Activist, Cultural Broker, Community Builder,
Mentor, Friend, Husband, Father, and Elder.

Contents

BICULTURAL PARENT ENGAGEMENT

1

Critical Voices in Bicultural Parent Engagement: A Framework for Transformation

Edward M. Olivos, Alberto M. Ochoa, and
Oscar Jiménez-Castellanos

For policymakers and educators alike, parent involvement often ranks high among the remedies proposed for solving the problems that plague our public schools, particularly those schools that serve working-class bicultural communities.[1] It is viewed as one of the most critical factors that influence student academic achievement and as an endeavor worthy of legislative legitimacy and financial and human investment (Henderson & Berla, 1994; Henderson & Mapp, 2002; U.S. Department of Education, 2004). And why shouldn't it be? Researchers have long claimed that the "evidence is consistent, positive, and convincing: families have a major influence on their children's achievement in school and through life" (Henderson & Mapp, 2002, p. 7). Indeed, given the body of literature on this topic, and the assertiveness of the findings, it is easy to see why educators and legislators alike find it so seductive to advocate for some form of connection between schools and parents/families and why parent involvement appears to be such a commonsensical component of successful students and schools.

Despite the fact that the concept of parent involvement in the public schools has been extensively studied and theorized about, it is still seldom understood (Boethel, 2003; de Carvalho, 2001; Henderson & Mapp, 2002; Olivos, 2006). A perusal of the literature often only raises more questions than answers and more doubts than reassurance. Thus, while the research literature on parent involvement appears to emphatically support integrating parents into the education system for improved student achievement and school accountability, certain key issues emerge that make broad assumptions about parent involvement problematic, particularly in how it relates to bicultural (i.e., linguistically and culturally diverse) parents and families (de Carvalho, 2001; Jordan, Orozco, & Averett, 2001; Lareau, 1989; Núñez, 1994; Olivos, 2004, 2006).

Problematic, for example, is the multitude of labels and definitions given to the concept of having students' parents and family members involved in the schools (Boethel, 2003). Terms such as *parent involvement, home-school collaboration, parent engagement, parent participation,* and *parent-school partnerships* (to name a few) have all been used to identify the many ways in which parents and families are involved in schools (Henderson & Mapp, 2002). These multiple terms beg the following questions: Do all these terms mean the same thing? Are all forms of parent involvement alike? Do all these terms have the same goals in mind? And if there *is* some general consensus on what parent involvement actually is and what it should accomplish, are parents and communities aware of them? If there is no consensus, then which group (school authorities, parents, both, or neither) has the power to define what parent involvement actually means and what it should achieve?

For the editors and the contributors of this book, all forms of parent involvement in public schools are *not* the same, nor are all parents treated equally by school authorities (Cline & Necochea, 2001; de Carvalho, 2001; Fine, 1993; Olivos & Ochoa, 2006a, 2006b; Ramirez, 2003; Shannon, 1996). For bicultural parents, we argue, meaningful and authentic participation in the schools is elusive, despite professed intentions by educators and decision makers to the contrary. Part of the reason for this is that all too often the power to define the nature of bicultural parents' involvement in schools rests in the hands of school officials, researchers, and policymakers and not in the parents themselves. That is, in bicultural communities, family and community involvement frequently implies helping "reach goals defined by the schools (administrators and teachers) that reflect only school values and priorities" (Jordan et al., 2001, p. viii). Furthermore, school officials and educational researchers have long identified only a narrow band of prescriptive behaviors that qualify as legitimate forms of parental involvement (Epstein, 2001). As a result, parents and families who stray from these accepted expectations become viewed as "different" (a palatable way to say "deficient") and school efforts become concentrated in changing the parents' behaviors and expectations rather than the schools' negative mindsets about them (Olivos, 2006).

When school authorities have the power to define what parent involvement is, they also, in tandem, define the expected outcomes of this involvement. Thus, through their position of power, school officials retain the rights to decide if the outcomes of parent involvement are to be educational, social, behavioral, political, or all (or none) of the above (de Carvalho, 2001). For many educators and policy-makers, however, improved student academic achievement is clearly the most important outcome of involving parents in schools and it is the most often referenced (Henderson & Berla, 1994; Henderson & Mapp, 2002; Houtenville & Conway, 2008; Jeynes, 2005; Lam, 1997; U.S. Department of Education, 2004). For working-class bicultural school communities, parent involvement is also often cited as a surefire way of addressing (and closing) the achievement gap (Boethel, 2003).

There are some educators and researchers, however, who contend that parent involvement should include more than individual student academic achievement (important as this may be) by focusing equally on the social and political aspects of involving parents in schools that will ultimately lead to broader social changes through civic engagement and a raised critical and political consciousness (McCaleb, 1994; Oakes & Rogers, 2006; Olivos, 2006; Olivos & Ochoa, 2006a, 2006b; Shirley, 1997) (see, for example, Shannon [Chapter 5]; Montero-Sieburth [Chapter 9]; or Terriquez & Rogers [Chapter 10] in this volume).

Thus, while individual student achievement is a worthy goal for involving bicultural parents in the schools, until those barriers that preclude bicultural parents from becoming meaningfully involved in the first place are challenged, these advantages will continue being reserved for only a select number of parents. Furthermore, Henderson and Mapp (2002) aptly point out that "while engaging families can help improve student achievement, it is not enough to overcome the deficits of low-quality schools" (p. 76), which is a problem that plagues low-income bicultural communities.

While there is an emerging, and promising, body of literature that looks at how schools may function to enhance asymmetrical power relations between themselves and certain parent groups, the preponderance of parent involvement policies and practices directed at bicultural parents and communities still conceptualize schooling inequality from a deficit perspective (Olivos, 2006; Valencia, 1997). That is, deficiencies in bicultural children's academic and social achievement are often presumed to originate in the home (i.e., with the parents) and in their social upbringing (Valencia & Black, 2002). This belief then leads to parent involvement practices and policies that focus on changing parental behaviors and expectations so that they become more congruent with educators' expectations (de Carvalho, 2001; McCaleb, 1994). As a consequence, the sole goal of bicultural parent involvement becomes "parents helping children learn at home, with most targeting a change in academic performance, including reading skills, mathematics skills, spelling, and homework completion" (Fishel & Ramirez, 2005, p. 371). For researchers, educators, and parents who are critical of this mindset (such as the contributors to this volume), these common practices are problematic in that they assume that all home-school relationships are neutral and always structured in the best interests of bicultural children and their families (Brantlinger, 2003; Cummins, 2001; de Carvalho, 2001; Fine, 1993; Lareau & Horvat, 1999; Olivos, 2004, 2006).

To assume that all parent groups are treated equally and that the goal of all parents and families should be to emulate middle-class Euro-American values are some of the most problematic of issues affecting the field of parent involvement in schools today (e.g., Comer & Haynes, 1991; Epstein, 2001). These models not only tend to ignore the diverse demographic reality of today's U.S. school system and the fact that many public school districts, particularly those in urban areas, now serve a bicultural parent and student majority, but also work to reinforce implanted beliefs that bicultural families must be changed to conform to existing school practices.

Further conceptual limitations to the concept of parent involvement in relation to bicultural parents are that the only goal of parental involvement in the public schools should be individual student results rather than community and school transformation (Fishel & Ramirez, 2005; Oakes & Rogers, 2006; Shirley, 1997); that the involvement of bicultural parents in the public schools is an apolitical act and that parents should diligently work to carry out all educators' requests within established bureaucratic protocols; or ignoring the social, political, historical, and economic context that encompasses the process of mass forms of education and the interpersonal relationships between school authorities and bicultural school communities. This topic is clearly explained by Johnson (Chapter 8), who argues from a parent perspective that Epstein's (2001) model does not go far enough to support bicultural parents in their understanding of the school system and in respecting their voice when it comes to raising concerns about school inadequacies. Montero-Sieburth shares a similar critique in Chapter 9 in her assessment that this commonly accepted, and seldom questioned, model tends to nestle the complex experiences of bicultural (immigrant) parents into a framework that is based on White, middle-class parents.

One of the goals of this book is to raise critical questions that will problematize how the current conceptualizations about parent involvement in public schools serve to replicate the status quo. It seeks to ask the following questions: What exactly is meant by parent involvement? How does this concept change when applied to bicultural parents and communities? What does it look like and what does it entail? Are all forms of parental involvement the same? If not, what are the differences? Do all parents have equal access and opportunity to participate in schools? If not, where are the challenges? And can the impact bicultural parents have on the public schools be effectively measured? That is, while student achievement and improved social behavior is a worthy goal, can the involvement of bicultural parents in schools lead to broader social changes, political consciousness, civic engagement, or involvement in policy development and decision making? By raising questions such as these, the editors and authors of this book aim to create a critical dialogue about the theory and research that drive the parent involvement phenomenon.

Changing Demographics in the United States and in U.S. Schools

There can be no doubt that the U.S. demographic and linguistic landscape is rapidly transforming. The past 2 decades have seen one of the largest movements of people both in terms of international immigration and national migration. Our nation is not only becoming increasingly various in racial, linguistic, and social diversity (i.e., social class, family composition, etc.), but is also becoming much more urban as people flock to the major cities to search for greater economic opportunities. These unprecedented demographic changes are most evident in the U.S. public school system. It's estimated by the National Center for Education Statistics (NCES) of the U.S. Department of Education (Planty et al., 2008), for example, that during the 2006–2007 academic year, over 40% of all students in U.S. public schools were from non-White families. Moreover, SchoolDataDirect (2008) reported that 40% of all students enrolled in the public school system came from low-income or poor families in 2007, as indicated by student participation in federal free or reduced-price school lunch programs. Additionally, in 2008–09, approximately 5.3 million, or 10.8%, of the U.S. student population were identified as English language learners (National Clearinghouse for English, 2011).

Much of the change in the national and the U.S. public school demography can be attributed to immigration and to the rapidly growing Latino population (Fry, 2008; Kane, 2010). During the 1st decade of 2000, Latinos accounted for most of the population increase in the United States and by 2008, Latino students in U.S. public schools constituted 19.8% of the student population, or 1 in 5 of all students (Fry, 2008; Fry & Gonzales, 2008). Furthermore, according to the PEW Hispanic Center (2008), this demographic trend is likely to continue well into the 21st century. It is projected that by 2050, the Latino student population will increase by over 150% (to approximately 28 million students), while the non-Latino school-aged population will grow by only 4%.

The growing influence of the Latino community in U.S. schools can also be witnessed in this book. The bulk of the chapters presented here specifically address this community's role in the functioning of schools as well as the challenges and potential schools face in authentically interacting with this large bicultural group. Chapters by Moreno, Lewis-Menchaca, and Rodriguez (Chapter 2) and by Wlazlinski and Cummins (Chapter 4), for example, speak to the participation of Latina mothers in the home and the school context. Moreno et al. explore how parent involvement among culturally diverse families may not easily translate/transfer to the school context. Drawing from their own research with Mexican American mothers, the authors demonstrate how these mothers' literacy activities within the home can be a complex and dynamic process, one that is not well captured by many of the current parent involvement models. The chapter by Wlazlinski and Cummins, meanwhile, documents how a collaborative home-school project enabled Latino parents and preservice teachers to learn from each other in the context of writing family life histories in an effort to challenge mind-sets that perpetuate coercive power relations.

Shannon (Chapter 5), Montero-Sieburth (Chapter 9), and Terriquez and Rogers (Chapter 10) also look at the relationship between Latino parents and the schools but through larger social interactions. Shannon, for example, documents how Latino parents in one particular school struggle to maintain their children's interests in a school that is mostly responsive to the White parent community. Montero-Sieburth, on the other hand, documents the power of Latino parents to become transformative change agents through the use of action research. In her chapter she documents how these bicultural parents, after being trained to use qualitative research methods and to focus on leadership development as part of their own learning about schools, responded to the education their children receive. She further highlights how these parents' development does not fit the universally cited Epstein (2001) model of parent involvement. And finally, Terriquez and Rogers document the role schools may play in developing civic engagement among immigrant Latino families. They argue that Latino immigrant parents participate civically through engagement with public schools, particularly when certain conditions prevail, and they participate in powerful ways when supported by grassroots community groups.

The editors of this book acknowledge that the prominence of the Latino experience described here is not meant to minimize the experiences of other bicultural groups, nor is it presented to oversimplify the multiple levels of inequality across racial and ethnic communities that exist in our society. The intent of the editors is to examine and illustrate salient concepts of parent involvement that focus on schools' conceptions of parent involvement and strategies for building better relations between bicultural families and schools (Moreno, Menchaca, & Rodriguez); cultural competency and culturally proficient schools and practices (Lindsey & Lindsey); the function of coercive power relations that frame the experiences of subordinated communities and the importance of collaborative scripting of identity (Wlazlinski & Cummins); the dynamics of parent engagement and asymmetrical social and political relations (Shannon); the application of deficit thinking and the denial of equal encouragement in actualizing parent involvement and guiding principles of democratic schooling for a deliberate democracy (Pearl); constructive pluralism as an approach that advocates for parent-teacher-school engagement (Grant & Potter); the presentation of seven types of parenting skills from the perspectives of parent advocacy (Johnson); using participatory action research for parent engagement in transformative change (Montero-Sieburth); meaningful civic engagement and development of immigrant parents (Terriquez & Rogers); and five levels of democratic and transformative parent engagement (Ochoa, Olivos, & Jiménez-Castellanos).

Bicultural Parent Involvement in the Public Schools

It is clear to us that the effects of bicultural parents' participation in the public schools are complex. While predictable historical shifts in balance have always occurred between the home and schools during times of school reform; changing demographics; or broader social, political, and economic movements (Cutler, 2000; Dalla, Defrain, Johnson, & Abbott, 2010), it is clear that the current relationship between educators and bicultural parents is becoming much more galvanized around the concept that the underachievement of bicultural students can be traced back to their parents and communities, who apparently are not holding up their end of the deal (Olivos & Ochoa, 2008; Valencia & Black, 2002). Indeed, educators who work with bicultural children often express concern about uninvolved parents, positions which often reflect these educators' implicit personal beliefs about race, class, and social standing (Brantlinger, 2003; Darder, 1991; Lightfoot, 1978; Souto-Manning & Swick, 2006). Bicultural parents are viewed by educators as conspicuously absent at important meetings, overly submissive in their involvement at the schools, and critically lacking in cultural and social capital to help their children (Brantlinger, 2003; Lareau, 1989). Bicultural parents, for their part, view educators as overly rigid and inaccessible, uncompromising, and exceedingly sensitive to critiques or questions (Olivos, 2006; Ramirez, 2003; Shannon, 1996).

Existing parent and family involvement paradigms tend to exclude "the valuable and legitimate interaction patterns of many [bicultural] families" (Souto-Manning & Swick, 2006, p. 188). They also tend to reinforce the power of school authorities while limiting the decision-making authority of families and communities. This becomes quite apparent in the restrictive band of acceptable behaviors educators allot them and is best exemplified when bicultural parents are periodically invited to school discussions, but whose actual opinion and involvement is not actually crucial to decision making. For bicultural parents, this scenario creates what Shannon (1996) refers to as the "paradox of minority parental involvement."

The fundamental nature of this paradox is the no-win situation bicultural parents are often placed in. They are criticized by school personnel for their lack of involvement and low presence at the school yet are actively dismissed or repressed when they demonstrate acts of leadership, advocacy, or activism on behalf of their children or their community. In addition, whereas White parents are seen as the key to their children's success, ethnically diverse and low-income parents are often viewed as barriers to their children's advancement (Brantlinger, 2003; Lareau, 1989; Valencia & Black, 2002). Shannon (1996) aptly conveys the following in her assessment of educators' relationship with bicultural parents:

> Parent involvement for [bicultural] parents can be paradoxical. Traditionally, they are not involved and teachers complain. However, teachers also complain about the aggressive parent involvement of majority, middle-class Anglo parents. If minority language parents choose to become involved, they may be perceived . . . to be aggressive. Unfortunately, the majority parents' aggressiveness is tolerated, whereas the minority parent's [sic] action may be not only ignored and dismissed but also attacked as irrational (p. 83).

Núñez (1994) believed that in order to develop clarity concerning bicultural parent involvement in the education of their children, two distinct arenas of parent involvement had to be explored. The first concerns the direct effect that bicultural parents have on their children as their primary source of nurture and socialization; while the second concerns their role in influencing the education at the school.

In regard to the former, past research in the field has argued that the home of the bicultural child is a rich sociocultural context of learning and cognition, even if it "differs" from that of the dominant culture (Allen, 2007; Delgado-Gaitan, 1990; Lopez, 2001; McCaleb, 1994). In fact, it is suggested that even in the "poorest" of homes, "school-like" literacy and learning activities are present (Clark, 1983; Dalla et al., 2010; Delgado-Gaitan, 1990; Taylor & Dorsey-Gaines, 1988). Moreover, the bicultural family provides moral and social support for bicultural children in ways often not recognized by school employees (Lopez, 2001; Stanton-Salazar, 2001). This support may come in the form of encouragement, the teaching of values such as respect for the teacher and appreciation for education, or the sharing of culture-specific traditions and beliefs.

In addition to the social, moral, and academic support bicultural families provide their children in the home, it is similarly important to understand the role they can play in improving the quality and effectiveness of education at the school site. For the editors of and contributors to this book, this points to the need of having underrepresented parents become vigilant and active participants in school-related matters such as school policy, decision making, and accountability (Fine,

1993; Henig, Hula, Orr, & Pedescleaux, 1999; Lopez & Kreider, 2003; Mediratta, Fruchter, & Lewis, 2003; Oakes & Rogers, 2006; Shirley, 1997). They also mean that efforts must be made to critically examine ideologies and practices that hinder a collaborative relationship between school officials and bicultural parents. This includes looking at not only the obvious factors that preclude bicultural parents' presence in the schools (such as work obligations, child care, limited English proficiency) but also those mindsets and practices that function inconspicuously in the actions of educators and in the culture of schools to devalue the life experiences of bicultural children and the input of their parents. In other words, it means understanding and challenging those oppressive elements that exist in broader society (such as racism, classism, bias, exploitation, and racial profiling) that often infiltrate the school system through commonly accepted ways of doing things that limit the potential of bicultural communities and their children.

What Is Parent Engagement?

We contend that the public school system has up to now failed to meet the needs of bicultural children and their communities and assert that transformation of this system is needed (Olivos & Ochoa, 2006a, 2006b; Shirley, 1997). Inequality is reflected in the public school system through the low achievement outcomes of bicultural children and in the treatment bicultural parents receive at the hands of educators and administrators. It is also represented in the inertia found in the school system that binds educators into enforcing institutional beliefs that reinforce inequality by excluding bicultural parents from important input and decision-making authority (Olivos & Ochoa, 2008). Inequitable treatment by educators leads to inequitable relationships with bicultural students and bicultural parents, and ultimately to inequitable educational results. Underlying assumptions about individuals and groups lead to differential treatment. Furthermore, schools also function to legitimize the societal myths of meritocracy and equal opportunity—that for those who work hard and do well in school, societal rewards (good jobs and wealth) are waiting for them upon completion (Feinberg & Soltis, 2004; Persell, 1977).

We further argue that bicultural parents and members of bicultural communities will be the catalysts that will trigger the necessary transformation in schools. However, not all forms of parental involvement in the public schools are equal, nor is the treatment that bicultural parents receive at the hands of school officials. In this book, we will therefore present different perspectives that examine why and how bicultural parents participate in the school system. We will also explore how educators can create conditions that will enhance bicultural parent participation rather than deter it.

Not to be driven by naive dreams, we understand that schools are clearly structured in the images of the societies upon which they are built and all too often schools are blamed for the sins of a society. Schools are easy targets for criticism because they are underfunded and function under the ever-changing political dynamics of educational reform. That is, we are aware of the constraints of the public school system to create an egalitarian and equitable environment in the shadows of an inherently unequal society. Despite these reservations, however, we also acknowledge the contradictory nature of public education, which despite its oppressive practices against disempowered communities and students, does contain a great potential for change, particularly when led by the authentic, altruistic actions of educators and parents (Darder, 1991; Oakes & Rogers, 2006). In this transformative manner of parent involvement we envision a new dynamic in which bicultural parents assume key roles as catalysts and change agents in the inequitable institution.

Given the academic disparities between students who come from high-status communities and those who don't, we feel the need to differentiate between the various forms of parent involvement and the labels given to them. As mentioned, we acknowledge that not all forms of parental participation are the same and that the language we use to identify the range of practices found in the concept of parent involvement reflect their ideological underpinnings and inherent goals (Olivos & Ochoa, 2006a, 2006b). For this purpose, we begin with the notion that public schools belong to the community, based on our public and collective financing of public education through our payment of taxes (ranging from food products to property taxes). As such, all community members are stakeholders who have the right to oversee their investment—by being engaged and making sure that their children have due process, academic rigor, and access to career options (Jiménez-Castellanos, 2008). However, because of the significant power imbalances and relations that exist between the priorities of the schools and those of low-income communities, we call for parents to be "engaged" with the schools and not simply involved or included. We therefore use the term *parent engagement* in the title of this book to differentiate from the often used generic label of *parent involvement*.

We view the term *parent involvement* as synonymous with school activities and practices designed to involve parents (or better yet, keep them busy) in support of the school and its daily tasks as defined by its leadership. These activities or practices are often driven by a bureaucratization that buffers the school from the bicultural school community. Parent involvement in these instances takes the form of assisting the school by being present (or visible) in selected school-sanctioned activities (Allen, 2007). Parents symbolically support the school through their representation in school requirements, for example, by providing their signature(s) to meet state and federal compliance requirements. Parents also participate in manners that allow school officials to train them on preferred behaviors or proper social capital that is required of their children to have access to the core curriculum. The generic term *parent involvement* therefore conjures up a passive, one-way connection that benefits the school and places the accountability of student success and failure exclusively on the parent/family.

In contrast, parent engagement, in our view, is a school-community process designed to bring or construct an open relationship between school personnel and the parent community in support of the student's social and academic development. Parent engagement takes the form of "critical partners" in the education process that is focused on building welcoming and trusting relationships, building leadership skills, and creating spaces of belongingness and awareness of how to navigate the school system and seeks to promote cultural, social, linguistic diversity and inclusion. Parent engagement can be generalized as an active, two-way connection that is an inclusive, ongoing, and engaged process through mutual agreement and that has direct benefits to the student/family. Furthermore, parent engagement is used by both the parent and the school to address the developmental skills of the child to match their career aspirations and their social democratic participation (Shirley, 1997).

In sum, the main purpose of this book is to move the idea of parental participation in schools for bicultural parents from an "accommodationist" perspective to a more "transformational" one through *engagement* rather than mere involvement (Shirley, 1997). Parental engagement, as defined by Shirley (1997), "designates parents as citizens in the fullest sense—change agents who can transform urban schools and neighborhoods" (p. 73).

The goal of parental engagement is to fulfill what research has begun to document, that when schools work together with families to support learning children tend to succeed not just in school, but also throughout life (Boethel, 2003; Henderson & Berla, 1994; Henderson & Mapp, 2002; Lareau, 1989; Jordan et al., 2001; PIQE, 2010; Ritblatt, Beatty, Cronan, & Ochoa, 2002).When parents are engaged as critical partners, parent and community engagement is linked to learning (Henderson & Mapp, 2002); when families are engaged as advocates for student progress, their children perform better and have higher school retention (PIQE, 2010; Ritblatt et al., 2002); and when schools work with community organizers, they get results (Henig et al., 1999; Lareau, 1989; Oakes & Rogers, 2006; Shirley, 1997).

In actualizing a transformative parent engagement process, the authors advocate for the use of a proactive or responsive participatory action research (PAR). PAR fosters social equality when participants value partnerships and cross-role cooperation (between parents, teachers, administrators, and community stakeholders). In the PAR process each participant is active in providing input that is relevant, has a voice in shaping new actions, and is committed to working on proactive school-community outcomes.

To address these critical issues, this book is divided into the following sections (or parts):

- *Multicultural Perspectives*—This section contains work that engages the bicultural parent population through an additive lens. That is, racial, ethnic, and linguistic diversity in schools is not seen as something that needs to be overcome and parents are not viewed as being barriers to their children's achievement. To the contrary, bicultural parents are seen as strengths and their cultural backgrounds are viewed as necessary assets for academic and social achievement.
- *Critical Perspectives*—The chapters in this section provide what we identify as "critical perspectives" in that these works begin to engage the issues of racism, classism, and conflicting personal interests. The critical perspectives acknowledge the sociopolitical and economic factors at play in the engagement of bicultural parent communities. In other words, it places bicultural parent engagement within a political context. This section of the book also begins to articulate considerations for a "transformational paradigm" of bicultural parental engagement. Two chapters in particular provide direction for actualizing democratic schooling. Pearl (Chapter 6) provides guiding principles for democratic schooling and the role that bicultural parents need to undertake in changing education from its current undemocratic nature characterized by systematic denial of encouragement of particular bicultural students to a democratic education. Grant and Potter's work (Chapter 7) advocates for the engagement of groups of diverse parents and the school staff in order to bring about a more democratic and socially just education. They call for a constructive pluralistic approach to parent-teacher/school engagement that brings together and unites the different stakeholders (e.g., school staff, parents, and students).
- *Operationalizing Transformative Parent Engagement*—This final section contains three chapters that operationalize in some form or another a transformative approach to bicultural parental engagement. They document work being done in local communities to engage bicultural parents in school matters beyond accommodation. They speak specifically to civic engagement, community organization, and the use of PAR.

We acknowledge the critical perspectives the contributing authors present in regard to bicultural parental engagement. The voices reflect an ongoing dialogue started by researchers such as Delgado-Gaitan and Trueba (2001), Fine (1993), Lareau (1989), Lightfoot (1978), McCaleb (1994), Núñez (1994), and others to visualize a form of parental engagement that addresses social and institutional inequities in order to transform them. Their work, in our estimation, presents nuanced and multilayered perspectives that challenge current manners of interacting with bicultural parents with the primary purpose of reforming education and society. Our ultimate goal is the transformation of schools into authentic institutions of learning and tools for social growth.

Discussion Questions

1. In the largest urban and rural cites of our nation, how are bicultural parents' voices incorporated into the life and engagement of schools? What has your experience been?
2. What theory and research drives the importance of parent involvement? What are the conceptual limitations to the concept of parent involvement in relation to bicultural parents?
3. What is meant by the notion that not all forms of parent involvement are equal? What are the differences? Where are the challenges? Why is parent involvement seldom understood?
4. What is the difference between parent involvement and parent engagement? What are the salient differences between the two?
5. What constitutes a socioconstructivist approach to parent engagement that values bicultural parents' perspectives and engagement?
6. What is proactive and responsive participatory action research (PAR)? How is PAR a tool to engage bicultural parents to be a catalyst for educational and social change?
7. What educational, social, and political perspectives are presented in the readings of this book on bicultural parent engagement?

Note

1. We use the term *bicultural* rather than *minority* because, in the words of Darder (1991), the latter term "linguistically, and hence politically, reflects and perpetuates a view of subordinate cultures as deficient and disempowered" (p. XVII).

Suggested Readings

Arum, R., Beattle, I. R., & Ford K. (2010). *The structure of schooling.* (2nd ed.). Thousand Oaks, CA: Sage.
Freire, P. (2004). *Pedagogy of indignation.* Boulder, CO: Paradigm.
Green, G. P., & Haines, A. (2011). *Asset building and community development.* Thousand Oaks, CA: Sage.

Sadan, E. (1997). *Empowerment and community planning: Theory and practices of people-focused social solutions.* Tel Aviv: Hakibbutz Hameuchad.

Skria, L., McKenzie, K. B., & Scheurich, J. J. (2009). *Using equity audit to create equitable and excellence schools.* Thousand, Oaks, CA: Corwin Press.

Stanton-Salazar, R. (2010). A social capital framework for the study of institutional agents and their role in the empowerment of low income students and youth. *Youth and Society, XX*(X) 1–44.

Starbuck, G. H. (2009). *Families in context* (2nd ed.). Boulder, CO: Paradigm.

Taylor, E., Gillborn D., & Ladson-Billings, G. (2009). *Foundations of critical race theory in education.* New York: Routledge.

Wayne A. (Ed). (2009). *Rethinking multicultural education: Reaching for racial and cultural justice.* Milwaukee, WI: Rethinking Schools.

Wepner, S. B. (Ed). (2010). *Collaborative leadership action.* New York: Teachers College Press.

Zinn, H. (2003). *A people's history of the United States: 1492–Present.* (Zinn Education Project Edition). New York: Harper Perennial Modern Classics.

References

Allen, J. (2007). *Creating welcoming schools: A practical guide to home-school partnerships with diverse families.* New York: Teachers College Press.

Boethel, M. (2003). *Diversity: School, family, and community connections.* Austin, TX: National Center for Family and Community Connections with Schools.

Brantlinger, E. (2003). *Dividing classes: How the middle class negotiates and rationalizes school advantage.* New York: Routledge.

Clark, R. (1983). Family life and school achievement: Why poor Black children succeed or fail. Chicago: University of Chicago Press.

Cline, Z., & Necochea, J. (2001). ¡Basta ya! Latino parents fighting entrenched racism. *Bilingual Research Journal, 25*(1&2), 1–26.

Comer, J. P. (1996). *Rallying the whole village: The Comer process for reforming education.* New York: Teachers College Press.

Comer, J. P., & Haynes, N. M. (1991). Parent involvement in schools: An ecological approach. *The Elementary School Journal, 91*(3), 271–277.

Cummins, J. (2001). *Negotiating identities: Education for empowerment in a diverse society.* Los Angeles: California Association for Bilingual Education (CABE).

Cutler, W. W. (2000). *Parents and schools: The 150 year struggle for control of American education.* Chicago: University of Chicago Press.

Dalla, R. L., Defrain, J., Johnson, J. M., & Abbott, D. A. (2010). *Strengths and challenges of new immigrants.* New York: Teachers College Press.

Darder, A. (1991). *Culture and power in the classroom: A critical foundation for bicultural education.* Westport, CT: Berson & Garvey.

de Carvalho, M. E. P. (2001). *Rethinking family-school relations: A critique of parental involvement in schooling.* Mahwah, NJ: Lawrence Erlbaum.

Delgado-Gaitan, C. (1990). *Literacy for empowerment: The role of parents in children's education.* New York: Falmer Press.

Delgado-Gaitan, C., & Trueba, E. (2001). *The power of the community: Mobilizing for family and schooling.* Lanham, MD: Rowman & Littlefield.

Epstein, J. L. (2001). *School, family, and community partnerships: Your handbook for action.* Thousand Oaks, CA: Corwin Press.

Feinberg, W. F., & Soltis, J. F. (2004). *School and society.* New York: Teachers College Press.

Fine, M. (1993). [Ap]parent involvement: Reflections on parents, power, and urban public schools. *Teachers College Record, 94*(4), 682–710.

Fishel, M., & Ramirez, L. (2005). Evidence-based parent involvement interventions with school-aged children. *School Psychology Quarterly, 20*(4), 371–402.

Fry, R., & Gonzales, F. (2008). *One-in-five and growing fast: A profile of Hispanic public school students.* Washington, DC: Pew Hispanic Center.

Henderson, A. T., & Berla, N. (Eds.). (1994). *A new generation of evidence: The family is critical to student achievement.* Washington, DC: National Committee for Citizens in Education.

Henderson, A. T., & Mapp, K. L. (2002). *A new wave of evidence: The impact of school, family, and community connections on student achievement.* Austin, TX: Southwest Educational Development Laboratory.

Henig, J. R., Hula, R. C., Orr, M., & Pedescleaux, D. S. (1999). *The color of school reform: Race, politics, and the challenge of urban education.* Princeton, NJ: Princeton University Press.

Houtenville, A. J., & Conway, K. S. (2008). Parental effort, school resources, and student achievement. *Journal of Human Resources, 43*(2), 437–453.

Jeynes, W. H. (2005). *Parental involvement and student achievement: A meta-analysis.* Retrieved from http://www.hfrp.org/publications-resources/browse-our-publications/parental-involvement-and-student-achievement-a-meta-analysis

Jiménez-Castellanos, O. (2008). *Beyond equality, equity and adequacy: Intra-district resource allocation's impact on school achievement.* Unpublished doctoral dissertation, San Diego State University/Claremont Graduate School, San Diego, CA/Claremont, CA.

Jordan, C., Orozco, E., & Averett, A. (2001). *Emerging issues in school, family, and community connections.* Austin, TX: National Center for Family and Community Connections with Schools.

Kane, W. (2010, November 13). Latino kids now majority in state's public schools. Retrieved from *San Francisco Chronicle,* http://sfgate.com/cgi-bin/article.cgi?f=/c/a/2010/11/13/MNIG1GBD0C.DTL

Lam, S. F. (1997). *How the family influences children's academic achievement.* New York: Garland.

Lareau, A. (1989). *Home advantage: Social class and parental intervention in elementary education.* Philadelphia: Falmer Press.

Lareau, A., & Horvat, E. M. (1999). Moments of social inclusion and exclusion: Race, class, and cultural capital in family-school relationships. *Sociology of Education, 72*(1), 37–53.

Lightfoot, S. L. (1978). *Worlds apart: Relationships between families and schools.* New York: Basic Books.

Lopez, G. R. (2001, April). *On whose terms? Understanding involvement through the eyes of migrant parents.* Paper presented at the Annual Educational Research Association (AERA), Seattle, WA.

Lopez, M. A., & Kreider, H. (2003). Beyond input: Achieving authentic participation in school reform. *Evaluation exchange: A periodical on emerging strategies in evaluating child and families, 9*(2). Boston: Harvard Family Research Project.

McCaleb, S. P. (1994). *Building communities of learners: A collaboration among teachers, students, families, and community.* Mahwah, NJ: Lawrence Erlbaum.

Mediratta, K., Fruchter, N., & Lewis, A. C. (2002). *Organizing for school reform: How communities are finding their voices and reclaiming their public schools.* New York: New York University Press.

National Clearinghouse for English Language Acquisition. (2011). *The growing numbers of English learner students 1998/99–2008/09.* Retrieved from http://www.ncela.gwu.edu/files/uploads/9/growingLEP_0809.pdf

Núñez, R. (1994). *Schools, parents, and empowerment: An ethnographic study of Mexican-origin parents' participation in their children's schools.* Unpublished doctoral dissertation, San Diego State University/Claremont Graduate School, San Diego, CA.

Oakes, J., & Rogers, J. (2006). *Learning power: Organizing for education and justice.* New York: Teachers College Press.

Olivos, E. M. (2004). Tensions, contradictions, and resistance: An activist's reflection of the struggles of Latino parents in the public school system. *High School Journal: Chicana/o Activism in Education; Theories and Pedagogies of Trans/formation, 87*(4), 25–35.

Olivos, E. M. (2006). *The power of parents: A critical perspective of bicultural parent involvement in public schools.* New York: Peter Lang.

Olivos, E. M., & Ochoa, A. M. (2006a). Operationalizing a transformational paradigm of parent involvement: Parent voice and participation. In K. Cadiero-Kaplan, A. M. Ochoa, N. Kuhlman, E. M. Olivos, & J. Rodriguez (Eds.), *The living work of teachers: Ideology and practice* (pp. 199–217). Covina, CA: California Association for Bilingual Education (CABE).

Olivos, E. M., & Ochoa, A. M. (2006b). Toward a transformational paradigm of parent involvement in urban education. In J. Kincheloe, P. Anderson, K. Rose, D. Griffith, and K. Hayes (Eds.), *Urban education: An encyclopedia* (pp. 196–217). Westport, CT: Greenwood.

Olivos, E. M., & Ochoa, A. M. (2008). Reframing due process and institutional inertia: A case study of an urban school district. *Equity and Excellence in Education, 41*(3), 1–14.

Parent Institute for Quality Education (PIQE). (2009). *Parent institute annual report.* Retrieved from http://piqe.org/Assets/Corporate/AnnualReports.htm

Persell, C. H. (1977). *Education and inequality: The roots and results of stratification in America's schools.* New York: The Free Press.

Planty, M., Hussar, W., Snyder, T., Provasnik, S., Kena, G., Dinkes, R., KewalRamani, A., & Kemp, J. (2008). *The condition of education 2008* (NCES 2008-031). Washington, DC: National Center for Education Statistics, Institute of Education Sciences, U.S. Department of Education.

Ramirez, A. Y. F. (2003). Dismay and disappointment: Parental involvement of Latino immigrant parents. *Urban Review, 35*(2), 93–110.

Ritblatt, S. N., Beatty, J. R., Cronon, T. A., & Ochoa A. M. (2002). Relationship among perceptions of parent involvement, time allocation, and demographic characteristics: Implications for policy formation. *Journal of Community Psychology, 7*(5), 519–549.

SchoolDataDirect. (2008). *United States public schools and districts: An overview.* Retrieved from http://www.schooldatadirect.org/app/location/q/stid=1036196/llid=162/stllid=676/locid=1036195/stype=/catid=-1/secid=-1/compid=-1/site=pes

Shannon, S. (1996). Minority parental involvement: A Mexican mother's experience and a teacher's interpretation. *Education and Urban Society, 29*(1), 71–84.

Shirley, D. (1997). *Community organizing for urban school reform.* Austin: University of Texas Press.

Souto-Manning, M., & Swick, K. J. (2006). Teacher's beliefs about parent and family involvement: Rethinking our family involvement paradigm. *Early Childhood Educational Journal, 34*(2), 187–193.

Stanton-Salazar, R. D. (2001). *Manufacturing hope and despair: The school and kin support networks of U.S.-Mexican youth.* New York: Teachers College Press.

Taylor, D., & Dorsey-Gaines, C. (1988). *Growing up literate: Learning from inner-city families.* Portsmouth, NH: Heinemann.

U.S. Department of Education. (2004). *Parental involvement: Title I, part A. Non-regulatory guidance.* Washington, DC: Author.

Valencia, R. R. (Ed.). (1997). *The evolution of deficit thinking: Educational thought and practice.* London: Falmer Press.

Valencia, R. R., & Black, M. S. (2002) Mexican Americans don't value education! On the basis of the myth, mythmaking, and debunking. *Journal of Latinos and Education, 1*(2), 81–103.

Part I

Multicultural Perspectives

2

Parental Involvement in the Home: A Critical View Through a Multicultural Lens

Robert P. Moreno, Kristal Lewis-Menchaca, and James Rodriguez

Parental involvement has long been viewed as a vehicle for academic success, particularly in addressing the achievement gap experienced by Latino and other racial and ethnic minority students. The current view holds that the more parents are "involved" in their child's schooling, the better the child will perform. Moreover, it has often been assumed that parents who are not involved simply do not care about their child's education. In this chapter, we will outline some of the problems with this line of thinking as it pertains to ethnically and racially diverse families. In particular, we will examine how parent involvement among culturally diverse families may not easily translate/transfer to the school context. Drawing from our own research with Mexican American mothers, we will show how parents' involvement within the home can be a complex and dynamic process, but one that is not well captured by many of the current parent involvement models. This chapter is organized into three sections: (a) first we will provide a brief overview of our current understanding of "parent involvement" and point to some of its shortcomings with respect to culturally diverse families; (b) drawing from our own research, we will give specific examples of the complexities that exist with parent involvement in culturally diverse families that can create gaps and conflicts between home and school; and (c) we will discuss some strategies for building better family-school relations between diverse families and schools.

Before we proceed, however, we should note that we use the term *parental involvement* (as opposed to *parental engagement*) for two reasons. First, we do so for the sake of consistency with previous publications (Moreno, 2004; Moreno & Chuang, 2011; Moreno & Valencia, 2011). Second, and more important, we understand the term to refer to a set of behaviors and activities that parents partake in to facilitate their children's success in school. As such, our use of the term does not imply passive participation on the part of parents in relation to the school. On the contrary, we share the view of others who argue that the ideal relationship between parents and schools is one of mutual trust and reciprocity (Delgado-Gaitan, 2004; Olivos, Ochoa, & Jiménez-Castellanos, this volume).

Understanding the Issues

An in-depth review of the parent involvement research is beyond the scope of this chapter; however, it may be useful to provide a brief contextual overview to better understand some of the issues regarding parents' involvement with their children's education.

Although parents have been involved in their children's education in some form or another since the inception of public schooling, the 1960s sparked a particular interest in parental involvement patterns. Social and developmental scientists began to demonstrate that parents' attitudes, beliefs, and behaviors were important predictors of children's intellectual and educational achievement (Bloom, 1981) and may play a role in the existing educational inequality among Whites and certain racial/ethnically diverse groups (Coleman et al., 1966). In addition, early childhood education programs such as Head Start began to incorporate parental involvement in their programming (Berger, 1981; Rich, 1987; Zigler & Styfco, 2004).

Initially, there were two competing conceptualizations of parental involvement. One perspective viewed parental involvement as a matter of "parental control" and advanced an advocacy orientation in which parents act as educational partners and decision makers. The long-term focus of this advocacy orientation was to develop a more inclusive educational system and change the structural conditions that perpetuated poverty. The second perspective was oriented toward "parent education." Those who held the parent education perspective believed that low-socioeconomic status (SES) parents were lacking parenting skills and a basic understanding of their role as their child's first teacher. It was these skills, or the lack thereof, that was at the root of various educational and social problems encountered by low-income families. The theories that framed this orientation were based on cultural and environmental deficit models, particularly the inadequate socialization of children by their parents (for a discussion, see Pearl, 1997). Parental involvement was therefore based on providing parents with the "correct" values and skills to interact with their children (Valentine & Stark, 1979). Over the years, parent involvement has been conceptualized and reconceptualized numerous ways, each with some combination of both the parent education and control perspectives (with varying degrees of emphasis). One of the most prominent and influential models was that developed by Joyce Epstein and her colleagues.

Epstein's model focuses on the family's involvement in the school as well as the school's involvement with the family and both being involved with the community. This triangular partnership between family, school, and community is complex and relies on involvement between all three to better support academic success. The degree of overlap between these three contextual influences enriches student learning (Sheldon & Epstein, 2002). At the core of Epstein's model are six types of involvement:

1. *Parenting.* Educate parents about their child's development. Assist parents in establishing a conducive environment for learning in the home. Encourage parents with developing proper parenting skills and to use and provide familial support. It is also necessary for schools to understand their families' backgrounds, cultures, and goals for children.

2. *Communicating.* Information regarding school programs and student progress must be communicated to families in clear ways and should vary based on each family's needs. Communication from school to home and from home to school should be created so that parents, families, and teachers and other school staff can easily keep in touch.

3. *Volunteering.* Improve opportunities for families to volunteer in schools by providing recruitment, training, and alternate schedules so that parents can participate. Provide opportunities for educators to work with volunteers who support students and their school.

4. *Learning at home.* Teachers should assign homework that facilitates discussion and participation from family members. Involve parents in learning activities at home. Examples of activities include homework and setting academic goals.

5. *Decision making.* Families should be participants in school decisions via parent involvement groups such as PTAs/PTOs, school councils, and committees. Encourage communication between teachers and family members to share information.

6. *Collaborating with the community.* Use resources and services from local businesses for families, students, and schools. Provide opportunities for students, staff, and families to provide services to the community.

According to Epstein (1990), a comprehensive partnership program will include elements of and provide opportunities for each of the six types of involvement. Each school's partnership program will be unique based upon the goals and specific needs of families, the school, and the community. Research has shown that this paradigm of involvement is significant in decreasing truancy issues, reducing behavioral and discipline problems, and increasing academic scores as well as family and community involvement (Epstein, 2005; Epstein & Jansorn, 2004; Epstein & Sheldon, 2002; Sheldon & Epstein, 2002, 2005).

Although Epstein's model is widely employed, its utility may be limited as it pertains to ethnically and racially diverse groups. For example, Ingram, Wolfe, and Lieberman (2007) postulate that the majority of schools would like to increase parent involvement. Their question therein lies in the process of involving parents and the ability to translate that involvement into student achievement. They sought to uncover the specific constructs of parent involvement that resulted in improved academic achievement using Epstein's model. Their research focused on three Chicago public schools that reported high levels of poverty, high minority populations, and high scores on standardized achievement exams. All three schools scored in the state's top third on the Illinois Standards Achievement Test (ISAT). The researchers chose schools that were considered to be highly effective at serving an at-risk population. The study focused on examining the specific ways the schools involved parents through the lens of Epstein's model in order to construct a model that would increase parent involvement and overall school effectiveness.

The researchers' findings suggest that Epstein's model is unable to clarify the characteristics and impact of parent involvement for high-risk and high-achieving populations. Only two of Epstein's six types of involvement (Parenting and Learning at Home) were deemed applicable. Epstein's Parenting typology states that parents provide an environment at home that encourages learning. The participants' responses indicated specific parenting practices that promoted learning and acceptable behavior while at school. Epstein's Learning at Home typology includes parents' involvement in learning activities such as homework or outings that promote learning. The participants' responses indicated that parents were consistently involved in learning activities with their child. Ingram et al. (2007) suggest that improving academic achievement for high-risk populations is a result of effective parenting strategies and learning-at-home activities. In this study, the remaining four typologies of Communicating, Volunteering, Decision Making, and Collaborating with the Community, did not represent a large influence on the parents. The participants' responses indicated that they rarely communicated with their children's teachers. The parents also stated that they always felt encouraged to volunteer by teachers and administrators but that they were rarely able to do so. The participants rarely helped with classroom activities and rarely collaborated in community activities (Ingram et al., 2007). According to the answers to open-ended questions, three roles were identified as important by parents but are not captured by or aligned with Epstein's six typologies. The participants' responses indicated that having high expectations, providing the best education possible, and teaching the importance of a good education are important parental roles. Finally, the majority of parents were aware of and able to define the impact of their involvement in their child's educational experience (Ingram et al., 2007).

Although Epstein's model has been the foundation for much research, Auerbach (2007) claims that it fails to capture the unique situations and limitations that many low-income parents and ethnically diverse parents encounter when attempting to become involved in their child's educational experience. It also negates the nonstandard, but situationally and culturally relevant ways that these parents participate in their child's education. According to Auerbach (2007), the invisible strategies employed by low-income and ethnically diverse parents are unnoticed or ignored if they are not displayed within the mainstream typologies put forth by Epstein. For marginalized bicultural families from historically underserved groups and communities, involvement may not manifest itself through school-based partnerships that rely on parental activity at the school site. Rather, Latino parents are primarily engaged in their children's education at home, out of the school's view (Moreno & López, 1999). Given that these activities are less visible, educators may erroneously assume that parents are not involved and by extension, do not care about their children's education.

The Complexities of Parent Involvement at Home

Although more recent conceptions of parent involvement incorporate both parent education and collaboration approaches, they appear to fall short on addressing issues that are unique to specific cultural groups that have been underserved by educational systems. As suggested above, the most active context in which parent involvement occurs is within the home. However, this only magnifies the lack of understanding surrounding how Latino parents interact with and teach their children in the home. Not only is Latino parental involvement not well understood, but Latino parental involvement practices are not incorporated into existing parent involvement models like those proposed by Epstein. In this section, we illustrate important differences in Latino parent-child teaching interactions and discuss how these differences may be used to facilitate greater involvement and continuity between home and school.

Before we proceed, it is important to note that early research on parent-child teaching interactions portrayed low-income and ethnically/racially diverse parents in a negative light. The teaching styles of ethnic/racial minorities were assessed by the degree to which they approximated their White counterparts. Differences in teaching patterns were viewed as deficits. More recent work has moved beyond gross comparative assessments. In our work, for example, we have conducted observational studies that examined the nature of Latina mothers' teaching interactions. Through our work, we found that Latina mothers do, in fact, differ in the way they teach their children (as compared with their White counterparts); however, these differences constituted effective strategies in their own right. In general, Latina mothers teach their children using a more "direct" teaching style. They tend to minimize their use of superfluous questioning. Despite the difference, Latina mothers were effective in their instruction. What made these finds all the more surprising was that these differences were identified even when Latina mothers' level of education and acculturation was taken into account (Moreno, 1997).

Although our research provided us with an initial understanding of instruction in the home, we needed more insight into how Latina mothers teach their children school-related tasks. If effective instruction is socioculturally rooted and not "universal," then our view was that before educators could encourage and facilitate parent involvement at home, it would be important to understand the nature of the interactions. Thus, we conducted a study where we asked Latina mothers to teach their children the alphabet.

Briefly, in this study we asked five Latina mothers to video-record their instruction of the alphabet to their preschool children (for details, see Moreno, 2002). All mothers reported that they were bilingual; however, Spanish was the predominant language used in the household. Each of the mothers who participated in the study emigrated from Mexico, but their children were born in the United States. All families were composed of two-parent households. The mother was asked to "teach your child the alphabet." It was emphasized to the mothers that the goal of the 2 days was to instruct the child such that he or she could become fully competent in the task (e.g., identify and label the letters of the alphabet). The mothers were asked to videotape all instruction sessions over a 48-hour period and were provided with all the videotape equipment and training necessary to record their interactions (i.e., video camera, tripod, etc.). This style of data collection was used to minimize the intrusiveness of an outside recorder and to allow the mothers more freedom to control the time, duration, and instructional techniques they used in each situation. It also allowed mothers to incorporate the teaching interactions within their typical schedule. It should be noted that at no time were the mothers given any instructions on how to teach the alphabet, nor were the mothers given any instruction about in which language they should teach (English or Spanish). Teaching letters of the alphabet was the selected task because it is well within the capabilities of normal preschool-age children, and children's knowledge of the alphabet is an important indicator of school readiness (Snow, 2001).

The results of the study revealed two important aspects of teaching that may be useful in understanding and facilitating parent involvement within Latina households—social organization and language use.

Social Organization. The social organization of the activity pertains to the individuals involved (directly or indirectly) in the interaction. In this case, mothers were free to organize their teaching in any manner they saw fit. In each case, the family consisted of the target child and at least one other sibling. As a result, each mother had to decide (explicitly or implicitly) what to do with the other siblings. For example, in the case of Christina, José, Luis, and Olga, Christina (mother) organized the teaching material on top of the coffee table. Christina sat at the table with her children: José, the target child (4 years old), and his two siblings Luis (6 years old) and Olga (2 years old). Although Christina did not specifically invite the other children to participate, she did not exclude them from the area.

During much of the teaching interaction, Christina's strategy appears to be to guide José through a series of matching trials. With the letters of the alphabet written on a separate sheet of paper, she asks José a series of questions such as "Busca esa letra allí" [Look for that letter] (she is pointing to the letter *A*) and José would look for the letter.

With this instructional strategy, Christina coordinates her instruction of José with her interactions with Luis and Olga. For example, throughout the session, Olga is constantly grabbing the letters of the alphabet and other teaching materials so she can "see" what is going on. Luis, on the other hand, is intent on displaying how smart he is by shouting out the answers to the questions before José can answer. Although it is clear that, at times, Christina loses patience with Luis and Olga, she never excludes them from the teaching interaction. In this case, the teaching event was organized as a family activity, not as an isolated dyad. The other siblings (Luis and Olga) were part of the instructional process and the context in which the "real" instruction resided. For example, Luis often serves as the "teacher's helper" by giving Christina examples of words that begin with a particular letter (in Spanish) and locating various teaching materials. In a brief conversation with Christina, she shared that she feels that it is important for all her children to be exposed to school activities. She interprets the activity as a family activity and she acknowledges Luis and Olga's interest to be a part of the instructional activity.

Another mother, Linda, takes a different approach when teaching her son Johnny (4 years old) and his three siblings (Pamela, 7 years old; Richard, 3 years old; and Melissa, 1–1/2 years old). She organizes her teaching event at the dining-room table. She sits down with Johnny. Linda asks Pamela, the eldest, to take Melissa out of the room. Linda also quickly escorts Richard to the back of the apartment (where the bedrooms are located) to watch TV. Before returning to the dining room she locks the door that separates the dining room from the rest of the apartment. Richard's response is to bang "endlessly" on the door and yell and scream that he wants to come out. This goes on steadily for approximately 6 minutes. Despite the noise, Linda continues to teach Johnny the letters of the alphabet.

Unlike Christina, Linda organizes the teaching event as a dyadic one. At the beginning of the event, she quite explicitly removes Pamela, Richard, and Melissa from the teaching interaction. However, this is not without its consequences. Linda's decision to lock Richard out of the room results in Richard's crying throughout the teaching interaction. Although the mother proceeds with her teaching of Johnny, she does so in a less than ideal situation. As with the first case, the teaching event does not happen in isolation of the other family members. The influence of the other family members is apparent, even if they are not in the immediate area.

The cases of Christina and Linda illustrate that the process of teaching your child is not a simple one. When mothers are in naturalistic and "everyday" conditions, they must coordinate not only the teaching interaction between themselves and their "child," but also that of other family members. As we see in the case of Christina and her children, the mother must juggle her instruction of José while managing the "intrusions" of the other two children. The mother is no longer (if ever) managing a dyad, but rather coordinating a mixed-age small group. In the case of Linda and her family, we see that she takes what might be considered a more typical approach. She organizes her instruction with Johnny as a dyadic interaction. However, this comes at a cost—extended crying of her 3-year-old, Richard, who was not included in the teaching session. These examples illustrate the coordination that is necessary for mothers to instruct a relatively straightforward task. In addition to her ability to teach the content, a mother must also possess the competence to coordinate the social conditions of the household.

Understanding the social context of the home under which these types of activities occur is crucial if we are going to facilitate parental involvement activities. In contrast to White families, Latinos have larger families and tend to have a more familial orientation. As such, educators may be more likely to increase learning activities in the home if they provide family-based activities and strategies that involve multiple family members with children at various age levels (such as those constructed by Christina and her children), thus avoiding dyadic base activities that may be less appropriate for larger Latino families (as in the case of Linda and her children).

Language Use. The issue of language use pertains to the process by which mothers used English or Spanish in their instruction. In the course of the study, not only did we avoid telling the mothers how to organize their teaching sessions, but also we refrained from telling them what language to use. This choice was left entirely to the mothers. As a result, the mothers had to decide which alphabet to teach. This is important because, although similar, the English alphabet does not contain certain Spanish letters (i.e., *ch, ll, rr,* or *ñ*). Mothers had to choose and in some cases negotiate whether they would teach in English or in Spanish, or a combination of the two. The following are three examples of how mothers addressed the language issues in their instruction.

The first example of is that of Alicia and her daughter, Gina. Alicia and Gina sit at the dining-room table with a variety of letters scattered on the table. Alicia picks a letter up from the table and asks Gina to label the letter and provide a word that begins with the selected letter (she does not seem to follow any discernible order).

ALICIA: *¿Ésta?* [This one? She points to the *B*]
GINA: *Ya le dije.* [I already said it.]
ALICIA: *Otra vez, para [que] se graben.* [One more time so it sticks.]
GINA: B *de "baby."* [B for "baby."]
GINA: *¿Cómo se dicen en inglés?* [How do you say them in English?]
ALICIA: B *de "baby."*
ALICIA: E
GINA: E
ALICIA: E *de "elefante"* [E for "elephant."]
GINA: E *de "elefante." ¿Y cómo se dicen en inglés?* E *de . . . ?* [E for "elephant."
    And how do you say it in English?]
ALICIA: Elephant.
GINA: *No, en inglés.* [No, in English.]
ALICIA: *Por eso. Primero en español.* [That's why. But first in Spanish.]
ALICIA: D *de "dedo."* [D for "finger."]
GINA: D *de "dedo." ¿Y cómo se dicen en inglés?* [D for "finger." And how
    do you say it in English?]
ALICIA: *Dedo* [Finger.]
GINA: *No, en inglés.* [No, in English.]
ALICIA: *Aprenda en español y luego en inglés.* [Learn in Spanish, and
    then in English].

As instruction progressed, Gina asked her mother what words meant in English (*¿Y cómo se dicen en inglés?*). Alicia clearly defined the task as a Spanish one. In doing so she prioritized one language over the other (*Aprenda en español y luego en inglés*).

This contrasts with the following example of Concha and her son Ernesto. Concha chose to teach the English alphabet. However, although the letters were labeled in English, she conducted the entire social interaction in Spanish.

In this scenario, Concha (mother) organizes the teaching event at the kitchen table and sits down with Ernesto. Concha teaches the alphabet primarily through identification and matching of letters. With a pile of letters on the table she asks Ernesto a series of questions.

CONCHA: *Búscame la "A"* [Look for the letter "A" for me. The "A" is
      pronounced in English]
ERNESTO: *¿Ésta?* [This one?]
CONCHA: *No.* [No.]
ERNESTO: *Aquí está.* [Here it is.]
CONCHA: *¡Bravo!* [Bravo!]
CONCHA: *Ahora ésta—B* [Now for the *B.*]
ERNESTO: *¿B?*
CONCHA: B—*la* B [*B*—the *B.*]
ERNESTO: [Shows an incorrect letter]
CONCHA: B!—*mira como ésta acá.* [*B*—look, like this one over here.]
ERNESTO: *¿Ésta?* [This one? Shows a correct letter]
CONCHA: *Oh,* B. [Oh, *B.*]

Despite the intertwining of the two languages, her son, Ernesto, showed no signs of confusion and was able to follow his mother's instruction quite easily. Clearly, Concha is using Spanish as a tool to teach her child English.

In the final example, of María and Julio, the issue of language use is further complicated when the English language proficiency of the mother differed greatly from that of the child. María (mother) had constructed the teaching event on the living room floor. Using a labeling strategy, María was teaching Julio the alphabet in Spanish. She labeled the letters in Spanish and she also maintained the social interaction in Spanish.

MARÍA: *¿Julio, qué letra es?* [Julio, what letter is this? *A* is the correct response]
JULIO: A. [*A.*]
MARÍA: *Muy bien.* [Good.]

After a few trials, Julio becomes nonresponsive. By the time they reach the letter *E* (they are proceeding in order), it is apparent that Julio does not know the correct Spanish response.

MARÍA: *¿Qué letra es?* [What letter is this? The Spanish *E* is the correct response.]

JULIO: *E.* [in English]

MARÍA: [long pause] *¿Qué letra es?* [What letter is this? the Spanish *F* is the correct response]

María asked her son to identify letters in Spanish, but Julio, apparently not knowing the correct response in Spanish, responded with the English label. At that point the mother paused and looked confused and then simply moves on to the next letter in the alphabet (*F*). Throughout the teaching event, María continued to label the letters in Spanish. Over time, it became clear that Julio knows very few letters in Spanish. Most of the letters he does know are in English. However, it seemed as if María was unsure if her child was "supposed" to answer in English.

The complexity of the teaching process becomes even more salient when we consider the conditions under which mothers select which language to use (English or Spanish). Given the lack of specificity in our directions, we were aware that mothers would have to make a choice regarding their language use. Our expectation was that mothers who were proficient in English would teach in English, and those who were proficient in Spanish would teach in Spanish. This view was a gross oversimplification. Language choice was not based solely on mothers' language proficiency, but on a number of linguistic and social factors that interactively defined the teaching context. This included the nature and purpose of the task itself, the child's own language proficiency and preferences, mothers' assessments of the child's proficiency, and mothers' perceptions of what was expected.

Not only did the mothers have to decide in what language they were going to teach, they had to decide which alphabet they were going to teach. In the case of Concha and her son, Ernesto, Spanish was used as a tool to teach English letters. Although Concha taught her son how to label and identify the letters in English, all her instructions were given in Spanish (*Búscame la* A). Even when she praises her son, she does so in Spanish (*¡Bravo!*). This approach allowed her to manage the interaction in the language in which she is most at ease, and at the same time teach the English alphabet. This is reminiscent of previous work that demonstrated how Spanish-speaking students used their Spanish-speaking skills to become better English readers (Moll & Diaz, 1987).

The cases of two other mothers, María and Alicia, raise a different issue. In each case the mother has selected to teach her child how to label and identify the Spanish letters, thus defining the task. Over time, however, the child challenges the definition of the task. In the example of Alicia, the issue of language selection was raised by her daughter (*¿Cómo se dicen en inglés?*). In response, Alicia makes it explicit that the goal of the task is to learn the Spanish letters first, and in doing so prioritizes the languages (*Aprenda en español y luego en inglés*).

In the case of María and her son Julio, the issue comes into play in a more subtle fashion. As with Alicia, María has selected to teach the Spanish letters; however, presumably to maximize his ability to respond correctly, Julio begins to identify the letters in English. The persistence of her son to answer in English seems to disrupt María's instruction. She becomes more hesitant with her son's answers as she seems to decide how to respond.

With respect to parent involvement, these interactions point to the fact that Latino parents are very much involved, but these interactions increase in their complexity because of their multilingual home and community context. In contrast to monolingual English-speaking families, many Latino families must in some way negotiate the use of Spanish and English. When Latino parents are faced with being involved in their child's education, what language can and should they use? As illustrated in the cases above, the answer may depend on a number of issues, such the parents' attitudes and values regarding English and Spanish. This would include their ability to negotiate and prioritize the language of instruction with their child (*Learn it in Spanish, and then in English*), their level of English proficiency, as well as the knowledge and skill to use one language to inform another. Again, if we are going to facilitate parental involvement activities in multilingual families, then the issue of language use must be dealt with in a supportive way.

Collectively, these examples highlight a level of linguistic and sociocultural complexity that must be taken into consideration in examining Latino parental involvement. Unfortunately, the prevalent models of parent involvement provide only a broad overview of various types of involvement (learning at home, volunteering at school, etc.), but are not well positioned to tap into the micro-interpersonal processes that are fundamental to how parents interact with their children in the context of schooling across culturally diverse families. As such, they offer us little instrumental guidance on how to understand and facilitate involvement.

Bridging the Gap Between Home and School

In addition to the more micro processes, a key variable often ignored in this area is the families' level of acculturation. Although it is of minimal importance for the vast majority of Whites, acculturation is crucial for understanding Latinos and other immigrant groups (Marín & Marín, 1991; Rueschenberg & Buriel, 1989). Among Mexican Americans, for example, parents' level of acculturation seems to play an important role in their level of involvement in their children's schooling (Delgado-Gaitan, 1990; Stevenson, Chen, & Uttal, 1990). Rueschenberg and Buriel (1987) found a positive relation between parental acculturation status and their involvement with their children's schools.

The role of acculturation should not be regarded as a solitary or isolated indicator, but rather as a barometer that provides insights into various psychological and behavioral constructs. Indeed, acculturation can serve as a window to dynamic processes and cultural assets that are often unrecognized and underused in the education of bicultural children. The failure to understand acculturative processes and cultural assets contributes to a lack of educational responsiveness, resulting in lower levels of effectiveness. In the case of bicultural children and families, it is critical to recognize their full arsenal of cultural assets and to seize upon opportunities to mobilize and use those assets in parent involvement programs. At the same time, we must be vigilant in negating programs that fail to recognize these assets and that perpetuate gaps between home and school.

We offer an example from our findings. We found, as have others, that despite low levels of acculturation, Latina mothers possess their own cultural attitudes and beliefs, as well as an "immigrant optimism" that serves as a "resource" for their own self-efficacy and competence. Unfortunately, this optimism can be attenuated by limited awareness of school activities and procedures. The language barrier that exists in many schools can explain this, in part. The combination of limited English proficiency among less acculturated mothers with low levels of Spanish proficiency among school personnel results in minimal communication between home and school. Thus, despite the high regard for the education of their children, the ability of Latina mothers to transfer this interest to effective support for their children's learning is compromised (Gutiérrez & Sameroff, 1990, Gutiérrez, Sameroff, & Karrer, 1988, Moreno & López, 1999). Too often the failure to communicate and to use mothers' attentiveness results in a gap between home and school. This gap can and must be addressed to promote learning, growth, and achievement among culturally diverse children and families.

If we are going to successfully use parent involvement as a vehicle to increase academic achievement across a diversity of families, parent involvement must be reconceptualized to include key factors such as acculturation and cultural practices among diverse families. Parent involvement models must incorporate culturally driven micro-interpersonal processes while simultaneously recognizing and understanding the values, practices, and challenges that face culturally diverse families. Parent involvement models must be educationally and culturally responsive to Latino families in order to increase participation rates and effectiveness.

We argue that schools are far from neutral institutions and, in many instances, are not responsive to Latino families. By their selective use of particular linguistic structures, curriculum, organization structures, and assumptions about home environments, schools "invite" certain segments of the community and discourage others (Lareau, 2000; Valenzuela, 1999). This selectivity results in varying degrees of educational responsiveness and effectiveness to different segments of the community. In the case of Latino families, this selectivity and lack of responsiveness and effectiveness explains, at least in part, the gap between school and home for Latinos. An argument can be extended that selectivity and lack of responsiveness and ineffectiveness can also help to explain the achievement gap for Latinos and other diverse communities.

One way that schools and educators have tried to increase parent involvement and bridge the gap between home and school is by promoting the notion of "parents as teachers." This perspective emphasis is that parents are their child's "first teacher." This view tries to highlight the importance of parents in their child's education. This perspective also tries to extend a school framework into the home, whereby the home is a learning environment that should parallel the classroom. When the values and culture of the school are shared and intersect with the home, this perspective is less problematic. However, when the home and school culture is disparate, this may be problematic, as this perspective privileges teacher-child interactions as the ideal. More often than not, the favoring or imposition of the school culture perspective leads to indifference toward the home culture and results in unresponsive and ineffective parent engagement. Also, opportunities to embrace and use the home culture as an asset in the educational process are missed. In some instances, the home culture may be actively negated and altered to reflect the prevailing school culture.

If we are to increase parent involvement among culturally diverse populations, we must move beyond the "teachers as parents" model to a more balanced collaborative approach that recognizes and uses assets of the home and school. Such an approach is more likely to be responsive and effective. In addition to emphasizing parents' role as teachers, we propose adopting a parallel model of "teachers as *compadres*," or teachers as co-parent. If schools embrace the notion of teachers as *compadres*, then the caregiving role of teachers becomes explicit. Just as the notion of "parents as teachers" implies a particular teaching role for parents, "teachers as *compadres*" implies a specific investment in the well-being of the child.

We believe that this would foster and facilitate a more reciprocal process between the home and school, with the overall well-being of the child as the focus. Thus, the overall well-being of the child becomes a shared goal. This, in turn, is more likely to foster a mutually respectful inclusive community, rather than a shuttling of children between different worlds where there is a stark division of labor between home and school. Increased reciprocity combined with the shared goal of the child's overall well-being would promote the recognition and understanding of the home culture, leading to increased home-school responsiveness and effectiveness.

If we are to be more inclusive in understanding family-school relationships, we will need to expand the ways in which we think about and assess the nature and extent of parents' involvement in their children's education. We must reconceptualize how we think about and how we approach parent involvement to maximize home and school assets. This reconceptualization and its implementation is likely to increase responsiveness to Latino and other diverse families and the effectiveness of our efforts. While general classifications of parent involvement behavior can be helpful, it is limited in its ability to guide us to a solution to the ultimate goal—the academic success and well-being of our children. Rather, we need an approach that will be more informed and inclusive regarding the nature of culturally diverse children and families that are not part of our educational system. A more responsive framework and approach will promote greater parent involvement; increase the effectiveness of parent involvement programs; and ultimately enhance learning, achievement, and the overall well-being of diverse children and families.

Discussion Questions

1. What is the primary goal of parent involvement? Can schools be successful without parent involvement? Why?
2. Can Epstein's model better account for parent involvement among ethnically and culturally diverse families? If so, how?
3. What are the micro-interpersonal processes used by parents as they interact with their children that go unnoticed by educators?
4. What teacher training strategies might be necessary to foster a "teachers as *compadres*" approach?
5. To increase parent engagement across a diversity of families, how can parent involvement be reconceptualized? What social and cultural practices need to be considered?

Note

Partial support for this chapter was provided to the first author by American Educational Research Association/Institute of Education Sciences.

Suggested Readings

Epstein, J. L., & Jansorn, N. R. (2004). School, family, and community partnerships link the plan. *Education Digest, 69*(6), 19–23.

Lareau, A. (2000). *Home advantage: Social class and parental intervention in elementary education* (2nd ed.). Lanham, MD: Rowman & Littlefield.

Valdes, G. (1996). *Con respeto: Bridging the distances between culturally diverse families and schools*. New York: Teachers College Press.

Valencia, R. R. (2002). *Chicano school failure and success* (2nd ed.). New York: Falmer Press.

References

Auerbach, S. (2007). From moral supporters to struggling advocates: Reconceptualizing parent roles in education through the experiences of working-class families of color. *Urban Education, 42*, 250–283.

Berger, E. H. (1981). *Parents as partners in education: The school and home working together.* St. Louis, MO: C. V. Mosby.

Bloom, B. S. (1981). *All our children learning: A primer for parents, teachers, and other educators.* New York: McGraw-Hill.

Coleman, J. S., Campbell, E. Q., Hobson, C. J., McPartland, J. M., Mood, A., Weinfeld, F. D., & York, R. L. (1966). *Equality of educational opportunity*. Washington, DC: Government Printing Office.

Delgado-Gaitan, C. (1990). *Literacy for empowerment: The role of parents in children's education.* New York: Falmer Press.

Delgado-Gaitan, C. (2004). *Involving Latino families in schools*. Thousand Oaks, CA: Corwin Press.

Epstein, J. L. (1990). School and family connections: Theory, research, and implications for integrating sociologies of education and family. *Marriage and Family Review, 15*, 99–126.

Epstein, J. L. (2005). A case study of the partnership schools comprehensive school reform (CSR) model. *Elementary School Journal, 106*(2), 151–170.

Epstein, J. L., & Jansorn, N. R. (2004). School, family, and community partnerships link the plan. *Education Digest, 69,* 19–23.

Epstein, J. L., & Sheldon, S. B. (2002). Present and accounted for: Improving student attendance through family and community involvement. *Journal of Educational Research, 95*, 308–318.

Gutiérrez, J., & Sameroff, A. (1990). Determinants of complexity in Mexican American and Anglo American mothers' conceptions of child development. *Child Development, 61,* 384–394.

Gutiérrez, J., Sameroff, A. J., & Karrer, B. M. (1988). Acculturation and SES effects on Mexican American parents' concepts of development. *Child Development, 59*, 250–255.

Ingram, M., Wolfe, R. B., & Lieberman, J. M. (2007). The role of parents in high-achieving schools serving low-income, at-risk populations. *Education and Urban Society, 39,* 479–497.

Lareau, A. (2000). *Home advantage: Social class and parental intervention in elementary education* (2nd ed.). Lanham, MD: Rowman & Littlefield.

Marín, G., & Marín, B. V. (1991). *Research with Hispanic populations*. Newbury Park, CA: Sage.

Moll, L., & Diaz, S. (1987). Change as the goal of educational research. *Anthropology and Education Quarterly, 18*(4), 300–311.

Moreno, R. P. (1997). Everyday instruction: A comparison of Mexican American and Anglo mothers and their preschool children. *Hispanic Journal of Behavioral Science, 19*(4), 527–539.

Moreno, R. P. (2002). Teaching the alphabet: An exploratory look at maternal instruction in Mexican American families. *Hispanic Journal of Behavioral Sciences, 24*, 191–205.

Moreno, R. P. (2004). Exploring parental involvement among Mexican American and Latina mothers. In R. M. De Anda (Ed.), *Chicanas and Chicanos in contemporary society* (2nd ed.) (pp. 81–97). Lanham, MD: Rowman & Littlefield.

Moreno, R. P., & Chuang, S. S. (2011). Challenges facing immigrant parents and their involvement in their children's schooling. In S. S. Chuang & R. P. Moreno (Eds.), *Immigrant children: Change, adaptation, and cultural transformation* (pp. 239–254). Lexington, MA: Lexington Books.

Moreno, R. P., & López, J. A. (1999). The role of acculturation and maternal education in Latina mothers' involvement in their children's schooling. *School Community Journal, 9*, 83–101.

Moreno, R. P., & Valencia, R. R. (2011). Chicano families and schools: Challenges for strengthening family-school relations. In R. R. Valencia (Ed.), *Chicano school failure and success: Past, present, and future* (3rd ed.) (pp. 197–210). New York: Routledge Press.

Pearl, A. (1997). Cultural and accumulated environmental deficit models. In R. R. Valencia (Ed.), *The evolution of deficit thinking: Educational thought and practice* (pp. 132–159). The Stanford Series on Education and Public Policy. London: Falmer Press.

Rich, D. (1987). *Schools and families: Issues and actions*. Washington, DC: National Education Association.

Rueschenberg, E., & Buriel, R. (1989). Mexican American family functioning and acculturation: A family systems perspective. *Hispanic Journal of Behavioral Sciences, 11*(3), 232–244.

Sheldon, S. B., & Epstein, J. L. (2002). Improving student behavior and school discipline with family and community involvement. *Education and Urban Society, 35*(4), 4–26.

Sheldon, S. B., & Epstein, J. L. (2005). Involvement counts: Family and community partnerships and mathematics achievement. *Journal of Educational Research, 98*, 196–207.

Snow, C. E. (2001). Language and literacy: Relationships during the preschool years. In S. W. Beck ad L. N. Olah (Eds.), *Language and Literacy: Beyond the here and now* (pp. 161–186). Cambridge, MA: Harvard Educational Review.

Stevenson, H. W., Chen, C., & Uttal, D. H. (1990). Beliefs and achievement: A study of Black, White, and Hispanic children. *Child Development, 61,* 508–523.

Valentine, J., & Stark, E. (1979). The social context of parent involvement in Head Start. In E. Zigler & J. Valentine (Eds.), *Project Head Start: A legacy of the war on poverty* (pp. 291–313). New York: Free Press.

Valenzuela, A. (1999). *Subtractive schooling: U.S.-Mexican youth and the politics of caring.* Ithaca: State University of New York Press.

Zigler, E., & Styfco, S. J. (2004). *The Head Start debates.* Baltimore: Brookes.

3

Culturally Proficient School Communities: Connecting Bicultural Parents to Schools

Delores B. Lindsey and Randall B. Lindsey

Cross, Bazron, Dennis, and Isaacs (1989) developed the initial concepts of *cultural competence* and *cultural proficiency* for meeting the needs of diverse mental health clients. The standards of cultural competence provide the framework for the Parent and Community Communication and Outreach Rubric, presented in this chapter, and are "a set of congruent behaviors, attitudes, and policies that come together in a system, agency, or amongst professionals and enables that system, agency, or those professionals to work effectively in cross-cultural situations" (p. iv). It is the intersection of personal leadership and systems approaches that heightens the potential effectiveness of the worldview implicit in cultural proficiency.

This chapter provides school leaders with a systems approach to create a climate and infrastructure that foster, support, and expect parent engagement in schools. *Culturally proficient leadership* is a systemic approach to foster the construction of cultural democracy in schools. Cultural proficiency occurs in schools when leaders align their own values and behaviors *and* the school's policies and practices in a transformative manner to provide equitable access to learning opportunities and outcomes. When conceptualizing and constructing this approach, we called upon the work of many other authors who share our passion for making our democracy more inclusive and who see our public schools as central to that process. This chapter includes:

- related literature that explores the relationship between parents and schools,
- cultural proficiency as an approach for recognizing the bicultural nature of the relationship of parents to schools, and
- the Parent and Community Communication and Outreach Rubric, to guide educational leaders in using the essential elements of cultural competence and proficiency as standards for their leadership practices and for school policies.

There is no lack of studies and educational tracts that speak to the need for heightened parent involvement in schools. However, current thinking seems to place most of the changes to be made at the feet of parents. In this chapter we review some of the major elements of parent involvement as a means of presenting a rationale for aligning *espoused theory* with *theory in action*. Inger (1992) noted, "There is considerable evidence that parent involvement leads to improved student achievement, better school attendance, and reduced dropout rates, and that these improvements occur regardless of the economic, racial, or cultural background of the family" (p. 1).

Educators and education researchers often identify lack of parent involvement as one of the main external barriers of student achievement. Sheldon and Epstein (2005) report that using activities that require parent-student interactions can (a) create a line of communication between parents and teachers, (b) increase family involvement, and (c) help improve student achievement. Battle-Bailey (2004) asserts that teachers must engage parents and keep them involved in their student's learning; involvement alone is insufficient for improving student achievement. Battle-Bailey recommends specific, daily reading strategies that provide a means for parents to support literacy efforts at home, monitor reading progress, and help to sustain student interest in reading and literacy. Quezada, Diaz, and Sanchez (2003) indicate that multiple benefits occur when parents are actively involved in their children's education. They posit that parent participation increases academic and language achievement, improves behavior, and improves attitudes toward school and parent-child relationships. Although all incidences of parent participation are important, Canales and Harris (2004) caution school leaders to view parent involvement as being more meaningful than just assisting in the classroom, attending ceremonies, or helping supervise a field trip.

The topic of parent involvement received renewed attention over the past decade partly because of the Goals 2000: Educate America Act and the Improving America's Schools Act (IASA). Goals 2000 was a response by the U.S. government to the need for public school reform to encourage high standards at the state level. As described by Gonzalez (2002), the "new Title I," which contains IASA, was designed to encourage states to raise academic standards for all students, including

English language learners (ELLs) and children with disabilities. In 2002 the No Child Left Behind Act (NCLB) mandated that states and school districts continue standards-based reforms identified in Goals 2000 and intensify them through ambitious new requirements designed to close the achievement gap that "exists between low-income, minority, and ELL students and their more affluent, White and English-proficient peers" (Gonzalez, 2002, p. 4).

If there is a virtue in NCLB and its many state-level counterparts for school reform, it may be that the requirement of disaggregated data has made public what activists have been proclaiming, namely, the achievement disparities that exist among cultural groups of students in our schools. Caution needs to be taken, however, to ensure that the use of such data does not reinforce dominant-group stereotypes that perpetuate oppression and that, rather, the data are used to transform the manner in which school people and educational researchers view and work with bicultural communities and their children. Likewise, it is fundamental to view parents/guardians as more than instrumental extensions of the school and instead, to focus on the cultural supports extant within bicultural communities.

School- and Community-Centered Perceptions of Parent Participation

Even though many educators assume that parents know what schools mean by involvement in their child's education, the reality is that both groups have different perceptions of the often-used term *parent participation*. These different interpretations may lead to tension or conflict even though both parties have the same goals in mind: student success and achievement (Olivos, 2006). Lawson (2003) uses the terms "communitycentric" and "schoolcentric" to describe these contrasting perceptions.

- *Communitycentric.* "Parents involved in activities that meet the basic needs of their children as going to school well fed, rested, and clean."
- *Schoolcentric.* "Parents involved in activities that are structured and defined for parents by schools." (p. 79)

Different theories of action operate between teachers' and parents' perceptions of parent participation. Lawson (2003) notes that educators see their role as training parents in skills to use at home to enhance their children's ability to perform well in school. In seeming contrast, parents' theories of action are embedded in broader worldviews and expectations that their children and community can do better. Similarly, Scribner, Young, and Pedroza (1999) found through interviews with teachers in high-performing bicultural schools in Texas that they defined parent involvement as participation in formal activities, such as school events and meetings, or working as a teacher assistant or tutor. Again, in seeming contrast, parents described being involved in informal activities at home, such as checking homework assignments, reading and listening to children read, obtaining tutorial assistance, providing nurturance, instilling cultural values, talking with children, and sending them to school well fed, clean, and rested.

Educators and parents often assign different meanings and interpretations to the concept of "parent participation." Thus, the ultimate goal is for educators and parents to have comparable views about parent participation in order to support each other's efforts through communication, collaboration, and cooperation. Lawson (2003) compares teachers' and parents' theories of action as two lines:

> Both run parallel and in near opposition to each other simultaneously. They are parallel because both teachers and parents are child focused. They are also nearly oppositional because teachers' schoolcentric and parents' communitycentric frames of reference consistently put them at odds with each other. (p. 122)

Bridging Home and School Cultures

Given the various perceptions that exist among parents and educators, successful and accurate communication between home and school is critical for bridging this relationship gap between home and school. Pena (2000) finds three elements fundamental to effective parent involvement:

- taking time to gain parental trust,
- engaging parents to develop shared understanding of parent involvement, and
- exploring the relative strengths and weaknesses of educators and parents.

Parental interest and input needs to be central when planning parent activities. Delgado-Gaitan (1994) holds that educators must consider parents' interests and input as they plan and develop ways in which to engage parents. She argues that "parents who are knowledgeable about the school's expectations and the way in which the school operates are better advocates for their children than parents who lack such knowledge" (p. 1). As an example, in her study, Delgado-Gaitan describes bicultural parents' forming an organization to be supportive advocates of their children through school. Their organization is dedicated to developing knowledge about the school, which they share with other parents. The major implication from this study is the unleashing of parent empowerment. School leaders hold the potential and opportunity to engage parents in ways that support their efficacy as a sense of power. Delgado-Gaitan describes this power as "the capacity to produce intended, foreseen and unforeseen effects on others to accomplish results on behalf of one self." She goes on:

> How one utilizes power determines the extent to which individuals or organizations access valued resources. Many definitions characterize the notion of empowerment. The most common is related to self-esteem … the idea that empowerment means that people feel good about themselves. Empowerment is an ongoing, intentional process centered in the local community, involving mutual respect, critical reflection, caring and group participation through which people lacking an equal share of valued resources gain greater access. (p. 2)

Effective and meaningful partnerships between parents and schools requires sensitive, respectful, and caring school leaders willing to learn about the positive nature and culture of the community as well as identify barriers that have impeded progress in school-community relations. Johnstone and Hiatt's (1997) case study of a school-based parent center in a low-income bicultural community reveals parent surveys as a means to assess parents' and educators' needs prior to developing programs. Both parents and school personnel identified the principal as the key to establishing parent involvement as a school priority. In a related study focused on the critical role of school administrators and parent involvement, Cotton (2003) identified productive, proactive behaviors of principals of high-achieving schools as engaging parents and community members to help in the classroom, taking meetings to neighborhoods, arranging for teachers to ride school buses in order to meet parents, and using schools to serve as community centers.

Ibañez, Kuperminc, Jurkovic, and Perilla (2004) offer school leaders the use of the terms "cultural attributes" and "cultural adaptations" to guide their work with parents:

> Specifically, immigrants and their families bring with them culturally distinctive ways of perceiving and making sense of their reality (cultural attributes), but they also create new ways of understanding their surroundings (cultural adaptations). (pp. 559–560)

Their study examines perceived school experiences linked to achievement motivation. The findings from a sample of immigrant and U.S.-born Latino students across language-acculturation levels and generational status suggest that "perhaps, the key to motivating all Latino youth regardless of acculturation or generational status is based on relationships—relationships within the school and family micro-systems" (p. 566). The implications of this and other studies support the need for school leaders to create an environment in which parents feel free to express their concerns without the fear of being criticized or ignored, and school leaders play a critical role in creating such an environment.

Gonzalez, Huerta-Macias, and Tinajero (1998) indicate that outstanding school leaders lead by example, are responsible for implementing a culture of respect and recognition, and have a clear understanding of instructional practices that result in high expectations for all students. Outstanding school leaders substitute the conservative educational philosophy that promotes assimilating and "Americanizing" students with an "equal educational opportunity" perspective that recognizes the strengths and needs of minority students (Slavin & Calderon, 2001).

Culturally proficient school leaders view the school as being *of* the community, not just *in* the community. These leaders possess an inclusive worldview and are intentional in their use of the four tools of cultural proficiency to affect the culture of the school and the manner in which the school interacts with the community and the school's diverse constituency.

Closing the Achievement Gap Through Cultural Proficiency

Educational achievement gaps and the concomitant disjuncture of schools and bicultural communities represent historical and persistent patterns. If these gaps are to be closed, well-intended and well-informed educators and laypersons must make concerted efforts. The *achievement gaps* and *disconnection of schools and community* must be viewed as *our* issue. *Our* must include educators, educational policymakers, parents, scholars, and interested activists. The issue of the academic underperformance of bicultural children is nothing new. When focusing on our practices as educators, we can make a difference for our students and their communities if we pay attention to who they are and what their particular needs are, rather than to our needs or the needs of the school system. As indicated in the opening to this chapter, Cross and his colleagues (1989) provide the tools of cultural proficiency to guide us in responding to issues arising from the diversity in our schools and other organizations.

Cultural proficiency is about being effective in cross-cultural situations. Cultural proficiency is concerned with educating all students to high levels through knowing, valuing, and using their cultural backgrounds, languages, and learning styles within the context of our teaching. A central tenet of cultural proficiency holds that change is an *inside-out* process in which a person is, first and foremost, a student of his or her own assumptions. One must be able to recognize one's own assumptions in order to retain those that facilitate culturally proficient actions and to change those that impede such actions. Similarly, educators apply this *inside-out* process to examine school policies and practices that either impede or facilitate cultural proficiency. It is this ability to examine one's self and the organization that is fundamental to addressing educational disparity issues.

Cultural proficiency provides a comprehensive, systemic structure for school leaders, parents, and interested community members to discuss issues facing their schools. The four tools of cultural proficiency provide the means to assess and change one's own values and behaviors and a school's policies and practices in a way that better serves our society. Cultural proficiency has little to do with the outcomes we intend with our policies and practices and everything to do with the outcomes we actually get. The Parent and Community Communication and Outreach Rubric in this chapter presents the tools of cultural proficiency to be used to examine the levels of parent involvement in your school. If a self-study using the rubric leads educators to data or outcomes that are unacceptable, the tools of cultural proficiency will help refocus the lens of intentions to get outcomes that better serve the needs of students.

The Four Tools of Cultural Proficiency

Cultural proficiency is a mindset, a worldview. For those who commit to culturally proficient practices it represents a paradigmatic shift from viewing others as problematic to viewing how one works with people different from one's self in a manner to ensure effective practices. Cultural proficiency is composed of an interrelated set of four tools, which when used authentically, provides one with the opportunity to improve one's own practice in service of others. Just as cultural proficiency is *not* a program, the tools of cultural proficiency are *not* strategies or techniques. The tools provide you with the means by which to perform your professional responsibilities in a culturally proficient manner. Being culturally competent or proficient is exemplified by how one interacts with parents and community members.

The tools of cultural proficiency—the barriers, the guiding principles, the continuum, and the essential elements—combine to provide you with a framework for analyzing your values and behaviors as well as your school's policies and practices. The following is a description of the appropriate use of the four tools, which are named in this list:

- Identifying the Barriers to Cultural Proficiency provides persons and their organizations with tools to overcome resistance to change.

- The Guiding Principles of Cultural Proficiency serve as a means for a person or organization to identify their core values as they relate to issues of diversity.
- The Cultural Proficiency Continuum provides language to describe unhealthy and healthy *values and behaviors* of persons and *policies and practices* of organizations. In addition, the continuum can help you assess your current state and project your desired state. Movement along the continuum represents a shift in thinking from holding the view of *tolerating diversity* to *transformation for equity.* This is not a subtle shift in worldview; it is paradigmatic.
- Taking action by using the Parent and Community Communication and Outreach Rubric

Planning and implementing a culturally proficient parent involvement component is a three-step process. First, school leaders must provide opportunities for school and community members to examine current processes and procedures. The Barriers to Cultural Proficiency help bring to the surface deeply held assumptions and values that may serve as obstacles to bicultural students and their families. The Guiding Principles provide core values foundational to working effectively in bicultural schools and communities. The Cultural Proficiency Continuum and the elements of cultural proficiency provide the structure for self and organizational assessment toward culturally proficient parent involvement practices. Finally, the Parent and Community Communication and Outreach Rubric offers the opportunity to further assess and plan for action toward new behaviors that recognize and include students' and families' cultural attributes within appropriate cultural adaptations of the school environment.

Step One: Identifying the Barriers to Cultural Proficiency. Whether one begins the study of cultural proficiency with the barriers, the guiding principles, the continuum, or the essential elements is somewhat immaterial. However, what is germane is that for one to be effective with the tools of cultural proficiency, one must engage in personal and organizational self-analysis or self-study. Consideration of the barriers to, as well as the guiding principles of, cultural proficiency is fundamental to understanding one's own underlying assumptions and motivation. The barriers and guiding principles serve as the yin and yang of cultural proficiency. The former defines the resistant forces and the latter the supporting forces. For school leaders, understanding both forces is fundamental to developing effective personal and systemic leadership practices.

In the manner that the guiding principles provide a moral compass for culturally proficient actions, there are barriers to achieving culturally proficient actions. The barriers to cultural proficiency are

- resistance to change,
- systems of oppression, and
- a sense of entitlement.

These barriers are often manifested in statements such as *It is not I who needs to change. I have been a successful educator for years; these kids/parents just need to get a clue!* Similarly, it is rare to find the person who doesn't acknowledge that racism, ethnocentrism, classism, and sexism exist in our society, but what they often fail to see is that when one group of people loses rights and privileges because of systemic oppression, those rights and privileges accrue to others in often unacknowledged or unrecognized ways. It is when one recognizes one's entitlement that one has the ability to make choices that benefit the education of children and youth.

A conversation gap exists among most educational policymakers and educators when focusing on the achievement issues of bicultural students. The gap in conversation, often unrecognized and unacknowledged, results from educators not having the perspective to see roadblocks that have been, and are, placed in the way of bicultural students and parents. This selective invisibility leads to a sense of privilege and entitlement for members of the dominant group. Whereas systems of oppression impose barriers for bicultural members, concomitant systems of privilege and entitlement impose barriers for members of the dominant group. The barriers erected by a sense of privilege and entitlement involve a skewed sense of reality that can impede one's ability to pursue ethical and moral avenues in meeting the academic and social needs of bicultural members.

The position of privilege often fosters biased or ill-informed assumptions on the part of educators about parents from nondominant groups. Typical of such assumptions are comments such as the following:

- Their parents won't come to parent conferences because they don't care about the education of their children.
- Why try to help them, they will just end up as gangbangers, just like their dad!
- Why should I learn anything about their culture? This is our country; let them learn about us!

Educators who make comments like these are in need of different lenses, tools, and structures to help them understand their students and the barriers they face and the unique learning needs they have in order to be successful in school. Educators must engage in intentional conversations about how bicultural parents and students behave and learn. Cultural proficiency is an approach for surfacing educators' assumptions and values that undermine the success of some student groups and a lens for examining how we can include and honor the cultures and learning needs of all students in the educational process. Culturally proficient school leaders honor the cultural attributes of students and parents and provide opportunities for appropriate cultural adaptations to the school's environment.

Step Two: The Guiding Principles of Cultural Proficiency. The guiding principles provide a moral framework for the examination of the core values of schools and how espoused theory and theory in action differ when schools are undergoing academic self-study (Argyris, 1990; Schein, 1989). The guiding principles of cultural proficiency and school-based examples of each principle are the following:

- *Culture is a predominant force in people's and organization's lives.* For members of the dominant group, the cultural norms and expectations of schools are somewhat intuitive. School is a source of educators' power and privilege. The culturally proficient leader is mindful of the bicultural role that parents must play in being part of the school community and fosters an understanding of the values and behaviors of all parties, including those of the school. Holidays, religious observances, heroes, and historical figures are among examples of culture that affect educators, students, and parents.
- *People are served in varying degrees by the dominant culture.* Culturally proficient leaders are intentional in involving members of the dominant group, dominated groups, and emerging groups into processes of change that affect children and youth. Profiles of who is represented in the curriculum, achievement gaps, and transition rates into colleges and universities are examples of those best served by dominant-group members who predominate in the writing of curricular materials and provide the greatest number of educators.
- *People have group identities and individual identities.* Culturally proficient leaders strive to guarantee the dignity of each person and that person's culture.

Each educator, parent, guardian, student, and community member is an individual person with an identity that makes him or her unique. At the same time, these individuals have a gender identity, have a sexual orientation, may be a member of a religious group, knows his or her racial/ethnic background, and most likely is a member of formal and informal groups. In our elementary schools we know the 2nd graders from the 5th *graders.* Likewise, in our secondary schools we can often distinguish the athletes from the Spanish Club participants (though there may be some overlap).

- *Diversity within cultures is vast and significant.* Within the categories *Latino, Hispanic, Asian,* and *African American* there are numerous ethnic, religious, gender, and social-class groups, among others. Within school districts we often speak of the organizational cultural differences among schools or among the grade levels or departments within the same school. Culturally proficient leaders work with colleagues to foster inclusive environments of trust and safety for educators, students, and parents.
- *Each cultural group has unique cultural needs.* Among the many cultural needs we experience in our schools are varied learning needs, different holidays to celebrate, and gender roles that differ. Members of the dominant group can be assured that their history and culture will be reflected in the school curricula, whereas that is often not the case with members of bicultural groups. Culturally proficient leaders work with their colleagues to make necessary adaptations in how schools provide services to bicultural communities.

In Lindsey and colleagues (2005), the authors note:

> Understanding and acknowledging the five principles and choosing to manifest them in your behavior are demonstrations of culturally proficient leadership. The choice you make to align your leadership actions with the five principles of cultural pro- ficiency communicates a strong message throughout your school's community that you value diversity and fully expect that every individual will do the same. Indeed, the guiding principles are attitudinal benchmarks that enable you and others to assess progress toward acknowledging and valuing cultural differences, and while this assess- ment yields crucial information, it is insufficient by itself in provoking the develop- ment of culturally proficient behaviors. (p. 52)

The guiding principles provide a framework for how the diversity of students informs professional practice in responding to student learning needs. A school or district's mission, vision, or belief statement is a good place to see if the stated val- ues align with predominant behaviors in the school/district. Most likely you will encounter phrases such as *all students, valuing diversity, 21st-century education,* or *responsible citizen.* The challenge is to align stated values with the behaviors of educators. The cultural proficiency continuum and essential elements of cultural competence provide a framework for aligning personal values and organizational policies in service of bicultural communities.

Step Three: The Cultural Proficiency Continuum. Culturally proficient educators are attentive to the barriers that restrict their and their fellow educators' effectiveness and are intentional in their use of the guiding principles as core values to performing their work. The continuum and essential elements are tools that allow educators to assess their own and their colleagues' behaviors, as well as the school's organizational practices. The continuum provides the opportunity to locate unhealthy and healthy behaviors and practices. The five essential elements serve as standards in developing healthy behaviors, policies, and practices for working with bicultural communities.

The first three points of the continuum (Cultural Destructiveness, Cultural Incapacity, Cultural Blindness) focus on *them* as being problematic and the next three (Cultural Precompetence, Cultural Competence, Cultural Proficiency) focus on our *practice* The first three points on the continuum may find us referring to our students as *underperforming*, while the next three would find us referring to the ways in which we are *underserving* our students and their communities (the inside-out approach). The six points of the continuum are represented across the top of Table 3.1, with brief summary descriptions. The following five rows of the continuum will be explained in greater detail below.

The continuum provides culturally proficient leaders with a frame of reference for viewing their work. Using the continuum as a component of the mental model of cultural proficiency, leaders can assess their and their colleagues' behavior and be intentional in choosing future actions. The five essential elements of cultural competence provide guidance in selecting those future actions.

Step Four: Taking Action by Using the Parent and Community Communication and Outreach Rubric. Culturally proficient leaders use the Parent and Community Communication and Outreach Rubric (Table 3.1) to assess where they and their school are with regard to parent and community communication and outreach. Once they locate their place, or range of places, on the rubric they look across the rubric to garner ideas for future directions. It must be noted that the rubric is not a stand-alone tool or activity. Deep consideration of the barriers and guiding principles, or similarly stated values, must precede use of the rubric for it to be effective.

Table 3.1 presents the Parent and Community Communication and Outreach Rubric. Under the first column are operational descriptions of parent and community outreach and communication for each essential element. The guide for how to read the rubric follows the rubric.

Table 3.1. Parent and Community Communication and Outreach Rubric

	Cultural Destructiveness	Cultural Incapacity	Cultural Blindness	Cultural Precompetence	Cultural Competence	Cultural Proficiency
Operational Definitions for Essential Elements of Cultural Competence				*Operational definitions for points of the continuum*		
	Seeking to eliminate vestiges of the cultures of others	Seeking to make the culture of others appear to be wrong	Refusing to acknowledge the culture of others	Being aware of what one doesn't know about working in diverse settings. Initial levels of awareness after which a person/organization can move in a positive, constructive direction or can falter, stop, and possibly regress	Viewing one's personal and organizational work as an interactive arrangement in which the educator enters into diverse settings in a manner that is additive to cultures different from the educator's	Making the commitment to lifelong learning for the purpose of being increasingly effective in serving the social justice needs of cultural groups. Holding the vision of what can be and committing to assessments that serve as benchmarks on the road to student success
1. Assessing Cultural Knowledge—extent to which community involvement facilitates the identification, assessment, and development of cultural identity	Ignore, intimidate, or punish the expression of needs of diverse parent/ community groups.	Help culturally diverse parent and community members by purposefully assimilating them into the dominant culture.	Parent, community, and school leaders are from select communities without regard to different cultural groups.	Recognizing the importance of knowing about each other's cultures, parent, community, and school leaders may learn about each other in authentic ways.	Parent, community, and school leaders learn about each other's cultures in order to bridge the gaps between and among home, community, and school cultures.	Parent, community, and school leaders continually scan the environment in order to be responsive to ever-changing community demographics.

(continued)

Table 3.1. (continued)

	Cultural Destructiveness	Cultural Incapacity	Cultural Blindness	Cultural Precompetence	Cultural Competence	Cultural Proficiency
			Operational definitions for points of the continuum			
2. Valuing Diversity—extent to which parent and community diversity is valued	Actively prevent involvement of different cultural groups in making decisions about programs and services that meet the needs of all students.	Identify parents and community members to remediate their cultural deficiencies.	Parent and community involvement is responsive to legal mandates without respect to different cultural groups.	Recognizing the need to involve culturally diverse community groups in decision making; may include some but not all groups appropriately.	Involve representative constituencies of parents and community members as partners in making decisions about programs and services that meet the needs of all students.	Representative constituencies of parents and community members advocate closing achievement gaps and develop and model advocacy for social justice practices.
3. Managing the Dynamics of Difference—extent to which community involvement efforts develop the capacity to mediate cultural conflict between and among diverse parent/community groups and the school	Sabotage involvement of some parent groups by instigating competition for scarce resources that results in intergroup conflict.	Ignore parent and community groups that are working to address issues important to them.	Facilitate groups working together to find common ground on divisive issues.	Recognizing emerging intergroup conflict, staff and community leaders may develop conflict resolution strategies or identify *key liaisons* within diverse cultural groups.	Create a culture that encourages multiple perspectives and builds capacity for and practices dialogue between and among all community, parent, and school groups.	Staff, parents, and community groups work together to anticipate the needs of the ever-changing community and associated issues.

4. Adapting to Diversity—extent to which people and schools change to meet the needs of the community	Parents or school staff prevent changes intended to benefit culturally different community and student groups.	Parents and school staff consider meeting the needs of culturally different groups as divisive.	Parents and school staff do not acknowledge the need to meet the needs of culturally different community groups.	Recognizing differences between home and school cultures, parent community and school leaders may begin to address the needs of diverse community populations.	Parents and school staff work together to identify and address the needs of diverse cultural populations.	Staff, parents, and community work together to meet the needs of all cultural groups and anticipate and plan for changes within the community.
5. Institutionalizing—extent to which people and schools integrate knowledge about diverse community and organizational cultures into daily practice	School staff create policies and practices that systematically exclude culturally different parent groups from being involved in important decisions about the education of their children.	Changes to meet diverse student needs are seen as against the status quo and the assimilation of different cultural groups.	School staff supports and sponsors traditional parent and community organizations, and governmental mandates, believing they serve all cultural groups.	Recognizing parent and community needs as they arise and may develop structures to respond to the needs.	Creates structures that address the diverse cultural needs of the school, parents, and community groups and assesses effectiveness in meeting those needs.	Parent and community groups provide ongoing meaningful contributions to decisions, policies, and practices that serve the diverse needs of the community.

Source: Lindsey, Graham, Westphal, & Jew (2008)

How to read Table 3.1, the Parent and Community Communication and Outreach Rubric:

- Note that the rubric is composed of rows and columns.
- Each of the rows is one of the five standards referred to as an *essential element of cultural competence.*
- There are seven columns. At the top of the first column is the title "Operational Definitions for Essential Elements of Cultural Competence." A brief description of the element is given in the context of the topic, working with parents and community.
- Each of the next six columns is one of the six points of the Cultural Proficiency Continuum.
- The fifth column of these six is titled "Cultural Competence." Each of the descriptors in that column covers one of the essential elements of cultural competence. The language is in active voice and describes actions that can be taken today in schools.
- The sixth column of the six is titled "Cultural Proficiency." The description is future focused and measurable.

The rubric provides leaders with a template for action. To reiterate, the development of the rubric is not a "stand-alone" activity for school leaders and their communities. The rubric is an action tool to assessment progress toward clearly defined goals focused on improving student achievement. Effective use of the rubric is dependent upon deep level conversations that emerge from using the four tools for cultural proficiency.

Breaking the Cycle of Social Injustice

What will it take to build a system of learning that liberates and supports thinking for all learners irrespective of ethnicity, gender, class, or sexual orientation? We believe it will take educators like you and like us who are deliberate and purposeful about breaking the cycle of social injustice throughout the educational system.

School districts across the United States are filled with well-intentioned teachers, counselors, and administrators who do good work, but are unaware that their beliefs, values, and assumptions may, in fact, serve as barriers for many learners. Those barriers may manifest themselves as traditional structures, schedules, and procedures for parent involvement. Cultural proficiency is a systems approach that asks leaders to closely examine why we do what we do. In other words, the question for culturally proficient leaders becomes, In what ways might our infrastructure and daily practices honor or dishonor the cultural attributes of our students and their families?

Cultural proficiency is an approach that challenges educators to surface and examine those deeply held assumptions about how students are served in the classrooms and in their communities. Educators must be willing to have difficult conversations, confront the issues of racism and socioeconomic disparity, and develop the skills to lead and support each other to do whatever it takes to liberate the goodness and genius of all children for the world (Lindsey, Martinez, & Lindsey, 2007). Culturally proficient schools exist within a community of members who recognize the cultural attributes of both home and school and are willing and able to adapt the school environment in support of students and their families.

Discussion Questions

1. Describe the shift from traditional parent involvement programs to culturally proficient parent involvement as described in this chapter. What do you see as the fundamental differences between traditional and culturally proficient parent involvement? In what ways are educators' and parents' roles changed by this shift?
2. In what ways might this chapter inform your work with parents in your school community? What practices would you change? Why? What new practices would you need to learn? How will the new practices benefit parents in your school? How will the new practices benefit the students in your school?
3. Using the Parent and Community and Outreach Rubric, describe current practices in your school and community and place them on the rubric. How might you use the rubric to inform your future practices?

Suggested Readings

Hilliard, A. (1991). Do we have the will to educate all children? *Educational Leadership*, *40*(1), 31–36.

Lindsey, R. B., Graham, S. M., Westphal, C. R., & Jew, C. L. (2008). *Culturally proficient inquiry: A lens for identifying and examining educational gaps*. Thousand Oaks, CA: Corwin Press.

Nieto, S. (2008). *Affirming diversity: The sociopolitical context of multicultural education* (5th ed.). New York: Longman.

Olivos, E. M. (2004). Tensions, contradictions, and resistance: An activist's reflection of the struggles of Latino parents in the public school system. *High School Journal, 87*(4), 25–36.

Trumbull, E., Rothstein-Fisch, C., Greenfield, P. M., & Quiroz, B. (2001). *Bridging cultures between home and school: A guide for teachers.* Mahwah, NJ: Lawrence Erlbaum.

References

Argyris, C. (1990). *Overcoming organizational defenses: Facilitating organizational defenses.* Englewood Cliffs, NJ: Prentice Hall.

Battle-Bailey, L. (2004). Interactive homework for increasing parent involvement and reading achievement. *Childhood Education, 81*(1), 36–41.

Canales, P., & Harris, J. (2004). Migrant service coordination: Effective field-based practices. In C. Salinas & M .E. Franquiz (Eds.), *Scholars in the field: The challenges of migrant education* (pp. 61–76). Charleston, WV: AEL. (ERIC Document RC 024 216).

Cotton, K. (2003). *Principals and student achievement: What the research says.* Alexandria, VA: Association for Supervision and Curriculum Development.

Cross, T., Bazron, B., Dennis, K., & Isaacs, M. (1989). *Toward a culturally competent system of care* (Vol. 1). Washington, DC: Georgetown University Child Development Program, Child and Adolescent Service System Program.

Delgado-Gaitan, C. (1994). Consejos: The power of cultural narratives. *Anthropology and Education Quarterly, 25*(3), 298–316.

Gonzalez, R. (2002). *The No Child Left Behind Act: Implications for local educators and advocates for Latino students, families, and communities.* Issue brief No. No-8). Washington, DC: National Council of La Raza.

Gonzalez, M. L., Huerta-Macias, M., & Tinajero, J. V. (Eds.). (1998). *Educating Latino students: A guide to successful practice.* Lancaster, PA: Technomics Publishing Company.

Ibañez, G. E., Kuperminc, G. P., Jurkovic, G., & Perilla, J. (2004). Cultural attributes and adaptations linked to achievement motivation among Latino adolescents. *Journal of Youth and Adolescence, 33*(6), 559.

Inger, M. (1992). *Increasing the school involvement of Hispanic parents. ERIC/CUE Digest No. 80* (No. EDO-UD-92-3). New York: ERIC Clearinghouse on Urban Education, Teachers College, Columbia University.

Johnstone, T. R., & Hiatt, D. B. (1997, March). *Development of a school-based parent center for low-income new immigrants.* Symposium conducted at the American Educational Research Association Annual Meeting, Chicago.

Lawson, M. A. (2003). School-family relations in context: Parent and teacher perceptions of parent involvement. *Urban Education, 38*(1), 77–133.

Lindsey, D. B., Martinez, R. S., & Lindsey, R. B. (2007). *Culturally proficient coaching: Supporting educators to create equitable schools.* Thousand Oaks, CA: Corwin Press.

Lindsey, R. B., Roberts, L., & Campbell-Jones, F. (2005). *Culturally proficient schools: An implementation guide for school leaders.* Thousand Oaks, CA: Corwin Press.

Lindsey, R. B., Graham, S. M., Westphal, Jr., C. R., & Jew, C. L. (2008). *Culturally proficient inquiry: A lens for identifying and examining educational gaps.* Thousand Oaks, CA: Corwin Press.

Olivos, E. M. (2006). *The power of parents: A critical perspective of bicultural parent involvement in public schools.* New York: Peter Lang.

Pena, D. C. (2000). Parent involvement: Influencing factors and implications. *Journal of Educational Research, 94*(1), 42–54.

Quezada, R. L., Diaz, D. M., & Sanchez, M. (2003). Involving Latino parent: Getting Latino parents involved in educational activities with their children hasn't always been a priority for schools. *Leadership, 33*(1), 32–34.

Schein, E. (1989). *Organizational culture and leadership: A dynamic view.* San Francisco: Jossey-Bass.

Scribner, J. D., Young, M. D., & Pedroza, A. (1999). *Building collaborative relationships with parents.* New York: Teachers College Press.

Sheldon, S. B., & Epstein, J. L. (2005). Involvement counts: Family and community partnerships and mathematics achievement. *Journal of Educational Research, 98*(4), 196–206.

Slavin, R. E., & Calderon, M. (Eds.). (2001). *Effective programs for Latino students.* Mahwah, NJ: Lawrence Erlbaum.

4

Using Family Stories to Foster Parent and Preservice Teacher Relationships

Maria Lombos Wlazlinski and Jim Cummins

In the living room of the Martínezes' home, Katie, a senior preservice teacher, asked Ana Martínez, *"¿Cómo debemos contar su cuento?"* (How should we tell your story?). That afternoon, they were considering ways to write and present the Martínez family life history. This scenario was replayed in many more homes as 54 other preservice teachers fulfilled a course assignment entitled Family Narrative Project: Preservice Teachers and Latino Parents as Co-authors/Historias de la Vida de Familia: Estudiantes de Educacion y Familias como Co-autores.

As linguistic and cultural diversity increases throughout the United States (and elsewhere), teacher education programs are faced with the challenge not only of preparing teachers to instruct a diverse student body but also to work in partnership with bicultural parents whose knowledge of English and previous educational opportunities may be limited. The challenge for teacher education programs is evident in the fact that according to the National Center for Education Statistics (1999), only 20% of teachers expressed confidence in working with children from diverse backgrounds. Although some states have incorporated required English for Speakers of Other Languages (ESOL)–focused courses into preservice education, in general, teacher education programs seldom provide preservice teachers with opportunities to work effectively with parents from diverse backgrounds (Hiatt-Michael, 2001).

In this chapter, we describe a project that enabled bicultural parents and preservice teachers to learn from each other in the context of writing family life histories. The project was conceived and initially implemented in spring 2002 by Mae Lombos Wlazlinski in the context of the undergraduate teacher education program of Berry College's Charter School of Education and Human Sciences in Rome, Georgia. The Family Narrative Project or El Proyecto de Historias de la Vida de Familia was included as one of the requirements of an ESOL course that all preservice teachers had to take. The significance of the project derives from the fact that it challenged the pattern of coercive power relations that frames the experiences of subordinated communities in the wider society. The project provided a medium for the voices of bicultural parents and children to be expressed and heard, thereby promoting a process of *empowerment*, understood as the collaborative creation of power (Cummins, 2001).

Power Relations and School Achievement

Extensive research has been carried out by sociologists and anthropologists on issues related to ethnicity and educational achievement (e.g., Bishop & Berryman, 2006; McCarty, 2002; Ogbu, 1978, 1992; Portes & Rumbaut, 2001; Skutnabb-Kangas, 2000). These studies point clearly to the centrality of societal power relations in explaining patterns of minority-group achievement. Groups that experience long-term educational underachievement tend to have experienced material and symbolic violence at the hands of the dominant societal group over generations. Ladson-Billings (1995) expresses the point succinctly with respect to African American students: "The problem that African-American students face is the constant devaluation of their culture both in school and in the larger society" (p. 485). A direct implication is that in order to reverse this pattern of underachievement, educators, both individually and collectively, must challenge the operation of coercive power relations in the interactions they orchestrate with bicultural students and parents.

Societal power relations express themselves in the classroom and in teacher-parent interactions through the process of identity negotiation (Cummins, 2001). The ways in which teachers negotiate identities with students and their parents can exert a significant impact on the extent to which students will engage academically or withdraw from academic effort. The intersection of societal power relations and identity negotiation in determining patterns of academic achievement among bicultural students is expressed in Figure 4.1 (adapted from Cummins, 2001).

This framework proposes that relations of power in the wider society, which span a continuum from coercive to collaborative, influence both the ways in which educators define their roles and the types of structures that are established in the

Figure 4.1. Societal power relations, identity negotiation, and academic achievement

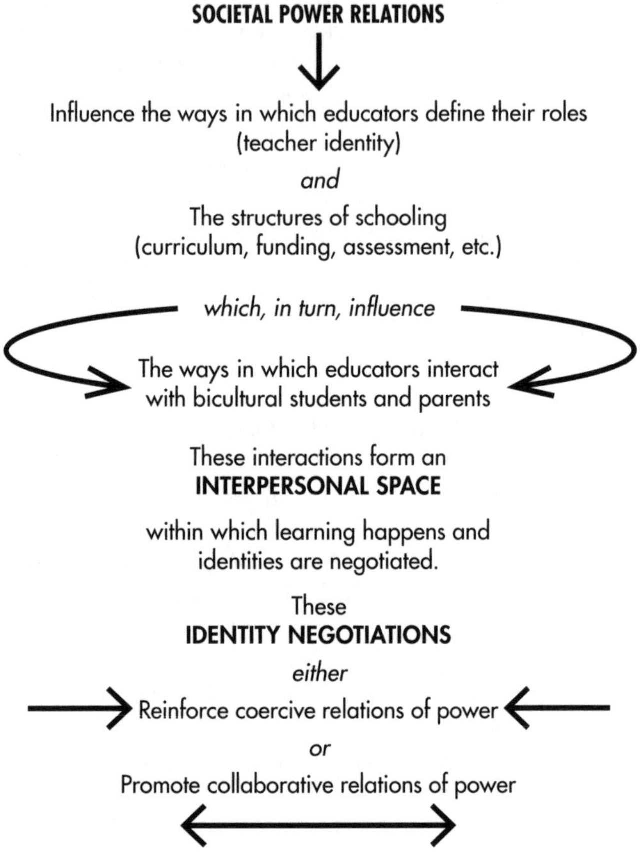

SOCIETAL POWER RELATIONS

↓

Influence the ways in which educators define their roles
(teacher identity)

and

The structures of schooling
(curriculum, funding, assessment, etc.)

which, in turn, influence

The ways in which educators interact
with bicultural students and parents

These interactions form an
INTERPERSONAL SPACE

within which learning happens and
identities are negotiated.

These
IDENTITY NEGOTIATIONS

either

⟶ Reinforce coercive relations of power ⟵

or

Promote collaborative relations of power

⟵⟶

educational system. *Role definitions* refers to the mindset of expectations, assumptions, and goals that educators bring to the task of educating culturally and linguistically diverse students. *Educational structures* refers to the general organization of schooling, including curriculum, assessment, and parental involvement; for example, to what extent does the school take concrete steps (e.g., provision of information in different languages, interpreters for meetings) to support the involvement of bicultural parents in their children's schooling?

Coercive relations of power refer to the exercise of power by a dominant individual, group, or country to the detriment of a subordinated individual, group, or country. For example, in the past, dominant-group institutions, such as schools, have required that subordinated groups deny their cultural identity and give up their languages as a necessary condition for success in the "mainstream" society.

Collaborative relations of power, by contrast, reflect the sense of the term *power* that refers to "being enabled," or "empowered" to achieve more. Within collaborative relations of power, power is not a fixed quantity but is generated through interaction with others. The more empowered one individual or group becomes, the more is generated for others to share, as is the case when two people care for each other or when we really connect with the students we are teaching. Within this context, the term *empowerment* can be defined as *the collaborative creation of power*. Students whose schooling experiences reflect collaborative relations of power participate confidently in instruction as a result of the fact that their sense of identity is being affirmed and extended in their interactions with educators. They also know that their voices will be heard and respected within the classroom. Schooling amplifies rather than silences their power of self-expression.

As illustrated in the case study of the Family Narrative Project (FNP) discussed later in this chapter, the same power dynamics operate in the interactions between teachers and parents. When parents feel respected by the teacher, they grow in confidence and in their understanding that they too are educators of their children. Children benefit from this in multiple ways: (a) as a result of their interaction with parents who feel empowered, (b) as a result of their direct participation in the parent-teacher partnership activities and interactions, and (c) as a result of their teachers' greater understanding of their background and experience.

Parental Involvement Through Experiential Narratives

There is a considerable literature on the importance of parental involvement for the success of culturally and linguistically diverse students (e.g., Ada, 2003; Ada & Campoy, 2004; Ada & Zubizarreta, 2001; Bernhard et al., 2006; Delgado-Gaitan, 1991; Epstein et al., 2002; Fashola, Slavin, Calderon, & Duran, 1996; McCaleb, 1997; Valdes, 1996; Wlazlinski, 2004). Yet the design and implementation of successful programs remains elusive, and particularly so in the case of partnership programs with bicultural parents.

The FNP drew its inspiration from previous work in the area of critical literacy and transformative education. Of particular importance was Ada's (2003) creative reading model. The model involves four phases. First is the *descriptive phase* in which readers focus on information contained in the text such as theme, characters, setting, and plot. Second is the *personal interpretive phase* in which readers relate the information to their own experiences, knowledge, and interests.

Third, the *critical/multicultural/anti-bias phase* orients readers to critically analyze issues or problems arising from the text. Readers might explore whose voices are included and whose are excluded from the text, how other cultures will interpret the message, and what the author's motives are in writing the piece. Finally, in the *transformative phase* readers evaluate the insights gained from the text in order to take action that will benefit society.

Ada's creative reading model was used in helping the preservice teachers involved in FNP to prepare for their collaborative writing with parents. The research strategy of narrative inquiry (Clandinin & Connelly, 1994) also informed the design and implementation of the project. Narrative inquiry strives for meaning and insight on the basis of a story constructed collaboratively out of the lives and experiences of both researcher and participant. Clandinin and Connelly argue that "people live stories, and in the telling of them reaffirm them, modify them, and create new ones. . . . Stories educate the self and the others" (p. 415). These reconstructed stories offer a means for participants to make sense of their experiences. In the case of the FNP, the collaborative construction of family stories enabled previously silenced voices to find expression and validation in a "mainstream" medium.

Based on her own practice as an elementary school teacher and influenced by the work of Alma Flor Ada (2003), Sudia McCaleb (1997) documented the empowering potential of family narratives for Latino parents and children. She points out that the collaborative creation of family books in which parents can share their experiences helps foster feelings of admiration and respect among their children:

> Children need to know that their parents are problem solvers. They need to hear about their struggles and to find out what knowledge and reasoning process their parents used to solve a problem. In this way, they can gain greater admiration and respect for their parents, even though their parents had little formal schooling. (pp. 108–109)

Also drawing inspiration from the work of Ada (2003) and Ada and Campoy (2004), Judith Bernhard and colleagues (Bernhard et al., 2006) documented the positive impact of an innovative language intervention program, entitled the Early Authors Program (EAP), involving the creation of bilingual books authored by students and family members. The EAP was first implemented in Miami-Dade County, Florida, with the goal of promoting early bilingual literacy in preschool children. In the course of the program, 1,179 children from 800 families in 32 early childhood centers were exposed to bilingual literacy development through writing and illustrating their own dual language books in which they themselves appeared as the protagonists. The books, which were written in English and the home languages of the children (usually Spanish or Haitian Creole), were based on family histories, the children's lives, and the children's interests. Parents, family members, and 57 educators also wrote books. In all, a total of 3,286 books were produced. The evaluation of the program used a pretest-posttest experimental design and random selection of children for both experimental and control groups. Bernhard et al. reported that the EAP students performed at a significantly higher level on a variety of language measures. Observations from the literacy specialists involved in the program highlighted the impact of the program on the self-esteem of children and family members. As expressed by one Spanish-English bilingual literacy specialist:

> I think that the program was absolutely an amazing experience, and I was honored and privileged to be a part of it. I see its value, and I really hope that the outcomes of what we feel have been very successful, really show as a success . . . because I see the success in the parents, I see it in the teachers, I see it in the students, . . . I feel that the growth on the emotional end of the Early Authors Program is huge with parents, caregivers, students, the literacy specialists themselves. I think that that's where the value lies. (p. 2398)

In short, the FNP built on previous theoretical and empirical work that pointed to family narrative creation as potentially empowering for parents, students, and teachers. Validation of parents' experiences and cultural knowledge clearly challenges the devaluation of community identity in the wider society and thus addresses the underlying causes of underachievement among bicultural students (Cummins, 2001). The FNP goes beyond previous projects by introducing collaborative family narrative creation at the preservice level.

The Story of the Family Narrative Project

In the spirit of narrative, the story of the FNP is recounted in the sections that follow by Mae Lombos Wlazlinski, coauthor of this chapter who designed the project.

Origins. The foundation for the FNP was laid in spring 2002. This was the 1st year Berry College School of Education awarded degrees in early childhood, middle grades, and secondary with ESOL endorsement. For the first time, students were required to take a course entitled ESOL Applications and Synthesis, which was scheduled during the last 7 weeks of the senior year. Not surprisingly, an ESOL methods and curriculum course was the last thing that students expected and desired. The timing was a serious mistake in programmatic planning, but the students had to take and pass it to graduate. The course requirements competed for space in students' lives with graduation preparation, program portfolio completion, job fairs, wedding plans, and so on. As part of the course, I created an assignment that required students to interview families from diverse backgrounds about their life in their home country, their life experiences in the United States, their difficulties dealing with school and teachers, and their aspirations for their children. This assignment was deeply resented and severely resisted.

I made the initial arrangements with families and the students followed up on them. English and Spanish interview questions were given to all students. Two bilingual interpreters provided assistance for those students who interviewed families who did not speak English at all. Children who could speak English assisted their parents with translation.

Paternalistic and dominant-culture attitudes were evident in some of the written transcripts of interviews and in the summaries written by students. However, also in evidence were themes such as students' disbelief of what parents had to go through to come to this country, admiration for their determination to work for a living, surprise at the families' pride in their homes, and satisfaction that the families regarded the United States as the land of opportunity. These initial results demonstrated the value of home-school collaboration for self- and social transformation (Wink, 2000) and also established the relevance of the assignment for teacher education.

Two semesters later, the FNP was born. When I introduced the FNP assignment, my goal was to demonstrate to my preservice students that it was not only possible but essential to communicate respectfully and effectively with bicultural families. Many students reacted initially that they could not possibly talk to Latino parents, because they did not speak their language. As a teacher educator, I thought if I did not provide the opportunity while the teachers and teacher candidates were in training, then how and when would they learn to have a dialogue with the families?

The goals of the FNP assignment were to (a) sensitize preservice teachers to the value of being able to communicate and establish respectful relationships with Latino parents, (b) create books that are cathartic and validating of life histories, and (c) provide professional growth opportunities to preservice teachers. The FNP also aimed to provide preservice teachers with the opportunity to become allies, partners who are "grateful for what [they] are learning and receiving in the process: a deepening ability to connect with other human beings" (Ada & Campoy, 2004, p. 27).

The FNP consisted of two phases. The first phase was the co-creation of story books by the parents and the preservice teachers. This involved life-history interviewing (Agosín, 1999), reading of story books with themes that were relevant to the family's experiences and immigration situation, and collaboratively writing the family history.

The story books, which were predominantly picture books, provided models for theme selection and presentation style for the family history books, or *historias*. The interview, on the other hand, shaped the plot of the *historias*. Interview questions, which were both in Spanish and in English, brought memories to the surface. Specifically, they elicited participants' experiences with the English language, language use at home, formal schooling, their children's teachers' attitudes toward them, immigration, work histories in the home country and in the United States, discrimination because of their ethnicity, and adjustment in the United States. Upon completion of the interviews, I subjected parents' responses to thematic data analysis (Bogdan & Biklen, 1998).

The next phase began after the preservice teachers and families had completed their books. During this phase, the preservice teachers reflected on and wrote about the significance of the assignment for their personal and professional development. As I had done with the parents' responses, I also subjected the preservice teachers' reflections to thematic data analysis. I created a list of thematic codes such as cross-cultural awareness, respect, and understanding of the parents, lessons learned, and sensitivity to students' and parents' needs.

Getting Started. Fifty-five preservice teachers were enrolled in my course, Methods and Materials of Teaching ESOL. These students worked with 51 families who agreed to participate in the project. All but six of the preservice teachers were graduating seniors and had already gone for job interviews. Some had interviewed in school districts that were largely populated by Latino students. The preservice teachers' ages ranged from 19 to 21. The Latino parents' ages were between 30 and 38.

In class, the preservice teachers and the instructor discussed an outline and rubric for the project, as well as the parent interview questions in English and Spanish, which asked parents about their life experiences. The parents' responses were intended to provide the plot for the book-writing project. We also clarified the procedures, and I explained my expectations. The preservice teachers asked questions and expressed their concerns. Their strong dislike for the project was palpable. However, a few preservice teachers came around and took the first step, which was to choose thematic picture books to read with the families and to use as a model for the family books that they would co-author. In the following days, other preservice teachers brought thematic picture books to class and asked for feedback concerning the appropriateness of the topic. I also provided a list of thematic book titles and brought in multicultural books from my personal library.

The preservice teachers arranged introductory meetings with the Latino families through the ESOL teachers in schools where they were doing their field experience, the migrant education coordinator, instructors of church-sponsored adult ESL classes, church staff, or neighbors. Three students chose to work with Latino families they already knew. To prepare themselves for the encounters with families, the preservice teachers learned basic conversational phrases in Spanish, which they used to establish affinity and break the ice. The preservice teachers and the family shared photographs and exchanged phone calls and emails.

Most of the preservice teachers had an easy time finding their families, setting up a schedule, and getting the project off the ground. However, a number of challenges had to be overcome. In the first place, some preservice teachers believed asking about the families' lives was an invasion of privacy. Also, only two students who were Spanish majors could go beyond basic Spanish to communicate with parents, with the result that some parents relied heavily on their children for translation. Finally, the project was supported by only a minority of ESOL teachers who served as cooperating teachers for the preservice program and was actively resisted by one school administrator in a school with a significant Latino population. Thus, the FNP was beyond the comfort zone not only for many of the participating preservice teachers but also for experienced professionals in the field.

The following assignment guidelines were provided to all participants:

1. Introduce yourself and try to get to know the family first. Welcome questions from the family about you.
2. Use the interview questions (I provided you) to guide you in getting to know and collecting information from the family. You should be able to ask additional questions as the situations allow.
3. After your interview, ask the family to look at some children's books whose themes include coming to America, survival in a foreign land, immigration, families, and cultural practices and traditions and tell them this will provide ideas for their books. Then ask parents how they would like to write their story; if they ask you to write it, tell your family that you will write their story up and come back to show it to them. Ask if there are pictures they would like to share or would some be interested in illustrating or drawing to decorate the pages of the book.
4. Come back with the typed-up text (16-size font is good). Read it to them and ask if there is anything they want to change. Ask if you were able to capture their intended meaning. At this time plan the layout of the book. Be ready to cut up the text into strips.
5. Arrange the strips and pictures according to the layout you and the family agreed to use.
6. Glue pictures and text strips down.

7. Design the book cover together.
8. Ask your family about their final thoughts about the total experience: how they feel about talking to you about their life story and creating the book.
9. Write a description of the whole process. Reflect on the whole experience and on how the assignment has helped your growth as a teacher.

Since the preservice teachers were "sponsored," endorsed, or introduced to the parents by a professor, an ESOL teacher, or a church staff member, they had a fairly easy time gaining the trust of the parents. Understandably, a few parents, as well as preservice teachers were guarded in the initial meeting, but all became comfortable with one another after the first encounter. In fact, many parents were more than happy to talk to the preservice teachers and help with the project. Preservice teachers met with the parents four times, on average, to complete the family storybooks. Preservice teachers wrote a progress report, 3 weeks into the process, so I would be alerted about possible difficulties.

Authoring Family Books. The family books can be classified into books coauthored by English language learners (children) and preservice teachers and those coauthored by parents and preservice teachers. The majority of the books, in content and form, were exceptionally well crafted.

The preservice teachers highlighted the following major steps in creating the family story books: (1) reading through picture and chapter books with parents (often with their children present) to get ideas for the books they would write; (2) parents narrating their life stories; (3) preservice teachers presenting an outline of the text to the parents, word-processing the text, and cutting up important sentences into strips to go with family photographs and printed pictures (usually obtained from the World Wide Web); (4) discussing with parents ideas for the design and layout of the cover as well as of the book itself; (5) creating mock copies of the books for parents to approve; (6) preservice teachers supplying book making materials; and (7) parents and preservice teachers creating the final copies. The sections that follow present some of the preliminary products of the bookmaking project.

Parent Interviews. Through telling their stories, Latino parents reconnected with and validated their experiences. They were not reluctant to share their stories, even if sadness or tragedy was involved, so others would learn. One parent stressed that "our neighbors should know about our story. Perhaps they don't know how difficult it was just to get here!" Another emphatically commented, "My children should not forget that we sacrificed for them so they can have a better life. I almost died trying to cross the river!" Finally, a father said, "I would like my new country to know who I am. I won't cause trouble here, I just want to work hard and send my children to school, so they will not be like me."

Book Selection. The following reflection captures the significance of the book selection component. Clearly, the first and second paragraphs of the reflection indicate the preservice teacher's thoughtful cultural selection and his knowledge of the importance of linking to personal background for relevance and scaffolding.

> *When approaching the types of books I wanted to give the Gómezes to read, I wanted to make an effort to give them books that they would instantly relate to and which would give them a good idea of the types of things we might want to put in their own book. I also wanted to give them some books that were on a level that would be easy enough for Mr. and Mrs. Gómez to read (since they have not acquired the language proficiency of their children). Luckily, since I have had previous experience working with them, I was able to use my existing knowledge to make these choices.*
>
> *The first book I chose was* Esperanza Rising *by Pam Muñoz Ryan. This book tells the story of a young girl and her family as they attempt to adjust to a new life in America. It also details their immigration experience. I felt that this was something that the Gómezes' children would definitely identify with and that it would help them recall their own experience for the writing of their own book. Since this is a chapter book, I felt that it might be too much to ask each of the children to read all of it. So, I gave them my copy of the book and split it up into four parts. Each child (Pablo, Manuel, Rosita, and Lorenzo) read a quarter of the book and shared it with their siblings. Finally, I discussed the books with the children and got their opinions on it. Like I had hoped, they connected what happened in the book to their own experiences and really opened up to me.*
>
> *The second book I selected was* A Day's Work *by Eve Bunting. This is the story of a young boy who lives in America. His grandfather comes to the country from Mexico and speaks no English. Nonetheless, the little boy helps his grandfather get a job as a gardener. Though he has difficulty in this, he has great integrity and work ethic and refuses to quit until he has done the job right. Mr. Gómez is also a man of integrity and great work ethic and I thought that he would probably get the most out of this book. He read it with the assistance of his daughter and seemed to really enjoy it. After reading it, he began to tell me about his own work experiences and*

what drives him every day. As we wrote the book, I could tell that what he had read really impacted the things he had to contribute to the book and I felt that this reading selection paid off.

The final book I selected was Coming to America: The Story of Immigration *by Betsy Maestro. This book tells the story of the millions of families from all over the world that have immigrated to America. It gives a simple but comprehensive history of immigration to the United States. I decided it would be the best book for Mrs. Gómez to read because she loves history and had talked with me at length about her interest in the citizenship process. After reading the book (mostly on her own but with some assistance from her children), I could tell that she felt that she had a better idea of how the system worked. It was also interesting to see how she related to people who had a different immigration experience from her own. Ultimately, I felt that the book gave me a good way of reaching out to her. I felt that her reading the book gave her the ability to contribute numerous anecdotes of her own to our book. Overall, I believe that these three books contributed to my understanding of the family and the creation of the story book.*

Designing the Books. Outlines, storyboards, and the page-by-page layout of the book helped preservice teachers make sense of all the information they collected from the family and create the design for the family book. Table 4.1 shows the outline for one family narrative. All names have been changed to preserve confidentiality.

A typical family story book coauthored by preservice teachers and parents included texts, images, and illustrations. Usually with the family photographs were strips of text introducing the father, the mother, and their children. The next pages might include a map of the home country, photos of events that had taken place in the home country, images of things the family missed, and cultural artifacts from their home country. Some also included thoughts about leaving their country and coming to America, the family's present home in the United States, and experiences of hardships and fulfillment in the United States. The family's dreams and aspirations were punctuated with pictures, which added life and color to the text.

Books co-created by preservice teachers and children reflected the playfulness of the young writers. Children's illustrations liberally scattered throughout the book made the pages come alive. In one family book, photographs and text chronicled the children's birth in the home country, the family's move to the United States, the children's school in the United States, the sadness of leaving friends behind, and the difficulty in adjusting to their new school and learning English.

Table 4.1 Family Narrative Project—Sample of Story Book Outline

Topics	Description
Coming to America	Description of home in Mexico Circumstances of departure Where the family came to in America
Starting Life in America	Early school experiences Finding jobs in America Parents' acquisition of English Moving again (to Chicago)
Land of Opportunity	Mr. Gómez loses his job Moving to Dalton Jobs in carpet mills Buying a house Attending Dalton Schools
Schooling in Dalton	Learning the English language Difficulties American culture Culture conflict Gangs
Jobs at Carpet Mills	Working at two different mills Working second shift Separation from family Missing their home Adapting
The Family Today	Mr. and Mrs. Gómez still work at the carpet mills David and Manuel are college students Gloria and Jaime are students at NW Whitfield High School Church and community life

Collaboration. Evidence of collaboration between parents and preservice teachers appears in the wording of the authorship, titles, and dedications, as illustrated in the following examples:

- Written by (name of parent), edited by (name of preservice teacher);
- Created with assistance by (name of preservice teacher);
- Written and illustrated by the Gamboa family and Mary Stuart.

Also, titles were either in English or Spanish or bilingual, and they reflected the story that was about to unfold: "The Agustin Family: Our Life, Our Journey"; "When and Why I Came to the U.S."; "A Family United from Mexico to America"; "Crossing the Border; La Familia Esquivel"; "I Love My Family"; "Adios Mi Patria"; "Mi Viaje de Familia"; "Miguel Comes to America"; "Looking Back, Looking Ahead"; "The Guerras Come to America"; "From Yesterday to Today: A Journey"; "A Columbian Girl's Travel to Georgia"; "La Familia Paniagua"; and "Across the Perilous Desert."

Dedications also previewed the stories. For example, a book co-authored by a preservice teacher and a woman who chose to honor her deceased father, a pastor, had the following dedication: "To all those individuals and families striving for a better life. May you find peace and happiness wherever you are. Trust in the Lord and seek Him first." The authors of "Crossing the Perilous Desert" wrote: "This book is dedicated to the families who live in Mexico and are dreaming of moving to the United States in hopes of pursuing the AMERICAN DREAM." In the following dedication, the preservice teacher expresses admiration for the family: "To the Navarrete family, for sharing their stories and time with a stranger. Your courage and hope are an inspiration."

Preservice Teachers' Reflections on the FNP

The preservice teachers reflected on the whole experience of participating in the project and how this course assignment had contributed to their growth as teachers. Their reflections indicate how the apprehension and unease that characterized the initial moments of the first meeting between them and the families were replaced by the enthusiasm and desire to know the person as another human being. They reveal preservice teachers tactfully pressing on with questions; sifting through responses; and making sense of stories, some in English and some in Spanish, by parents whose voices were no longer silenced. The following quote from a preservice teacher's reflection shows the family in command, giving directions about how they wanted their story presented.

On the later visits to their home, I took notes on their values, experiences in America, and the changes their family has undergone. I worked with them to make sure the text I created was accurate and reflected the elements they found most important. They also suggested pictures that might go in the book at this time. The two children translated back and forth and helped their mother to tell me that I should use another word. Using the information from these discussions, I assembled the book using the corrected text and visuals.

Examination of the preservice teachers' reflections provides evidence of what they have learned from the Latino parents with whom they co-authored family books, as well as their own professional growth.

The Role of Parents as Teachers

Bicultural parents have experiences that can teach important lessons of survival, courage, perseverance, sacrifice, humility, and resilience. The following quotes from the preservice teachers' reflections indicate that preservice teachers have become aware of the parents' positive attributes, which are worthy of emulation. In a very significant sense, Latino parents have become the teachers.

In the first two quotes, preservice teachers expressed dismay in relation to the racism and discrimination that parents faced. To hear firsthand from the victims of racism gave a new resolve to the preservice teachers not to be complacent.

I became very emotional when hearing about the hatred that they faced at work and around town. People would yell racial slurs at them, and would refuse to cooperate with them because they felt that they had stolen someone's job. I could not believe that at this day and age people could be so cruel, especially over things that cannot be controlled. I also did not realize that it was on such a large scale. I had hoped that ignorance had decreased since my parents' time. I am sad to say that it only changes form, and that hatred just switches from one group to the next.

I am unbelievably grateful to the Valdez family for sharing all of this with me. It was very difficult for them, but they were glad to do it. They told me that they did it because they hoped that it would make people understand them and their community better. They wanted everyone to understand that we are all the same on some level, and that there is no need to be so hateful. I feel that this will make me a more sympathetic teacher. I will understand more of what the family is experiencing, which will help me to meet the needs of that student better. I also feel that this has helped me develop my skills for dealing with parents on any level. I feel that I have changed so much because of the Valdezes, and I am grateful to them.

The following reflections indicated appreciation and admiration for the parents' tenacity, industry, and dedication to their families. The preservice teachers come to appreciate that parents work extremely hard not only for basic survival in this country but also for a better future for their children.

Now that the project is finished I am very glad that I had the opportunity to do this. I learned a lot about the Hispanic culture and about the hardships of coming to America illegally. She is a United States citizen now but it took some years for this to become a reality. I was not even sure what she was talking about when she first started describing how she came to America. I have heard of stories but they have been in newspapers, books, or magazines. I have never talked with someone that crawled under the fence from Mexico to America and then worked their way up to a decent life for themselves and their children. Her children are wonderful kids and did well when working on the project as well.

The story that you have just read is a prettier version of what she told me that day. I was captivated by her experiences, and it was enough of a catharsis for her to share that she ended up crying through some of it. When I told her that she didn't have to talk about it, she reassured me that I should include it if it would help someone else understand Latinos better.

Their story is inspiring and their passion for their children is contagious. I hope I would work hard and sacrifice great things for the people I love.

The Hernández family inspires me and challenges me to have a greater global worldview than ever before. Someday, I believe they will achieve their "Mexican Dream." I am proud to be part of their cultural experience.

The following quotations illustrate the mutual benefits preservice teachers and parents derived from the experience.

I asked the family how they felt about my asking questions and making a book with them about their lives. They said they really enjoyed doing this project. They said it allowed for them to know more about me, or Americans in general, and for me to know and understand more about their lifestyles and cultures. The father hopes that once I leave somebody else would come along to help his children.

I saw his parents one more time when they came in for a conference at the school, and they both thanked me for even taking the time to listen to their story. I told them that I was the one who was grateful that they even let me bother them with this project I had to do. It made me feel so good to see how much it meant to them that I wanted to learn about them. Overall, I am just happy to have been able to work with them and learn about another family's journey to the United States. Their story makes me appreciate my father's journey from Mexico to the U.S. especially because I will be the first to graduate in the U.S.

Preservice Teachers' Professional Growth

The importance of connecting bicultural parents with the teachers that will teach their children can best be illustrated in the quotations below. They demonstrate, in the preservice teachers' own words, the insight they gained on how to relate to bicultural parents and how to work with them as important resources and partners in education.

Teacher 1: I grew professionally and personally through this experience. I realized that just because you think you know somebody, you really do not until you sit down and speak with them. I also learned that just because immigrant families seem very happy in their new country does not mean that they do not long for their home country at times. Even though I will be teaching kindergarten next year, if I ever teach an upper-level elementary class I would love to have them write a book and complete this with their family whether they be an immigrant or not. I feel that it is important for children to understand where they came from and appreciate all that they have. I have learned to appreciate my childhood even more after completing this assignment. I look forward to sharing the finished project with the Gómez family.

Teacher 2: I believe the biggest area of growth due to this assignment is cultural sensitivity. I always felt that my cooperating teacher picked on Samuel in class. He wasn't a disciplined worker and has some behavioral problems. As soon as I began teaching Samuel, he became a different student simply because of the way I treated him. I treated him with respect and clearly set down my expectations of him. I discussed his work and his progress with him and he even came to me for help between classes. He was honored to help me fulfill a class requirement and learn about his history. This assignment helped me understand what kind of home life my students might have.

Teacher 3: Overall this was a great experience. I really feel that I will be more sensitive to the needs of my students now that I know the challenges some of them faced coming to America. Because of this project, I have also experienced growth as a professional. This gave me the opportunity to learn how to communicate with Latinos both as a professional completing a project and as a friend. I felt like my Spanish background really helped my understanding and sensitivity, but I also feel like I have learned from them. Even preservice teachers who were initially uncomfortable with or resistant to the project acknowledged its value in terms of getting to know their students' backgrounds and relating curriculum content to their prior knowledge.

Teacher 4: Even though it made me very uncomfortable, I appreciated this field experience. Seeing parents at home and hearing about the elements of their background that influence their family has helped emphasize the importance of understanding family history when teaching students of any classification. Cooperation with parents of all linguistic abilities and socioeconomic levels is central to creating rich educational experiences with children; they need to have learning supported at home for it to be most effective, and understanding their background helps the teacher prepare more connected and contextualized lessons.

Teacher 5: Sometimes, I felt like it was not my place to pry into their lives. To them, I was a complete stranger. When I become a teacher someday, I feel like it will be easier to communicate with parents. . . . Overall, I enjoyed being able to look into another family's life, to really see where they came from. As a teacher, it is our job to know each of our students. The better we understand their background, the better we can connect new information to their prior experiences.

The quotations above demonstrate the potential that projects like the FNP can have on preservice teachers in creating interpersonal space where identities can be negotiated and respected. It also serves to help preservice teachers better understand how societal power relations may be affecting the structure of schooling and the teachers' interactions with bicultural students and communities.

Forming Substantive Relationships Between
Parents and Preservice Teachers

The reflections of the preservice teachers clearly show that the FNP served as a catalyst for substantive relationships between parents and preservice teachers. Notwithstanding the discomfort some preservice teachers expressed because of difficulty of scheduling meetings with parents, not having a common language, getting past the concern that "this is an invasive assignment," all preservice teachers admitted that the assignment provided them with learning opportunities they would not normally have or seek.

Life stories become educational tools because participants, either as tellers or listeners, gain a deeper understanding of who they have been, who they are, and who they can become (Hones, 1998, p. 227). In other words, life stories express and explore identities. The present project has demonstrated that collaboration between educators and communities in the articulation and public validation of family identity is a process of *empowerment*—power was generated in the authoring of family histories for both the family (parents and children) and the participating preservice teachers.

Case studies document what has happened in a particular context. For policy purposes, the logic underlying case studies can be expressed simply: *Actuality implies possibility.* The documentation that a particular phenomenon *has* occurred logically implies that this phenomenon *can* occur. The fact that, in the FNP, preservice teachers successfully engaged in a process of repudiating the devaluation of identity that subordinated communities typically experience in the wider society implies that, even at the preservice level, educators *can* become agents in the collaborative generation of power.

Thus, we believe that the FNP case study entails some profound implications for both teaching in general and teacher education in particular. Specifically, it suggests that education and teacher education are not just about instructional techniques and strategies. Rather, relationships are at the heart of schooling. The negotiation of identities between educators and both students and parents will exert a significant impact on the extent to which students engage academically and the efficacy with which parents are enabled to support their children's academic progress.

The life stories described in the family books co-authored by preservice teachers and parents continue to be lived. Lives go on. Identities are continually being scripted in the interactions between educators and families. As implied in the note written on the last page of one of the family story books, education in general, and preservice education in particular, must nurture agency:

The story does not end here. The remainder of this book is left blank, so that the Natividads can continue to write their own story on its pages. Good luck, God bless, and thank you again.

In preparing teachers to be agents in the collaborative generation of equal power, and as our school communities continue to be more linguistic and culturally diverse, teacher education programs have an obligation to prepare teachers to work in diverse school communities, as well as to work in forming and maintaining partnerships with bicultural parents that yield access to educational opportunities for their children and community.

Discussion Questions

1. As linguistic and cultural diversity increases throughout the United States, what are the implications for teacher education programs and for creating partnerships with bicultural parents whose knowledge of English and previous educational opportunities may be limited?
2. What are societal power relations? What are patterns of coercive power relations that are experienced by subordinated communities in the wider society?
3. How can the voices of bicultural parents and children be expressed and heard, to promote a process of empowerment and as a collaborative creation of power?
4. Within a teacher preparation program, what assignments can challenge a candidate's level of comfort in getting to know diverse school communities and bicultural families? What types of resistance can such assignments encounter in the professional development of the teacher candidate?
5. What process can authentically engage teacher candidates with bicultural parents/families in documenting a family life story?
6. How can life stories become educational tools for gaining a deeper understanding of family and community identities?
7. What insights can be gained from engaging with bicultural parents in their homes and community that can have a long-lasting effect on how teachers interact and work in ethnically and linguistically parents and diverse school communities? In becoming an agent in the collaborative generation of equal power?

Suggested Readings

Baker, C. (Ed.). (1995). *The multilingual resources for children project: Building bridges; Multilingual resource for children.* Clevedon, UK: Multilingual Matters.

Cummins, J. (2000). *Language, power, and pedagogy.* Clevedon, UK: Multilingual Matters.

Durán, R., Durán, J., Perry-Romero, D., & Sanchez, E. (2001). Latino immigrant parents and children learning and publishing together in an after-school setting. *Journal of Education for Students Placed at Risk (JESPAR), 1532-7671, 6* (1), 95–113.

Igoa, C. (1995). *The inner world of the immigrant child.* Mahwah, NJ: Lawrence Erlbaum.

Schecter, S., & Cummins, J. (Eds.). (2003). *Multilingual education in practice: Using diversity as a resource.* Portsmouth, NH: Heinemann.

Trumbull, E., Rothstein-Fisch, C., Greenfield, P., & Quiroz, B. (2001). *Bridging cultures between home and school: A guide for teachers.* Mahwah, NJ: Lawrence Erlbaum.

Valdés, G. (2003). *Expanding definitions of giftedness: The case of young interpreters from immigrant communities.* Mahwah, NJ: Lawrence Erlbaum.

References

Ada, A. F. (2003). *A magical encounter: Latino children's literature in the classroom.* Boston: Allyn & Bacon.

Ada, A. F., & Campoy, F. I. (2004). *Authors in the classroom: A transformation process.* Boston: Pearson Education.

Ada, A. F., & Zubizarreta, R. (2001). Parent narratives: The cultural bridge between Latino parents and their children. In M. L. Reyes & J. J. Halcon (Eds.), *The best for our children: Critical perspectives on literacy for Latino students* (pp. 229–244). New York: Teachers College Press.

Agosín, M. (1999). U*ncertain travelers: Conversations with Jewish women immigrants to America.* Hanover, NH: Brandeis University Press.

Bernhard, J. K., Cummins, J., Campoy, F. I., Ada, A. F., Winsler, A., & Bleiker, C. (2006). Identity texts and literacy development among preschool English language learners: Enhancing learning opportunities for children at risk of learning disabilities. *Teachers College Record, 108*(11), 2380–2405.

Bishop, R., & Berryman, M. (2006). *Culture speaks: Cultural relationships and classroom learning.* Wellington: Huia, Aoteroa New Zealand.

Bogdan, R. C., & Biklen, S. K. (1998). *Qualitative research for education: An introduction to theory and methods.* Boston: Allyn & Bacon.

Clandinin, D., & Connelly, M. F. (1994). Personal experience methods. In N. Denzin & Y. Lincoln (Eds.), *Handbook of qualitative research* (pp. 413–427). Thousand Oaks, CA: Sage.

Cummins, J. (2001). *Negotiating identities: Education for empowerment in a diverse society.* Los Angeles: California Association for Bilingual Education.

Delgado-Gaitan, C. (1991). Involving parents in schools: A process of empowerment. *American Journal of Education 100*, 20–46.

Epstein, J. L., Sanders, M. G., Simon, B. S., Salinas, K. C., Jansorn, N. R., & Van Voorhis, F. L. (2002). *School, family, and community partnerships: Your handbook for action.* Thousand Oaks, CA: Corwin.

Fashola, O., Slavin, R., Calderon, M., & Duran, R. (1996). *Effective programs for Latino students in elementary and middle schools.* Baltimore: John Hopkins University, Center for Research on the Education of Students Placed at Risk.

Hiatt-Michael, D. (2001). *Preparing teachers to work with parents* (Report EDO-SP-2001-2). Washington, DC: ERIC Clearinghouse on Teaching and Teacher Education. (ERIC Document Reproduction Service No. ED460123)

Hones, D. (1998). Known in part: The transformational power of narrative inquiry. *Qualitative Inquiry, 4*, 225–248.

Ladson-Billings, G. (1995). Toward a theory of culturally relevant pedagogy. *American Educational Research Journal, 32*, 465–491.

McCaleb, S. P. (1997). *Building communities of learners: A collaboration among teachers, students, families, and community.* New York: St. Martin's Press.

McCarty, T. L. (2002). (Ed.). *Language literacy and power in schooling.* Mahwah, NJ: Lawrence Erlbaum.

National Center for Education Statistics. (1999). *Teacher quality: A report on the preparation and qualifications of public school teachers.* Washington, DC: Author. (ERIC Document No. ED427009)

Ogbu, J. U. (1978). *Minority education and caste.* New York: Academic Press.

Ogbu, J. U. (1992). Understanding cultural diversity and learning. *Educational Researcher, 21*(8), 5–14, 24.

Portes, A., & Rumbaut, R. G. (2001). *Legacies: The story of the immigrant second generation.* Berkeley: University of California Press.

Skutnabb-Kangas, T. (2000). *Linguistic genocide in education—or worldwide diversity and human rights.* Mahwah, NJ: Lawrence Erlbaum.

Valdes, G. (1996). *Con respeto: Bridging the distances between culturally diverse families and schools.* New York: Teachers College Press.

Wink, J. (2000). *Critical pedagogy: Notes from the real world.* New York: Longman.

Wlazlinski, M. (2004). Mi escuela es su escuela: Teachers and parents as invested and equal partners for the education of language-minority students. *NABE Journal of Research and Practice, 2*(1). Retrieved from http://njrp.tamu.edu/2004/PDFs/escuela.pdf

Part II

Critical Perspectives

5

Parent Engagement and Equity in a Dual Language Program

Sheila Shannon

In this chapter I focus on the dynamics of parent engagement in a school with a dual language program (DLP). The very structure of a DLP that calls for the student population to be half monolingual English-speakers and half dominant Spanish-speakers simultaneously involves two distinct parent communities (Shannon, 1999). These communities are positioned in U.S. society in dramatically asymmetric ways. The English language community tends to be White and middle class, while the Spanish language community is invariably Mexican, poor or working class, and immigrant. While the problem of asymmetric social and political status of parents in dual language programs has been alluded to (Amrein & Peña, 2000; Peña, 1998; Potowski, 2007; Valdés, 1997), few studies or discussions have focused on the magnitude of the problem and how it creates disparate parental relations and student outcomes.

In my experience as a researcher and educator in dual language education, I have found that the topics of racial, political, and socioeconomic disparities in DLP are unwelcome in most forums, including research conferences and local professional development opportunities. On the other hand, issues about language separation, curriculum (particularly, when to introduce literacy and in which language), models, and teacher and administrator qualifications typically grasp listeners' attentions. Talk focused on the power and privilege of certain parent groups is quickly avoided.

The school on which I focus in this chapter is one of several where I have witnessed this phenomenon of avoidance or denial. It seems that it is difficult to discuss inequity, racism, or classism in a society like that of the United States that is believed to be a postracial and proudly democratic nation. Indeed, some find it incredible that I see striking similarities between DLP in the United States and DLP in high-conflict areas of the world, such as Israel.

Bekerman (2004), Feuerverger (2001), and Glazier (2003) have each examined Israeli schools with dual language programs. These programs bring together Jewish, Hebrew-speaking children and Palestinian, Arabic-speaking children. Their investigations have revealed that the conflict between the groups in Israeli society persists in the schools. Glazier (2003) further notes that while the groups are in physical contact in the schools, they lack "engaging in one another's company" (p. 141). She insists that this engagement requires a kind of "cultural fluency—via sustained experiences of 'company'" (p. 144). Bekerman (2004) similarly calls for engagement that is multivocal and that involves "more than mere inclusiveness" (p. 605).

The social construction of the nation-state of Israel favors Jewish history and Hebrew as the national language and the marginalization of Palestinians and Arabic. Thus, the problem here is that in Israeli society Jews and Palestinians do not naturally engage in one another's company and not in any sustained way. Indeed, Palestinian and Jewish settlements, villages, and neighborhoods are segregated and in some cases this separation is fortified with walls and military intervention.

U.S. educators and parents may read about Israel and Hebrew/Arabic DLP and can easily discern the conflict. Moreover, parents of the White, English-speaking, middle-class children in DLP may readily empathize with the Jewish/Hebrew majority. Few, in my opinion, would equate the Palestinian/Arabic minority with the Mexican/Spanish minority in the United States despite the fact that since 9/11 and the establishment of a "homeland security" ideology, a wall between the United States and Mexico continues to be constructed, fortified, and militarized (Ellingwood, 2004). Indeed, for many high-status U.S. parents, alarm and dismay might be more noticeable reactions than understanding and empathy.

My point here is that in the United States the relationship between the White/English majority and the Latino/Spanish minority exists within a high-conflict area. The conflict arises from a feeling of ambivalence or resentment toward Mexican workers in the United States (Bacon, 2008; Chomsky, 2007). In my view, no immigrant in the United States, living and working with documents or not, misses the fact that he or she is welcome to work at low wages with no protection or benefits as long as he or she does not expect the rights and privileges of citizenship (Chomsky, 2007). In fact, even those who are citizens but of Latino descent are vulnerable to being treated as second class.

This situation of marginality and mistreatment of Latinos (namely, Mexicans) has grown out of a long history of exploitation of our neighbors to our south (Hernandez, 2010; Shannon, 2005). Similar to the Jewish and Palestinian asymmetrical phenomena, within the wall separating the United States from Mexico, White employers generally do not engage with Mexican immigrant workers as socially equal peers. Their contact with Mexican working-class people is limited to hiring Mexican immigrants for day labor; migrant farmwork; housekeeping in private homes and in the service industry; and factory labor in carpet mills, chicken farms, meatpacking plants, canneries, fisheries, the fast-food industry, forestry, and so on (Bacon, 2008; Shannon, 2008). However, there is no intent or effort to humanly interact with this community in a nonexploitative way.

There are an estimated 11 to 12 million undocumented people in the United States, and presumably a significant majority of them are of Mexican origin (Passel & Cohn, 2011). Five million of those people are school-aged children. Clearly, not all Spanish-speaking children in DLP are from families with undocumented parents, but in the current political climate in the United States, and with the prevailing attitudes toward Mexican immigrants, whether the families live here in some legal sense or not is a moot point. Identifying all Latinos as Mexicans and associating all Mexicans in the United States with the criminalized undocumented immigrant creates and legitimizes an us-versus-them dichotomy (Hernandez, 2010). In this dichotomy, "us" is right, White, and legal, with full rights and privileges. The "them" are groups and individuals of questionable citizenship status and thus not due basic human rights and privileges (Shannon & Escamilla, 1999). In my view, DLP must make this civics and history lesson as fundamental when conceiving programs and certainly when assessing how the parent groups are to be engaged in them.

Parent Engagement in Dual Language Programs

A brief look at what the literature has taught us about parent involvement in U.S. schools reveals that race and class are inevitable determinants of which groups of parents wield power and privilege (Brantlinger, 2003; Fine, 1993; Lareau, 1989; Olivos, 2006). Much of the research looks at parental involvement in general and some has a particular focus on the relationship between families and schools for particular groups, such as African Americans or Latinos. The conclusions generally point to the positive correlation between parents who are actively involved in their children's schooling and their children's academic success (Henderson & Mapp, 2002).

Here, I acknowledge the prodigious work of Joyce Epstein and her colleagues on parent involvement (Epstein & Sanders, 2006). However, Annette Lareau's work eclipses that body of research when it comes to looking at status and privilege, while Epstein has led the field in emphasizing the importance of preparing teachers to work with parents and families. Therefore, for examining parent involvement in dual language education, Lareau's (1989) groundbreaking study provides a rationale for understanding the differences in how parents of high and low social status are involved in their children's education.

Nearly 20 years after the initial study, and with some paradigmatic and demographic shifts in schools, Lareau and her colleagues found that the same dynamics prevailed. High-status parents participated in the education of their children by exercising their privilege, or what Lareau refers to, in Bourdieuian terms, as cultural capital (Weininger & Lareau, 2003). Further, they found that these same parents used their symbolic capital to demonstrate their superiority over the teacher. In contrast to these parents, however, they continued to find that low-status parents lacked these forms of capital and thus deferred to schools or did not engage in parent involvement activities, nor did they advocate for their individual children. This distinction between high- and low-status parents becomes crystallized in the DLPs I've studied and in the case study found in this chapter.

Low-Status Immigrant Communities in DLP. Children in many DLP programs tend to be immigrants or the children of immigrant parents. Undocumented immigrant children attend schools in the United States under the protection of the U.S. Supreme Court decision *Plyler v. Doe* (1982). The Court decided that laws in Texas at the time that prohibited children who had entered the country without authorization to attend public schools were unconstitutional.

Demographic trends in the late 1990s and early 2000s indicate that many immigrant and U.S.-born children of immigrant parents speak Spanish as their mother tongue. They generally receive the same education as has been designed for ordinary monolingual English-speaking children. Otherwise, since the implementation of the Bilingual Education Act of 1968—the first official federal recognition of the needs of students whose first language is not English—children from non-English-dominant backgrounds could also be provided with some form of bilingual education.

The differences in bilingual education programs revolve around how much Spanish is used for instruction and other formal school purposes and for how long in a child's educational career. Most programs unfortunately tend to fall short on both counts. Distinguished programs with high success rates involve as much as 50% Spanish throughout the day and the elementary grades (Greene, 1998; Lindhom-Leary, 2001; Ramírez, 1992; Thomas & Collier, 2002; Willig, 1985). In any case, bilingual programs have overwhelmingly been designed only for the child who speaks a language other than English. Often, these programs are perceived by educators, parents, and the children themselves as remedial and compensatory and not value-added, enrichment bilingual programs. In these bilingual programs, immigrant children become the "other" and subject to educational and language policies that devalue and restrict them (Darder, 1994; Foucault, 1977).

Dual Language Programs. Dual language programs are an increasingly popular alternative attempt to provide meaningful, successful, and equitable educational experiences for Spanish-dominant children. What distinguishes dual language programs is that the Spanish-speaking children are joined by English-speaking children in an educational program. The goals of this bilingual program are that both groups of children will become bilingual and biliterate. That is, each group is immersed in its second language for part of the day, either for instruction or for instruction about the second language. Additionally, each group also receives instruction in mixed groups in either language. In other words, during mixed or integrated groups both Spanish-speaking children (usually Latino) and English-speaking (i.e., White) children learn together. A key component of dual language programs is that there are equal numbers of Spanish and English speakers.

Dual language programs have grown exponentially over the past 40 years. In 2008, there were over 300 two-way programs in the United States with the majority of them at the elementary level involving Spanish and English speakers (Center for Applied Linguistics, 2008). These programs exist in over 24 states throughout the country with many concentrated in California and other southwestern states.

Equity in Dual Language Programs. Howard, Sugarman, and Christian (2003) conducted a comprehensive review of research about two-way programs. Their goal was to carefully question whether indeed they are successfully improving the educational experiences and outcomes of two-way programs, particularly for Mexican immigrant children. They found that "in many respects, the literature . . . indicates that much is going well in two-way immersion programs." They concluded, however, that the one issue that consistently emerged in all studies was that of "equity, and the tension that arises between the ideal of two-way immersion and the reality of [its] implementation in the United States, a monolingual English society" (p. 49).

There are different ways to conceive of inequity. In DLP, one could focus on academic outcomes and they may be different and inequitable when comparing the two groups of students. Another could be on linguistic outcomes, that is, to what extent the second language is acquired and used. This chapter focuses on inequity of parent engagement in DLP and the implications of this inequity.

DLP can be seen as, and can be, a win-win situation for both groups. They can also be examples of democratic education and challenges to English monolingualism and hegemony for U.S. children (Shannon, 2008). In terms of parent engagement, Scanlon and Palmer (2009) cite Rubio (1995) to say that DLP "schools foster strong levels of parent/caregiver engagement" (p. 392). Like many schools with programs that parents actually choose, one could expect high levels of parental presence and engagement. In DLP that is not necessarily the case as in many programs, such as the one featured in this chapter. In this example, "choice" was reserved for the White, English-speaking parents, whereas it was a school of necessity for the Spanish-speaking parents (i.e., the school provided second-language instruction and first-language support).

In surveys of parents with children in DLPs, both Parkes (2008) and Shannon and Milian (2002) found that while all parents had positive reasons for choosing a DLP school for their children, the differences between the English-dominant and Spanish-dominant parents' reasons fell between Ruiz's (1984) orientations of *language as resource* or *language as a right*, respectively. The former is an economic-orientation, or "value added," perspective of a bilingual program, whereas the latter is about the use and maintenance of a language other than English in an English monolingual society.

That the different groups of parents have different orientations toward what DLP means for their children, and that they may have different motivations for placing their children in the DLP (choice and value-added bilingualism versus necessity and maintenance of the mother tongue), means that their engagement might be different. Certainly that they are different groups in a hierarchical society will mean that they engage in the school and are engaged by school personnel in different ways.

The Interest Convergence Dilemma

Upon the 25th anniversary of the *Brown v. Board of Education* (1954) decision, Harvard law professor Derrick Bell presented his thoughts on why this decision was not necessarily a momentous civil rights victory for Blacks (Bell, 1980). The dilemma found in this victory, Bell argued, was that Whites tend to generally support legal decisions that ultimately serve their own interests whether or not they serve the interests of Blacks. *Brown*, of course, put an end to segregated schools and was seen by many as a landmark legal decision in the civil rights movement. It was also, according to Bell and others, an attempt to make racism less visible or problematic in the United States. Bell (1980) also argued that "Whites simply can't envision the personal responsibility and potential sacrifice inherent in Black's conclusion that true equality for Blacks will require the surrender of racism-granted privileges for Whites" (p. 22).[1]

Richard Delgado, a University of Pittsburgh law professor and critical race theorist, extended Bell's dilemma to Latinos. To do this he looked at the 1954 *Hernández v. Texas* decision upon its 50th anniversary (Delgado, 2006). He likened the multiple anniversaries of *Brown* and his fictitious one of *Hernández* as examples of what he calls "celebratory jurisprudence." Delgado warns that "celebration stills our critical instincts" (p. 55) and goes on to critically view why the Supreme

Court would rule as it did in *Hernández*. Much as with *Brown*, White's interests in the *Hernández* decision were motivated by international concerns (and remember that both cases were decided at the same time with the same judges). Delgado points to evidence that the U.S. government was concerned with the spread of communism in Latin America. If the United States wasn't taking care of Latinos within its borders it wouldn't be influential in how Latinos outside responded to communist movements within their own countries. Delgado (2006) provides thorough evidence that during this era, the Supreme Court judges and the U.S. government were concerned about the U.S. image abroad and that racism in the United States was a barrier to its leadership and domination in the world.

In the late 1990s, Guadalupe Valdés (1997) cautioned educators that two-way immersion programs (i.e., DLP) may create more injustices by providing White students with skills, like bilingualism, that give them even more advantages over the Latino students. White students acquire Spanish as an additional language, one they may not even use outside of school, while Latino children have little choice about learning English or making it at least their public language (Rodríquez, 1982).

This alternative educational program that involves bringing two politically asymmetrically related groups together for common goals is problematic on the fundamental basis of equity. Palmer (2009) states, for example: "If allowed to evolve without explicit attention to the dynamics of race and power, DLP [Two Way Immersion] can also serve as a textbook example of the interest convergence dilemma (ICD)" (p. 110).

DLPs brings together Whites and Latinos who would otherwise not find themselves together in the same schools or in the same programs. Just as desegregation put Whites and Blacks in the same schools and programs that they themselves would not necessarily have chosen (except through a color-blind "best school choice" motivation), DLPs offers a choice for Whites that some find irresistible (language as resource). Petrovic (2005) argues that "without careful implementation and without consideration of issues of power and privilege associated with the hegemony of English language both in and out of schools, dual immersion programs have the potential of becoming the Epcot Center of foreign language curriculum providing language majority students an opportunity to view live specimens of the second language" (p. 406). Skepticism aside, ICD requires us to determine what the interests in decision making are and in whose interest these decisions are being made. Whites are generally attracted to the neoliberal orientation of language as resource because they are English speakers. Spanish or any other language is extraneous. Latinos in DLP look for the attractions elsewhere (i.e., having their children retain their heritage language, having access to teachers they as parents can communicate with, etc.) because English is mandatory and its acquisition is constantly under scrutiny.

Converging and Diverging Interests in a
Dual Language Program

Escuela Bilingüe Kennedy (EBK) was a dual language elementary school located in a town in a western state. The school was closed in the 2nd half of the 1st decade of 2000, after having thrived for over 12 years. Local school mythology had put EBK in the pantheon of excellent bilingual programs in the state, a status only one other school shared at the time. EBK was begun by a group of teachers who sought out an innovative and promising model of bilingual education. The teachers presented the model to parents, both Latino immigrant parents and White parents, who would eventually be the petitioners for the program in the school district.

The community in which EBK was located is a prosperous town with much community and economic activity surrounding a large state university. The Spanish speakers were by and large Mexican immigrant families. Many of the families lived in a public housing project and adjacent trailer parks, attesting to their relative low economic status. Although some Mexican immigrants parents had high levels of formal education and held professional positions in Mexico, the majority did not. Some Mexican states, such as Chihuahua and Michoacan, were more highly represented in the community, but there was no distinct pattern of immigration. This community was attractive to Mexican immigrants for the available itinerant labor, work in the service industry and construction. Several of the para-educators were Mexican women from the community, as were the service workers at the school. This town was not always the first destination for the immigrants, or the last. Often children when asked where they were born would report New Mexico, Texas, or California.

The English speakers were mainly Whites whose parents had relatively high levels of formal education and held professional positions or were themselves involved in education. They lived throughout the town and vicinity and most lived in relative luxury. There were some parents, in the minority, who were mixed-race couples where one was Mexican or Latino and who were more likely than ordinary White parents to be bilingual. Another minority was formed by families headed by political activists interested in promoting social justice and exposing their children to diversity.

Those who lived outside the community (and some insiders) described it as a "granola" town, referring to the health and environment consciousness of many of the residents. The political climate was relatively liberal, compared with other communities in the state. At the same time, the Mexicans in the community were residentially and socially segregated from both the townsfolk in general and the university in particular. The campus did not attract significant numbers of Latino students and did not promote itself as a university committed to the higher education of the minorities in the community, the state, or the region.

Furthermore, undocumented high school graduates could attend the university only as out-of-state residents, making the tuition exorbitant and out of reach for the Mexican immigrants.

Engaging Parents: Teachers who were involved in the education of parents to get the school opened said that it was somewhat easier to convince the White parents of the value of the two-way program than the Mexican parents. The White parents saw the bilingual and biliteracy goals of the program to be added value for their children. Also, these parents expressed their desire to have their children in a school with a diverse population. The Mexican parents had to be convinced that a bilingual program with a larger portion of instruction in Spanish in the early grades would not interfere with their children's acquisition of English.

After just a few years, EBK became extremely popular and was perceived as an excellent program. Until shortly before the school closed, it always had a waiting list for English-speaking children.

The teachers at EBK, as well as most of the staff, had always been bilingual in Spanish and English. Instruction in Spanish was invariably carried out by native Spanish-speaking teachers and instruction in English by native English speakers. Two years before the school closed, most of the teachers who taught in Spanish were of Mexican origin. When a change in leadership occurred at the school and a new principal was hired, staffing changed dramatically.

School Leadership and Decision Making. For the first 10 years the school had two principals. The first was a Mexican American male who was bilingual and went on to provide leadership at a large urban school district and then an independent Catholic dual language school. The second was a Mexican American woman, bilingual, with extensive experience as a principal. She worked well with the staff and parents. She left the school to provide leadership for a new program in another district. A search committee was formed to select a new principal. Some teachers and staff on the committee were devoted to the former principal and had clear ideas of what kind of person should replace her. They believed that only a certain kind of person with skills, experience, and background could pick up where the former principal left off, maintaining the integrity of the DLP model that was established at the school and the relationship of the school community with the communities it served.

Two candidates made it to the final cut. One was Ms. García (pseudonym), a first-generation Mexican American bilingual woman with extensive experience in the bilingual classroom (a National Association for Bilingual Education [NABE] Teacher of the Year), although this would be her first position as a principal. The second was Ms. Baker, a European American who grew up in Costa Rica and is bilingual. This would be her 2nd year as a principal.

The selection of Ms. Baker as principal was controversial among the staff, the parents, and the school district. Some veteran teachers and staff members wanted Ms. García to be selected. When Ms. Baker was chosen over her, supporters of Ms. García raised concerns about racism and discrimination. Some teachers believed that Ms. Baker was chosen to appease White parents by having a principal who "looked" the part and was dominant in English. Members of the selection committee who had wanted Ms. García believed that due process was not followed and that their votes were ignored. Seven teachers and paraprofessionals went on to other assignments, saying that Ms. Baker's selection was a factor in their decision to move on. They included all the Mexican teachers.

Ms. Baker hired most of the replacements for the staff though an agency that recruits teachers from abroad and sponsors them. The Mexican teachers were replaced with teachers from Peru, Spain, and Colombia and a couple of White teachers fluent in Spanish they acquired in Spanish-speaking countries other than Mexico. With the new principal and new teachers, the EBK community tried to continue with the success that the school had experienced in the prior 10 years.

The theme of the interest convergence dilemma (ICD) runs throughout the change of leadership in the school. Leadership shifted to less-Mexican-oriented interests with a principal who was perceived as acting in the interests of the Whites along with a considerably larger number of teachers who were viewed similarly. Whether the strategy to shift leadership and interests to favoring Whites was deliberate is not the point. In my assessment, the shift of power to those already with power and privilege was an inevitable by-product of the decisions being made at EBK.

Equity Problems at EBK: Up until the last principal, the program at EBK was succeeding like other well-implemented dual language programs, as documented by a review by Howard et al. (2003). The model for two-way immersion was clearly designed and agreed upon. The teachers were highly qualified and considered among the best in the district. The environment at the school was one that valued Spanish and made Mexican culture relevant in the academic and social aspects of the program. Parents were equally integrated into the program and had highly positive attitudes—indeed, the parents themselves had petitioned for the school. And, as Howard et al. (2003) found in general for dual language programs, academic outcomes for all children, Latino and White, at EBK were higher compared with those in other programs.

The problem of equity, however, continued to be the one issue that no one seemed to know how to address or even how to talk about. For example, the very teachers who established the program were concerned that the Latino children always fell short when compared with the White children in terms of academics. At the same time, there was also a concern that while the Latino children acquired English to high levels of proficiency, the White children's Spanish rarely matched that of the Latino children's English. The question then became, Whose academic and linguistic interests are best being met at this school? No one seemed to know what the answers were and in whose interest it was to find them.

A Critical Incident at a Dual Language School

In previous years the Latino and White parents came together for school improvement team (SIT) meetings which were carried out bilingually. For the first half of the new principal's 1st year, however, the Latino parents were involved in a specially funded project, Families and School Together (FAST), which was meant solely for them and was highly successful in getting a large number of the parents involved. It also meant, however, that the Latino parents and the White parents were not meeting together. The SIT meetings were on the same night as the FAST ones, which heightened the sense of separateness.

What follows is a description of a critical incident that occurred during the first joint meeting of the Latino and White parents. The FAST group had convened its last meeting. Most of the Latino parents stayed for the meeting. As the White parents showed up, they immediately set about reconfiguring the room, placing chairs around in a circle. Most of the chairs were already occupied by the Latino parents, who simply got up and watched the White parents rearrange furniture.

About 20 people were in attendance, including four bilingual teachers, two para-educators, the principal, and the simultaneous translator. There were twice as many White parents as Latino parents. The group had decided to have two co-chairs: one a Spanish monolingual father and the other a bilingual Latina para-educator and mother.

The discussion was about spending funds to erect a marquee outside the school facing a busy street to advertise the school and give it more prominence. The school district had an open-enrollment policy, so advertising seemed a good strategy for increasing enrollment at EBK. At one point in the discussion a White mother interrupted with a complaint about how procedural rules were not being followed at the meeting. She insisted that these meetings were serious and thus formal rules needed to be followed. She directed her complaint to the bilingual co-chair, saying that she needed to state a motion and put it to a vote. The co-chair didn't know how to do that so the White mother, in a loud and demanding voice, asked her to repeat the procedures after her. The co-chair, looking humiliated and confused, got up and excused herself from the meeting. At that point the other co-chair began to discuss the problem, arguing that in Mexico parents did not meet with formal rules. A heated discussion was looming, but the principal interceded and said it was time to separate the groups for their discussion of the agenda items in their respective languages and then reconvene to make decisions. When teachers and parents alike protested that they should address the problem together, the principal said it was irrelevant.

The White parents continued with agenda items and then strayed into a discussion about how to improve relations between themselves and the Latino parents. One mother offered a plan to have a buddy system whereby families could get together outside school. She said that they could invite a Latino family over for dinner and then that family could reciprocate. Then she hesitated and explained that the Latino families might be intimidated by the houses that the White families lived in and feel ashamed about their own homes. They decided that was not a good idea.

At that point the mother who had insisted on Robert's Rules interrupted and asked, "Am I going to be the only asshole here? Is no one going to say anything about how these meetings are run? Why do we have a co-chair that is supposed to be bilingual not understand me?" Again, the principal shifted the discussion to the agenda. Apparently the discussion among the Latino parents was all about the incident. One father reported, "They use the agenda to silence me."

This critical incident illustrates the dilemma of interests converging at EBK. Obviously the two parent groups had distinct interests when it came to their engagement at the school. White parents were interested in managing resources, for example, putting up a marquee to advertise the school. The resources were diminishing at the school and the building was outdated and unattractive to potential parents who could choose any school in the district's open-enrollment system. Additionally, the promise of bilingualism was fading as high-stakes testing entered the arena. Parents could also choose schools even in the neighborhood that had high test scores, something EBK could not offer.

The era of chronic low scores for children who spoke a language other than English on standardized tests had dawned thanks to No Child Left Behind (NCLB). (This will be discussed in greater detail in this chapter). Thus, the image of school was deteriorating as educators and parents scrambled to do well on high-stakes state assessments. Furthermore, the Latino parents had just completed a state-funded program to cater to their needs and interests at the school that included nutritious lunches, free breakfasts, and a variety of services for low-income and immigrant families. One could say that the interests were diverging at EBK—equally a dilemma for a school meant for White and Latino students and their families.

Working to Name Racism, Inequality, and Social Injustice

By the following year, tensions at EBK were at a peak and the atmosphere at the school became more divisive. The dividing line was between Latinos and Whites—even White Latinos. The principal fueled that divide by targeting Latino parents and their sympathizers on her staff. She accused one Latina teacher of not paying equal attention to the White children in her 1st-grade class. These animosities appeared to grow daily.

To address the problems, a group applied for a grant to develop a graduate course on equity that teachers could volunteer to take after school. The principal continued to be an enormous obstacle to the teachers' quest for the examination and ensuring of equity, however. She believed that equity was not a problem and that political issues had no place in the school. No one other than a handful of teachers was willing to acknowledge that equity was a problem. As time progressed, however, the only way one could say that there wasn't a problem with equity at the school was to call it something else.

In the "equity class," participants read academic literature on the topic and had local experts come to discuss their work with them. Among the teachers were three Mexican women, five White women, a woman from Venezuela, and a Mexican American woman. Several para-educators of Mexican origin sat in on most of the discussions.

Ms. Baker permitted the class to take place after staff meetings with the idea that any teachers could sit in on the discussions if they chose to stay. The teachers kept journals and wrote reflections on the readings. Discussions eventually spilled over into each of the teacher's lives. Equity was a topic that they each needed to talk about as if to keep alive.

Equity came to be defined as keeping White privilege in check and elevating the status of Latinos and Spanish. One White teacher wrote about her feelings about racism targeted at the Latino families:

> All my life in education in the U.S., I have fought against myself in order to be able to show that I want each one of our children to have the opportunity to receive the best education that we could give them. Because of that I know, understand, and comprehend that we need leaders to keep on fighting against all the prejudice that exists against Mexicans.

The obvious missing participants in these meetings and discussions were parents—White or Latino. Parent engagement hobbled along on its own with regular SIT meetings and little else. However, one topic became of interest to some parents—high-stakes testing.

High-Stakes Testing and Converging/Diverging Interests

The testing program instituted by law (George W. Bush's No Child Left Behind legislation, 2002) was meant to hold schools accountable for student achievement. In the state in which EBK was located, the results of the test were used to rate schools on report cards that became public knowledge. Not only was the school rated, it was ranked against 10 nearby schools. Parents had access to this information and through open enrollment could choose a school based on its "grade." The test was not designed to measure what students in dual language programs were prepared to do in two languages. The tests were only appropriate for English monolingual students who received all their instruction in English. EBK students received half their instruction in each language, although more in Spanish in the primary grades. Naturally, these students' average scores would be lower than those for English-only schools and English-only students.

Although White parents reported reasonable ideas about why they had their children in a DLP, they might have reconsidered if they had believed that the report card grade for the school was important and an indicator of the quality of the program. White parents indeed began to demonstrate more than usual concern over their children's achievement in the classroom and never about how well their child was acquiring Spanish, interacting with Latino students, or using Spanish outside school. The following excerpt from an email from a White parent to a 3rd-grade teacher illustrates how interests began to shift in the DLP:

> Ms. T, I talked to Ms. Baker about the info I need. She gave me some of it, e.g., a little about the writing rubrics and how you do them and what they mean. These evaluations seem comprehensive and informative in terms of identifying areas where he needs to improve. It is still somewhat unclear to me how [my son] is doing in writing compared to what is expected of a third grader, i.e., is he progressing normally, a little behind, or performing strongly? I need to have that kind of information—both how he is doing compared with the 3rd grade "norm" (not just his class, but 3rd graders everywhere) *and* how he is doing compared with how his teacher (you, presumably) think he should/could be doing with his abilities. I see how he is doing at home in reading and writing, but this does not help me evaluate whether he is where he ought to be and if there are areas where he should/could do extra work at home to improve.
>
> I need this info from you, not just 2 times during the year, but frequently. I would like to know the results of the writing rubrics, reading evaluations, and math evaluations on an ongoing basis. There must be some way to make this information available without needing to spend a lot of

your time. Perhaps you could let parents know about the ongoing evaluation methodologies, what type of results come out of it, and how they can tap into that information. Let me emphasize that I need and expect to have this information on an ongoing basis.

When the interests of the White parents shifted to higher test scores, as this mother's detailed note illustrates, the former converging interests of bilingualism and biliteracy and multicultural fluency began to diverge. Latino parents, however, rarely expressed concerns about the standardized tests scores. For example, as one Latino father put it:

> *Es natural que nuestros hijos no sacan calificaciones muy altas porque están aprendiendo en dos idiomas.* [It is natural that our children do not have very high grades because they are learning in two languages.]

Reflections on Political Clarity of Parent Engagement

In this society, we expect schools to do for our children what our society fails to do. White English monolingual parents reportedly choose schools with dual language programs so that their children may become bilingual and will be exposed to children of "other" cultures while Latino parents hope that the programs will help their children maintain Spanish while they learn English (Shannon & Milian, 2002). From this case study I can say that, by and large, White English monolingual parents want what is in their children's best interest from dual language programs. They want them to learn Spanish coincidentally while succeeding academically in English. Their attitudes dramatically illustrate the interest convergence dilemma. When their interests were not being met at the point that the dual language program did not produce the desired high-stakes testing scores, for example, they lost interest. Of course, their interest had begun to wane before the high-stakes testing issue came to the fore; they tired of the conflicts between the Latino parents and their allies, parents, and teachers alike. They were accustomed to getting their interests attended to without conflict. It seemed that the dual language program would be successful only if the interests of the White parents were being recognized and attended to.

Furthermore, many of the White parents in this DLP showed no effort to engage in the company of the Latino parents at or outside the school. They did not demonstrate the cultural fluency that Glazier (2003) calls for. They modeled behavior for their children that reinforced the segregation and asymmetry of their places in society. They expressed fear and misunderstanding about the Latino families and their homes. It seemed as if the White parents wanted their children to be in a DLP but one that perhaps did not include Latinos. One could also say that the Latino parents did not engage with the White parents or show cultural fluency. But I would argue that it is not fair to expect the oppressed group, in this case Latinos (predominantly of Mexican origin), to even be able to engage with the White community when they are not viewed as worthy or equal (Shannon, 1996). And cultural fluency is an expectation for immigrants in a society that is fiercely monolingual English and expects cultural assimilation.

I am not suggesting that dual language programs be dismantled; rather, I am urging those who advocate for and promote such programs to be clear about the potential dangers of bringing together members of an oppressed group with members of a privileged group. I concur with Bartolomé (1994), who insists on "political clarity" on the part of educators, and, I would add, parents, when choosing programs. We could view dual language programs as great opportunities to teach about social justice but we have to recognize that Latinos in U.S. society are denied social justice on a grindingly daily basis.

Parent engagement in a DLP is a challenge precisely because the relative status, power, and privilege of one group are excessively higher than the other group's. There are responsibilities to having a higher status if one is to choose to participate in democratic projects such as a DLP. If the neoliberal tendency to capitalize and profit is part of the functioning of parent engagement in DLP, then it is not fair to have Latino immigrant families participate.

The EBK program (which I am most familiar with) is perhaps an extreme example of the coming together of two asymmetrically related groups. Perhaps a different scenario in which the English speakers are not middle class and with professional backgrounds and high levels of formal education might ameliorate the situation. But what if they are Chicano and Spanish is their heritage language or are African American and are perceived as speaking a nonstandard variety of English? There is no combination that would not demand the same attention to the historical and political constructions of intergroup relations. The rules must be explicit and everyone must be expected to play fairly.

Other than the high-stakes-testing discussion, academic achievement and closing the achievement gap have not been addressed here. Also, language acquisition and bilingualism are all valuable topics to explore in DLPs. Challenging racism, however, has to be a worthy goal in and of itself. DLPs demands attention to this goal because the parents of the English-speaking students are at an advantage and their interests, whatever they may be, could unwittingly (or deliberately) be made a priority. Finally, the exceptions to the homogenous portraits of White and Latino parents depicted here provide hope. White parents with genuine concerns about the rights of immigrant families, their experiences of success in schools, and their legitimate place in U.S. society were never absent. Courageous individuals stepped forward with a willingness to learn and understand. They also inspired others to do the same. Surely the spirit of dual language education appeals to the true democratic sensibilities of many parents who choose these programs for their children. Dual language education can help keep those sensibilities alive and flourishing.

Discussion Questions

1. In this chapter Shannon compares dual language education of Mexican/ Latino children and Whites in the United States to that of Jews and Arabs in Israel. In what ways do you feel this is a fair or unfair comparison and why?
2. If dual language programs are problematic in terms of equity and potential discrimination, are there ways to anticipate and prevent such problems from arising?
3. How can schools resolve the dilemma that parent involvement is desirable for its positive correlation with students' academic success and at the same time undesirable because high-status parents have the advantages of cultural and symbolic capital, as Weininger and Lareau (2003) argue?
4. What recommendations could be derived from this case study for federal policy regarding the education of the children of Mexican immigrants in the United States? How could such an educational policy be linked in some ways to immigration reform?

Note

1. Charles Black was a law scholar then professor at Columbia Law School and a critic of the neutrality of the *Brown* decision.

Suggested Readings

Acuña, R. (1996). *Anything but Mexican: Chicanos in contemporary Los Angeles.* Los Angeles: Verso.

Bartolomé, L. (1994). Beyond the methods fetish: Toward a humanizing pedagogy. *Harvard Educational Review, 64*(2), 173–194.

Bell, D., Jr. (1980). *Brown v. Board of Education* and the Interest-Convergence Dilemma. *Harvard Law Review, 93*(3), 518–533.

Delgado, R. (2006). Rodrigo's roundelay: *Hernández v. Texas* and the interest convergence dilemma. *Harvard Civil Rights–Civil Liberties Law Review, 4*, 23–65.

Valdés, G. (1997). Dual language immersion programs: A cautionary note concerning the education of language-minority students. *Harvard Educational Review, 67*(3), 391–429.

Weininger, E. B., & Lareau, A. (2003). Translating Bourdieu into the American context: The question of social class and family-school relations. *Poetics, 31*, 375–402.

References

Amrein, A., & Peña, R. (2000). Asymmetry in dual language practice: Assessing imbalance in a program promoting equity. *Education Policy Analysis Archives, 8*(8), 1–18.

Bacon, D. (2008). *Illegal people: How globalization creates migration and criminalizes immigrants.* Boston: Beacon Press.

Bartolomé, L. (1994). Beyond the methods fetish: Toward a humanizing pedagogy. *Harvard Educational Review, 64*(2), 173–194.

Bekerman, Z. (2004). Potential and limitations of multicultural education in conflict-ridden areas: Bilingual Palestinian-Jewish schools in Israel. *Teachers College Press, 106*(3), 574–610.

Bell, D., Jr., (1980). *Brown v. Board of Education* and the interest-convergence dilemma. *Harvard Law Review, 93*(3), 518–533.

Brantlinger, E. (2003). *Dividing classes: How the middle class negotiates and rationalizes school advantage.* New York: RoutledgeFalmer.

Center for Applied Linguistics (CAL). Retrieved from http://www.cal.org/twi/directory/

Chomsky, A. (2007). *"They take our jobs!" and 20 other myths about immigration.* Boston: Beacon Press.

Delgado, R. (2006). Rodrigo's roundelay: *Hernández v. Texas* and the interest convergence dilemma. *Harvard Civil Rights-Civil Liberties Law Review, 4*, 23–65.

Ellingwood, K. (2004). *Hard line: Life and death on the U.S.-Mexico border.* New York: Vintage Books.

Epstein, J. L., & Sanders, M. G. (2006). Prospects for change: Preparing educators for school, family, and community partnerships. *Peabody Journal of Education, 81*(2), 81–120.

Feuerverger, G. (2001). *Oasis of dreams: Teaching and learning peace in a Jewish-Palestinian village in Israel.* New York: RoutledgeFalmer.

Fine, M. (1993). [Ap]parent involvement: Reflections on parents, power, and urban public schools. *Teachers College Record, 94*(4), 682–710.

Foucault, M. (1977). *Discipline and punish: The birth of the prison* (A. Sheridan, Trans.). New York: Pantheon.

Glazier, J. A. (2003). Developing cultural fluency: Arab and Jewish students engaging in one another's company. *Harvard Educational Review, 73*(2), 141–163.

Greene, J. M. (1998). *A meta-analysis of the effectiveness of bilingual education.* Claremont, CA: Tomás Rivera Policy Institute.

Henderson, A. T., & Mapp, K. (2002). *A new wave of evidence: The impact of school, family, and community connections on student achievement.* Austin, TX: Southwest Educational Development Laboratory.

Hernandez, K. L. (2010). *Migra! A history of the border patrol.* Berkeley: University of California Press.

Howard, E., Sugarman, J., & Christian, D. (2003). *Trends in two-way immersion education: A review of the research.* (Report No. 63). Baltimore: Center for Research on the Education of Students Placed at Risk (CRESPAR).

Lareau, A. (1989). *Home advantage: Social class and parental intervention in elementary education.* Philadelphia: Falmer.

Lindhom-Leary, K. (2001). *Dual language education.* Clevedon, UK: Multilingual Matters.

Olivos, E. M. (2006). *The power of parents: A critical perspective of bicultural parent involvement in public schools.* New York: Peter Lang.

Palmer, D. (2009). Middle-class English speakers in a Two-Way Immersion bilingual classroom: "Everybody should be listening to Jonathan right now . . ." *TESOL Quarterly, 43*(2), 177–202.

Parkes, J. (2008). Who chooses dual language education for their children and why? *International Journal of Bilingual Education and Bilingualism, 11*(6), 635–660.

Passel, J. S., & Cohn, D. (2011). *Unauthorized immigrant population: National and state trends, 2010.* Washington, DC: Pew Hispanic Center.

Peña, R. A. (1998). A case study of parental involvement in a conversion from transition to dual language instruction. *Bilingual Research Journal, 22*(2, 3, & 4), 237–259.

Petrovic, J. E. (2005). The conservative restoration and neoliberal defenses of bilingual education. *Language Policy, 4*(4), 395–416.

Plyler v. Doe. (1982). *James Plyler, Superintendent, Tyler Independent School District, et al. v. John Doe, et al.* 457 U.S. 202; 102 S. Ct. 2382; 72 L. Ed. 2d 786; 1982 U.S. LEXIS 124; 50 U.S.L.W. 4650.

Potowski, K. (2007). *Language and identity in a dual immersion school.* Clevedon, UK: Multilingual Matters.

Ramírez, J. D. (1992). Executive summary. *Bilingual Research Journal, 16*(1–2), 1–62.

Rodríquez, R. (1982). T*he hunger of memory: The education of Richard Rodríquez.* Boston: Godine.

Rubio, O. (1995). "Yo soy voluntaria": Volunteering in a dual language school. *Urban Education, 29*(4), 396–409.

Ruiz, R. (1984). Orientations in language planning. *NABE: The Journal for the National Association for Bilingual Education, 8*(2). 15–34.

Scanlon, M., & Palmer, D. (2009). Race, power, and (in)equity within two-way immersion settings. *Urban Review, 41*(5), 391–415.

Shannon, S. M. (1996). Minority parental involvement: A Mexican mother's experience and a teacher's interpretation. *Education and Urban Society, 29*(1), 71–84.

Shannon, S. M. (1999). Language rights or language privileges? *TESOL Journal, 8*(3), 23–28.

Shannon, S. M. (2005). *La construcción social de la hegemonía del inglés en los EE UU.* Unpublished manuscript. University of Guadalajara, México.

Shannon, S. M. (2008). Mexicans in the Pacific Northwest: Lessons from progressive school leaders for progressive educational policy. *Journal of Educational Research and Policy, 8*(2), 16–40.

Shannon, S. M., & Escamilla, K. (1999). Mexican immigrants in U.S. schools: Targets of symbolic violence. *Educational Policy, 13*(3), 347–370.

Shannon, S. M., & Milian M. (2002). Parents choose dual language education in Colorado: A survey. *Bilingual Research Journal, 26*(3), 681–696.

Thomas, W., & Collier, V. (2002). *A national study of school effectiveness for language minority students' long-term academic achievement* (CREDE-9088OP2). Santa Cruz, CA: Center for Research on Education, Diversity, and Excellence.

Valdés, G. (1997). Dual language immersion programs: A cautionary note concerning the education of language-minority students. *Harvard Educational Review, 67*(3), 391–429.

Weininger, E. B., & Lareau, A. (2003). Translating Bourdieu into the American context: The question of social class and family-school relations. *Poetics, 31,*(2003), 375–402.

Willig, A. (1985). A meta-analysis of selected studies on the effectiveness of bilingual education. *Review of Educational Research, 55*(3), 269–317.

6

Engaging Bicultural Parents for Democratic Schooling

Art Pearl

Parents have always played a critical role in the education of their children. This role has not always dovetailed with the demands of a bureaucratic public school system that has in recent years become increasingly inflexible. Indeed, the more underserved the student is by the system, the greater the inflexibility appears to be. The underserved student is not only inadequately encouraged and often discouraged by overt prejudice in the school system but also often by well-meaning teachers whose deficit thinking, "blaming the victim" mentality, and inability to establish legitimate authority contributes significantly to the "achievement gap." To counteract this mentality of perceiving bicultural people and communities as second-class citizens and undoing the existing achievement gap, bicultural parents must work to change and transform current undemocratic school practices that deny them due process and access to equal opportunity. The activism of bicultural parents should lead to an educational system that provides equal encouragement and preparation for careers and democratic living.

As Jeffrey Stout (2002) has observed, "Nearly every nation makes grand democratic pronouncements nowadays" (p. 4). This, however, is definitely not reflected in our public education system. Indeed, for democratic education to serve as an alternative to current undemocratic policies and practices, more than just proclaiming democracy is needed. Defining democracy in terms of

fundamental principles is a necessary first step in an analysis of the role bicultural parents can play in assisting their children to obtain the empowering
benefits of a democratic education.

The democratic education proposed here is a strong (Barber, 1984) and deliberative democracy (Cohen, 1989; Dryze, 2002). Strong democracy in the sense
that governmental institutions, such as public schools, are vital to a functioning
democracy but only if school communities learn about democracy by actually
experiencing it in their children's schooling and only when schools accept as a
major responsibility preparing informed and responsible democratic citizens.
Deliberative democracy in schools promote the sense that school communities,
schools, and classrooms are viewed as places where the widest range of ideas about
vital issues such as racism and justice are exchanged and those voices rarely heard
or suppressed enrich the discourse. In democratic school communities and classrooms, deliberation is not an academic exercise but is a serious effort to advance
public good and influence policy and practice.

The democracy I propose for school communities and schools has seven fundamental principles that work toward actualizing democratic schooling:

1. *Authority* that is persuasive and negotiable and is distinguished from
    its enemies' authoritarianism and anarchy (Dahl, 1989), both of which
    plague the schools where many if not most bicultural students attend;
2. *Inclusion,* where all are welcomed as equally important contributing
    members of a learning community;
3. *Knowledge development,* sufficient to solve the important personal and
    social problems and a necessary component of deliberative democracy;
4. *Development of democratic citizenship skills,* critical for effective
    collective action;
5. *Inalienable rights* guaranteed to all in the Bill of Rights;
6. *An optimum learning environment* available for all; and
7. *Equality* that in schooling is manifest with all students equally
    encouraged to succeed in all of society's legal endeavors (Pearl & Knight,
    1999). In the words of Freire (1970), a democratic education equips
    school communities and students "to engage in action and reflection . . .
    upon their world in order to transform it. . . . The students—no longer
    docile listeners—are now critical co-investigators in dialogue with the
    teacher" (pp. 66, 68).

How each of these principles can be applied to school communities, schools,
and classrooms—and thus influence the education of bicultural students and their
parents—follows.

Legitimizing Authority in Schools

In a democracy, authority is consented to by the governed. No school administrator or teacher is elected; therefore, if that school administrator or teacher is to establish legitimacy either the student has been persuaded to accept that authority or the school administrator/teacher is willing to negotiate openly and fairly with students on issues of curriculum and classroom management. There are four possible responses to existing school/classroom authority: (1) Students actively accept and support the school/classroom authority, (2) students passively accept the authority, (3) students passively resist the authority, and (4) students actively resist the authority. Research into this area in recent years has been sparse, although this aspect of education was the major emphasis in looking at democracy and schooling in the 1930s. Kurt Lewin and his colleagues studied the effect of three types of school leadership/teachers: democratic, authoritarian, and laissez-faire (Lippitt, 1940; White, 1938; White & Lippitt, 1960). Although this research strongly favored democratic teaching, it was not without its critics; moreover, it has only remote bearing on school administrator/teacher legitimacy. Current research reveals from vastly different perspectives school administrator/teacher bias either directly as overtly expressed racial, ethnic, or gender prejudice or through the lens of lowered expectations informed by any of a variety of manifestations of deficit thinking Cochran-Smith, 1997; Cooper, 2003; Delpit, 1995; Oakes & Lipton, 1999; Ogbu, 1990; Solorzano, 1997; Trueba & Bartolomé, 2000; Valencia, 1997).

In my 13 years as a school board member in Northern California, I found many, many incidents of discriminatory practices in the disproportionate number of African American and Latino suspensions and expulsions and gained a not altogether favorable reputation by convincing a majority of my fellow board members to refuse to follow administration recommendations for expulsions. In the vast majority of the cases where we refused to expel students, these students went on to successfully complete their high school education. In working with an alternative high school in Santa Cruz, California, for students who had difficulties in the three comprehensive high schools, again a disproportionate, in this instance, number of Latino students, provided me with detailed litanies of perceived unfair treatment in the schools they had left.

However, revelations of school administrator/teacher bias or neglect have at best a correlation to school administrator/teacher legitimacy. School administrator/teacher legitimacy is based on parent and student perceptions. These perceptions may not be valid, but they nonetheless require a school administrator/teacher response. Failure to obtain legitimacy will inevitably lead to either passive or active parent and student resistance (Olivos, 2006). There is a high correlation between race, ethnicity, class, and in this instance, bicultural parent and student resistance. The seminal work by Willis (1977) ascribes the cause to working-class culture. McFadden (1995) attributes it more to a "rejection of the curriculum and pedagogy encountered by students than to a conscious resistance to the dominant ideology of society" (p. 297). Giroux (1983), on the other hand, views it as opposition to oppressive systems. The position taken here is that while resistance stems from many causes, one important ingredient is that school administrator/teacher legitimacy must be addressed as part of the arsenal in trying to eliminate the achievement gap as well as a necessary element in promoting parent and student engagement with the school.

Regardless of cause, it is not in the interest of bicultural parents and students to resist education. The consequences of resistance are, in accelerating importance, poor academic performance, shunting to the margins in special education or alternative schools, premature removal from schooling, or most devastating, the juvenile justice system. All these consequences damage opportunity for decent employment and opportunity for empowered citizenship. The goal of good education is therefore to generate sufficient support for the purpose of adequately and equally serving all segments of the society—especially bicultural school communities. It is not change for change's sake. The changes advocated here are toward democracy. One such necessary change is transforming school administrators and teachers from illegitimate authorities to legitimate ones.

The parents of bicultural students have an important role to play in transforming teaching. It begins with taking seriously student complaints about indifference, prejudice, or unfairness. Such discussion should include encouraging students to fully express their feelings, to try to elicit the evidence used to reach a conclusion of school administrator/teacher indifference or bias and to determine whether other students share this perception.

Past practices have shown us that efforts will be made to recruit the parent into being an ally of the system and to apply parental leverage to encourage the student to set aside his or her grievances, become "a team player," and do whatever is necessary to follow the leader. The mistake here is that submission to illegitimate authority will not lead to widespread educational success, nor will the student be getting the education that is needed for empowerment in a rapidly changing world. To whatever extent possible, bicultural parents need to be helped to ensure that their children's school administrators/teachers work hard to earn legitimacy by making a persuasive case for the topics they teach and to discuss the causes for their children's school/classroom resistance. More on the importance of what is being taught is presented later in this chapter. In far too many instances the only possible allies students will have when resisting school/teacher illegitimate authority will be their parents and thus it is important to support both agents equally.

Bicultural Parents' Role in Inclusive Education

If school authority depends on the perception of parents, inclusion is determined by the perception of how the school system at the school community level views parents, especially low-income bicultural parents.

Historically, the slow and very uneven progress toward developing democracy in the United States began with the American Revolution, which was inspired by reaction to abuses of authority. The Declaration of Independence, apart from its inspiring first and last paragraphs, is essentially a compilation of grievances against the king's malfeasance. But the elimination of an illegitimate authority did not result in a democracy. The constitution created by the founders did not endorse democracy. It endorsed slavery and in one of the negotiated compromises shockingly counted slaves as 60% of a human being to provide Virginia and other slaveholding states more congressional members (Berlin & Hoffman, 1983). The slaves did not get to vote; neither did women, nor did almost 80% of White males that didn't own property.

The spirit of democracy has been kept alive by the struggles for inclusion. This can be witnessed beginning with the elimination of property as a requirement to vote, through the long and bitter struggle to abolish slavery, to the prolonged effort to secure women's suffrage, to the ultimate granting of citizenship to Native Americans, to the right for workers to organize and culminating in the civil rights movements of the 1960s. All these struggles for inclusion, however, met with savage resistance, and all have been somewhat reduced by new exclusionary efforts.

At the time of this writing a hysterical effort is being mounted to deport over 10 million undocumented immigrants in the United States, while in other states in our nation efforts are being mounted to exclude the children of undocumented immigrants from citizenship. Furthermore, Arizona's tough new anti-immigrant law, S.B. 1070, gives police broad new authority to demand papers or other documentation of anyone they may suspect of being in the state illegally. Arizona's new anti-immigrant law is eerily familiar to this country's earlier Chinese Exclusion Act (Li, 2010).

In this climate, inclusion has become an even more pertinent issue. And nowhere is the issue of bicultural parent inclusion more vital than in public education. All efforts to reform education over the past 40 years have failed to eliminate the achievement gap, which is the persistent differences in academic achievement when African Americans, Native Americans, and Latinos are compared with "White" and Asian students. No Child Left Behind was supposed to address that problem. It has not and cannot (Ravitch, 2010). A manifestly undemocratic education cannot lead to a democratic result.

The persistence of the achievement gap has led to another major problem of exclusion, the vast underrepresentation of bicultural parents engaged with their school community, and the underrepresentation of bicultural teachers is evident. Yet where do bicultural parents fit in with the effort to undo exclusionary practices? Bicultural parents need to exert their voice and representation. The implication for schools is to engage parents in action and reflection in reconceptualizing the role of schooling in order to transform the educational and social context of their school communities into democratic living spaces—where all are welcomed as equally important members of the community.

The implication for bicultural parents is to play multiple roles to make inclusion a reality. At the classroom level parents need to find ways to maintain pressure on teachers to include all students in the class as celebrated members of a learning community. Just as parents take seriously student complaints about teacher bias so too should they take seriously students' feelings of exclusion. At the teacher level, parents need to continue to lobby for the inclusion of bicultural teachers, including support of paraprofessional career ladder programs. One way that parents can become part of the inclusion effort is to consider becoming para-educators in a career ladder program. At the school-site level, parents need to work closely with site administrators and assert themselves and participate in school site decision-making committees. At the school community level, parents need to engage in civic issues that directly affect the consciousness of schools.

Bicultural Parents and Knowledge Development for a Deliberative Democracy

The prevailing myth is that increased effort, better teaching, and equalized resources will result in the elimination of the achievement gap and also provide students from bicultural low-income schools with the education they will need for successful lives. Given existing educational conditions, however, that will not happen (Trueba & Bartolomé, 2000). The current curriculum prepares students for success in the 19th century. It is a curriculum primarily organized to satisfy powerful corporate interests. Its primary goal is to fit students into an existing stratified world. The logical result is social reproduction—the maintaining of the existing economic order with a small percentage of the population monopolizing economic resources (Bowles & Gintis, 1976; West, 1993). Such an education disempowers bicultural parents and students in particular.

In a world of ever accelerating change, the primary curriculum goal must be to provide low-income school communities and students with knowledge and with the ability to locate the knowledge to be able to participate meaningfully and equally in changing the world. In a remodeled curriculum for a 21st-century education, the bicultural student learns how to invent the future. In such an education, no topic is off the table. Students discuss issues of justice and racism, alternatives to war, solutions to environmental challenges, and the eradication of poverty. In such an educational experience, students replace passive lecturing on the evils of drug use, violence, and reckless sexual behavior with extensive research and active deliberation on how best to deal with such matters. In such an education students learn to contribute back to their school communities and to be citizens by practicing citizenship in school community–designed projects constructed to make a better classroom, school, or community.

Bicultural parents will need to recognize how the existing curriculum leaves the student unprepared for the realities of a world that constantly will be invented and reinvented. If bicultural low-income school communities are not prepared to be part of this reinvention process, they will live in a world that someone else invents (similar but even more fraught with threats and potential disasters than today), and it is unlikely they will be treated well or even fairly in such a world. It is the unfairness of the existing system and its political paralysis in addressing the palpable threats to human existence that make democratic education imperative.

Bicultural parents need to be a visible presence in pushing for schools and classrooms where students actively participate in deliberations about issues that affect their lives and engage in the development of knowledge that will serve them well as they enter a uncertain and challenging future. When their children complain about the irrelevance and dullness of the curriculum, bicultural parents should not rush to try to persuade them to suffer through it, but become allies in efforts to enliven the curriculum to solve community issues and problems.

Bicultural Parents and the Development of Democratic Citizenship Skills

Every aspect of education is influenced by politics. For the past 25 years antidemocratic forces have dominated education (Macedo, 2006). The cost of that domination is an undemocratic education that has ill served the vast majority of students and particularly bicultural students and school communities. Both bicultural parents and their children will need to develop the skills of citizenship that includes defending positions with logic and evidence, listening to the arguments of others, mobilizing constituencies, and developing coalitions. The political battles to be fought and won at every level require networks of bicultural parents working together at the school and classroom level; organizing influence at the district level, including representation on school boards; and coalescing with a range of others at the state and federal level.

As bicultural parents engage in learning the skills of a socially conscious citizen they will take an active role in their community and society and work to develop a new vision of education that will enable them to explore different ways of being active participants in the school community. Active citizenship can take the form of taking a more active part in school and classroom learning, to bicultural parents supporting each other's development, to improving structures in the school that develop active involvement, to taking active roles in the social and political development of their community. In the process they will learn about the power of cooperation, patience, fairness, respect, and personal and collective strength (McFadden, 1995; Olivos, 2006; Wenger, 1998).

Bicultural Families and Inalienable Rights Guaranteed to All

They that can give up essential liberty to obtain a little temporary safety deserve neither liberty nor safety. (Franklin, 1963)

The rights found in the first 10 amendments to the U.S. Constitution, the Bill of Rights, more than anything else has maintained the imperfect democracy of the United States. Throughout our history those rights have been threatened. In the early years of the Republic the threat was the Alien and Sedition Acts; periodically since then the threats have come in different forms. In one sense those rights are endangered at the moment with the Patriot Act and the suspension of habeas corpus, which permits persons to be held indefinitely without charge or trial and the invasion of privacy through eavesdropping on telephone conversations. In another sense targeted populations have never enjoyed the protection of the Bill of Rights. It was not until the 1960s that students were protected by the Bill of Rights. One can surmise that bicultural parents and children can rightfully claim that those treasured rights never have been extended to them (ACLU, 2010).

Those rights, deemed to be inalienable, are in reality very few. They include (1) the right of expression, which includes freedom of religion, speech, press, and assembly and the right to petition; (2) rights of privacy (not expressly found in the Bill of Rights but covered in what are called a penumbra of rights in the 4th and 14th Amendments); (3) a unique due process system that includes the presumption of innocence, the right not to testify against oneself, the right to a speedy trial, the right to counsel, and protection against cruel and unusual punishment; and (4) the right to movement. Because the rights under the Bill of Rights are currently threatened and because they have rarely protected most bicultural people, securing the aforementioned four should be the first order of business. Often, bicultural low-income parents when confronting a social or educational issue are reminded that they need to follow the law and be expected to collaborate with authority, including school officials and the hierarchy of the educational system. The assumed expectation is for bicultural parents to follow policy (fair or not) and be good citizens (Olivos, 2006).

School districts have denied due process rights to bicultural parents on the grounds that only the responsible deserve them. Such is not the intention of the Bill of Rights, nor should it be used as an excuse to deny parent communities and students their right to obtain a quality education.

Bicultural parents will find that the education of their children will run far more smoothly when they are protected by fundamental rights of our Constitution. Learning those rights will also help build a constituency for them. The goal should be not only to secure the Bill of Rights but also to work to extend these rights to those who never enjoyed their protection.

Bicultural Parents and Optimum Learning Environment for All

How is the persistence of the achievement gap to be explained in low-income bicultural school communities? Throughout the years and continuing into the present, the explanation placed the onus on the lagging group (Valencia & Black, 2002). At different times, different "deficits" were deemed to be the cause. Starting in the mid-19th century and continuing into the 1960s and supported by "science," genetics was deemed to be the cause of students' failure in schools and it was determined that it was a waste of time trying to teach persons whose inherited intelligence precluded more than that which was necessary to perform menial tasks.

Later, other explanations gained prominence—accumulated environmental deficits stemming from an impoverished early childhood or membership in a culture that disparaged intellectual activity (Valencia, 1997). It was never considered that students' academic underachievement stemmed from limited encouragement to succeed, particularly for those students who came from marginalized and oppressed communities (Pearl & Knight, 1999).

Previously and briefly mentioned was the illegitimacy of the classroom authority, exclusion, and an irrelevant curriculum, all of which could lead to markedly different academic achievement. However, my experience has been that students are differentially encouraged by the nature of the school community and classroom environment. In the case of the school environment, more than the importance of the physical environment—dilapidated buildings, limited textbooks, and even overcrowded classrooms, all of which do take their toll—is the psychological environment that can be changed by any teacher in any school building. This type of optimum learning environment has 11 components, and because they are experienced differently they can make it possible for two students, even from the same family, to experience the learning process differently in the classroom. The suggested 11 components are areas that bicultural school communities must advocate to have present in every classroom of their schools. Specifically, bicultural parents can work to improve the following factors of the learning environment of the school:

1. *Encouragement:* Encouragement to risk, to make mistakes. Only a rare few are so encouraged and some are firmly discouraged.

2. *Elimination of unnecessary discomfort:* This includes boredom, humiliation, and loneliness. Within a class some students experience these unnecessary discomforts far more than others.

3. *Meaning:* Meaning, to understand why learning a particular lesson is important, or knowing exactly what is expected by the teacher. Research indicates that a large number of students do not know what teachers want them to do (Corbett & Wilson, 1998).

4. *Feelings of competence:* Developing in students a sense of their own competence is a vital condition for personality development (White, 1959). Currently only a select few are so encouraged to that sense. Those that are not so encouraged learn quickly that they are "dummies" and begin to perceive themselves as teachers perceive them (Wigfield, Eccles, & Rodriguez, 1998). All students need to gain a sense of efficacy. This is especially true for students who are believed to be plagued with deficits of whatever kind.

5. *Belonging:* Ours is a society that systematically includes and excludes. Belonging is a critical human need (Goodenow, 1993). Humans hunger for companionship. So much of today's life is centrifugal and impersonal. Exclusion from welcomed membership in school or in a classroom does not terminate a student's desire for belonging. In a very crucial way building strong feelings of belonging to school is an effective antidote to gang membership.

6. *Usefulness:* Uselessness is a dreaded condition. Enforced uselessness is cruel punishment. Enforced uselessness is the essence of existing classrooms. School is preparation for a fantasized future of usefulness. One reason students find school so deadly is that they don't see themselves in the fantasized future. Schools, by and large, ask students to put their lives on hold. Conversely, democratic classrooms prepare students for future challenges, but at same time usefulness is built into daily classroom activity (Wenger, 1998). Ideally usefulness is curriculum

for problem posing and in solving important problems. But that is not the only way students can be useful in a classroom. Usefulness in school is achieved when all students are given a wide range of choices in providing services to others and also a wide range of choices in accepting the services of another.

7. *Hope:* The major enemy of survival in the United States for the majority of low-income bicultural communities is neither oppression nor exploitation but rather the nihilistic threat—that is, loss of hope and absence of meaning. For as long as hope remains and meaning is preserved, the possibility of overcoming oppression stays alive. The self-fulfilling prophecy of the nihilistic threat is that without hope there can be no future, that without meaning there can be no struggle (West, 1993).

   Hope begins with understanding the world. Hope begins with small victories. Hope requires vision. Hope requires community development projects that both provide support and act on the world to change it. Hope also means picking up students, dusting them off, and getting them back into learning and action. And hope is maintaining a sense of humor.

8. *Excitement:* Excitement is the thrill of discovery. Excitement is the challenge to go beyond previous accomplishments. Excitement is not knowing in advance how things will turn out. Excitement is everything school is not. Excitement is the 1st night in a school play. Excitement is a sporting competition, an art exhibit, a musical event, a community project, engaging in civic activities. Excitement is a science fair addressing community problems. Excitement is doing history rather than memorizing it.

9. *Creativity:* Creativity is the thrill of invention. Doing what no one has ever done before. It is part of a good community development project. It is art, theater, and music. It is being part of any knowledge development project. It is reliving Galileo at Pisa, Diego Rivera doing history in murals, Einstein in 1905, Picasso at Guernica, learning from Carrie Chapman Catt how to devise a winning plan for today.

10. *Ownership:* Ownership is doing things for oneself and the community and not for the teacher or the educational system. The lack of meaningful ownership is one of the many things that make high-stakes testing so tragic—and why so many students don't even try. Ownership has been found to be a more powerful predictor of school success than parent income (Christenson & Sheridan, 2001; Guthrie & Wigfield, 1997). Currently it is not easy to get students to see that what they are doing in school is for them—mainly because in most instances it isn't.

11. *Participation:* Participation in a vital, vibrant, mutually fulfilling community development project. It is the feeling that comes with being part of something important; the camaraderie that comes with that kind of community building; the feelings of support that come with being a part of a mutual support group, of being relied upon and knowing where and from whom you can get help and support; it is transforming. Such a feeling surpasses the gratification that comes with a sense of belonging or usefulness. Developing that kind of feeling is not for tomorrow; it will take time to build.

Bicultural Parents and Equality in Schools

All democratic societies claim equality; none even come close. Equality, like much of democracy, is sometime in the distant future. Philosophers are bogged down by definition. Conservatives define equality as identical treatment, and some liberals define it as equal results. The debate between them has no impact on life, in school communities or on the street. A viable equality that can be put into practice in our school communities is equal encouragement. In school equal encouragement would mean that all are taught by legitimate authority; all are included equally in the school and classroom as celebrated participants and learners; all are provided the knowledge and skills needed to solve problems, big and small; all are equally prepared to be informed and skilled democratic citizens; all are provided equally the protection of the Bill of Rights; and all benefit from an optimum learning environment.

Bicultural parents and students have been disproportionately victimized by undemocratic and often anti-democratic education. No one has more to gain from democratic schooling than bicultural school communities. Inertia, tradition, and those who benefit from existing undemocratic and often anti--democratic education stand in the way. Bicultural parents must be in the forefront of the struggle to make democratic education happen if their children are to derive the benefits from it. There needs to be a closer tie between democratic schooling principles and the engagement of bicultural parents. How do these issues tie into bicultural parents?

Helping Parents Help Their Children

Democracy is difficult—difficult to achieve, difficult to understand, and impossible to achieve if not understood. For parents to be effective advocates for their children, particularly when so much effort will be made by school authority to co-opt them to be agents of the school's undemocratic practices and policies, parents will need support and assistance. The creation of some form of partnership of the university-school community and parents is beneficial to all parties. Concerned university faculty can provide valuable consultation to assist parents in developing understanding of fundamental principles of democracy and the intricacies of educational polices in these times of federal and state ascendancy as ever more powerful agencies. Parents can be of invaluable assistance to faculty to provide them with the understanding of what actually is happening day to day, on the ground in schools and classrooms. Community advocacy organizations (legal, social, political, and economic) can serve as allies to parents in supporting their concerns and equity issues. With such assistance bicultural parents not only can join the "many parents and parent groups currently out in the public school system that have already taken their own individual transformational view of being involved in their children's schools" (Olivos, 2006, p. 118) but also can significantly advance such a movement.

University faculty, community advocacy organizations, and community leaders concerned with social justice and the continual denial of equal encouragement in ever new guises have a responsibility to help bicultural parents gain an understanding of what democratic education truly means and thus assist parents to be active participants in bringing democracy to their children's education. Partnerships of parents, community organizations, and university scholars do more than help parents; they bring new insights to the university and community. It is unlikely that without bicultural parents working cooperatively with concerned university faculty, community leaders, and organizations, vital change will occur either in higher education or in public schools.

One approach that universities and community organizations can actualize is to diversify the teaching profession given that bicultural families and children are vastly underrepresented in all the credentialed professions, particularly in education. In the case of California, over 70% of all students in public schools are classified as culturally linguistically diverse (CLD), while 70% of teachers are Euro-American (Ed-Data, 2011). That disparity dramatically underscores the magnitude of the exclusion of CLD from the teaching profession. The disparity of CLD teachers, like the achievement gap, has stimulated interest and various efforts to bring more CLD teachers into the profession, ranging from efforts to increase academic achievement, to building interest in teaching elementary, middle school, and high school CLD students (Pearl & Riessman, 1965; Rueda & Monzo, 2000).

But even more important is creating classrooms that are conducive to learning. As funds for education are increasingly scarce, classroom sizes are growing, particularly in the inner city or barrio schools. Education has became a political football to be kicked in almost every direction by those who wish to make political capital out of what needs to be recognized as a critical condition requiring something more than cute slogans devoid of meaning. Education needs money—money designed to meet the democratic goal of inclusion. A federal teacher supplement bill that would reduce all classrooms in the United States to no more than 15 students to a classroom could be mounted for roughly the same amount of money wasted on No Child Left Behind each year of its existence. A federal teacher supplement that emphasizes teacher diversity could put 750,000 persons into teaching roles. Such a supplement could include $5 billion open for bid to teacher education institutions toward creating and implementing courses for each rung of the career ladder. This would also allow an opportunity to rigorously document and evaluate the impact that CLD teachers, especially bilingual-bicultural ones, have on student performance.

Engaged Parents Create Democratic Schools

Bicultural parents play many important and vitally useful roles in providing support for their children. Contrary to myth, bicultural parents are concerned about and involved in their children's education (Macedo, 2006). Historically, low-income bicultural parents have not been included in important decision making. They are not to be found on school boards and rarely on school site committees. Moreover, the schools of today, straitjacketed by an obsession with "high-stakes" testing, have lost sight of their mission to prepare informed and responsible democratic citizens. The only adequate response to problems bicultural students have in school is movement in the direction of democracy.

Democracy in school communities occurs when students are in classrooms informed by democratic principles and when parents and students are prepared to be democratic citizens by practicing citizenship in the community and at every grade level. A school community based on democracy equally encourages all and thereby equalizes life chances by equalizing the distribution of credentials, but it is also a democracy that addresses poverty, among other important issues, to ensure that those without credentials can live fulfilling lives.

Democracy in school communities will not come easily, especially now that we have moved so dramatically in an opposite direction. An important, if not critical, element in the development of democratic schooling must be bicultural parents who can significantly contribute to the democratic education at the school by meaningful participation in important decision-making roles at the schools and in the community. This will not happen without strong political action at the community level, in which bicultural parents and their children work together to transform education. It is important that bicultural parents and students see each other as allies and that parents refrain from becoming the force for an education system that does not empower their children and school community.

All of us interested in meaningful reform must pressure schools in bicultural low-income communities to find ways to include and engage parents of children in those schools in vital decision making. We also need to find ways to help those parents understand the importance of democracy not only for their children's future but also for the well-being of their community and society.

Discussion Questions

1. What are the eight democratic principles that are proposed for guiding the actualization of democratic education?
2. What are the tensions that prevent the eight principles from being part of a proactive democratic education?
3. What are the perceived benefits of the seven democratic education principles for bicultural school communities? Schools? Bicultural parents? Students?
4. What roles can bicultural parents play to bring democratic education to their children?
5. How do the seven democratic schooling principles challenge schools to be more responsive to school communities and bicultural parents?

Suggested Readings

Benjamin B. (1984). *Strong democracy: Participatory politics for a new age.* Berkeley: University of California Press.

Diamond, L. (1997). Cultivating democratic citizenship education for a new century of democracy in the Americas. *Social Studies, 88*(6), 244–251.

Pearl, A., & Knight, T. (1999). *The democratic classroom: Theory to inform practice.* Cresskill, NJ: Hampton Press.

References

ACLU. (2010). *Immigrants' rights: No human being is illegal.* Retrieved from http://www.aclu.org/immigrants-rights

Barber, B. (1984). *Strong democracy: Participatory politics for a new age.* Berkeley: University of California Press.

Berlin, I., & Ronald Hoffman, R. (1983). *Slavery and freedom in the age of the American Revolution.* Charlottesville: Published for the United States Capitol Historical Society by the University Press of Virginia.

Bowles, S., & Gintis, H. (1976). *Schooling in capitalist America: Educational reform and the contradictions of economic life*. New York: Basic Books.

Christenson, S. L., & Sheridan, S. M. (2001). *School and families: Creating essential connections for learning*. New York: Guilford Press.

Cochran-Smith, M. (1997). Knowledge, skills, and experiences for teaching culturally diverse learners: A perspective for practicing teachers. In J. Irvine (Ed.), *Critical knowledge for diverse teachers and learners* (pp. 27–88). Washington, DC: AACTE.

Cohen, J. (1989). Deliberative democracy and democratic legitimacy. In A. Hamlin and P. Pettit (Eds.), *The good polity* (pp. 17–34). Oxford, UK: Blackwell.

Cooper, C. W. (2003, April). The detrimental impact of teacher bias: Lessons learned from the standpoint of African American mothers. *Teacher Education Quarterly, 30*(2), 101–116.

Corbett, H. D., & Wilson, B. L. (1998). Scaling within rather than scaling up: Implications from students' experiences in reforming urban middle schools. *Urban Review, 30*(4), 261–293.

Dahl, R. A. (1989). *Democracy and its critics*. New Haven, CT: Yale University Press.

Delpit, L. (1995). *Other people's children: Cultural conflicts in the classroom*. New York: New Press.

Dryze, J. S. (2002). *Deliberative democracy and beyond: Liberals, critics, contestations*. London: Oxford University Press. Retrieved from http://www.educationtosavedemocracy.org

Ed-Data. (2011). *Education data partnership: State of California education profile on K–12 schools*. Sacramento: California State Department of Education.

Franklin, B. (1963). Pennsylvania Assembly: Reply to the Governor, November 11, 1755. In L. W. Labaree (Ed.), *The papers of Benjamin Franklin, Volume 6: April 1, 1755 through September 24, 1756*. New Haven, CT: Yale University Press.

Freire, P. (1970). *Pedagogy of the oppressed*. New York: Seabury Press.

Giroux, H. (1983). *Theory and resistance in education: A pedagogy for the opposition*. South Hadley, MA: Bergin & Garvey.

Goodenow, C. (1993). Classroom belonging among early adolescent students: Relationships to motivation and achievement. *Journal of Early Adolescence, 13*(1), 21–43.

Guthrie, J., & A. Wigfield (Eds.). (1997). *Reading engagement: Motivating readers through integrated instruction* (pp. 168–182). Newark, DE: International Reading Association.

Li, C. (2010). *Arizona's new Chinese exclusion laws*. Retrieved from http://www.cristyli.com/?p=8045

Lippitt, R. (1940). An experimental study of the effect of democratic and authoritarian group atmospheres. In K. Lewin, R. Lippitt, & S. K. Escalona (Eds.), *Studies in Topological and Vector Psychology. University of Iowa Studies in Child Welfare, 16*(3), 43–195.

Macedo, D. P. (2006). *Literacies of power: What Americans are not allowed to know*. Boulder, CO: Westview Press.

McFadden, M. (1995) Resistance to schooling and educational outcomes: Questions of structure and agency. *British Journal of Sociology of Education, 16*(3), 293–308, 297.

Oakes, J., & Lipton, M. (1999). *Teaching to change the world.* Boston: McGraw-Hill College.

Ogbu, J. (1990). Minority education in comparative perspective. *Journal of Negro Education, 59,* 45–57.

Olivos, E. M. (2006). *The power of parents: A critical perspective of bicultural parent involvement in public schools.* New York: Peter Lang.

Pearl, A., & Knight, T. (1999). *The democratic classroom: Theory to inform practice.* Cresskill, NJ: Hampton Press.

Pearl, A., & Riessman, F. (1965). *New careers for the poor.* New York: Macmillan.

Ravitch, D. (2010). *The death and life of the great American school system: How testing and choice are undermining education.* New York: Basic Books.

Rueda, R., & Monzo, L. (2000). *Apprenticeship for teaching: Issues surrounding the collaborative relationship between teachers and paraeducators.* Santa Cruz: University of Southern California, Center for Research on Education, Diversity and Excellence.

Solorzano, D. (1997). Images and words that wound: Critical race theory, racial stereotyping, and teacher education. *Teacher Education Quarterly, 24*(3), 5–19.

Stout, J. (2002). *Democracy and tradition.* Princeton, NJ: Princeton University Press.

Trueba, E. T., & Bartolomé, L. I. (2000). Beyond the politics of schools and the rhetoric of fashionable pedagogies: The significance of teacher ideology. In E. T. Trueba & L. I. Bartolomé (Eds.), *Immigrant voices: In search of educational equity.* (pp. 277–292). New York: Rowman & Littlefield.

Valencia, R. R. (Ed.). (1997). T*he evolution of deficit thinking: Educational thought and practice.* London, UK: Palmer Press.

Valencia, R. R., & Black, M. S. (2002). Mexican Americans don't value education! On the basis of the myth, mythmaking, and debunking. *Journal of Latinos and Education, 1*(2), 81–103.

Wenger, E. (1998). *Communities of practice: Learning, meaning, and identity.* Cambridge, UK: Cambridge University Press.

West, C. (1993). *Race matters.* Boston: Beacon.

White, R. K. (1938). Democratic and autocratic group atmospheres. *Psychological Bulletin, 35,* 694.

White, R. K., & Lippitt, R. O. (1960). *Autocracy and democracy: An experimental inquiry.* New York: Harper.

White, R. W. (1959) Motivation reconsidered: The concept of competence. *Psychological Review, 66,* 279–333.

Wigfield, A., Eccles, J. S., & Rodriguez, D. (1998). The development of children's motivation in school contexts. *Review of Research in Education, 73–118.*

Willis, P. (1977). *Learning to labor: How working class kids get working class jobs.* Lexington, MA: D. C. Heath.

7

Models of Parent-Teacher/School Engagement in a Time of Educational Reform, Increased Diversity, and Globalization

Carl A. Grant and Aubree A. Potter

The general tendency of the postwar movements for the promotion of human rights has been to subsume the problem of . . . minorities under the broader problem of ensuring basic individual rights to all human beings, without reference to membership in ethnic groups. The leading assumption has been that members of . . . minorities do not need, are not entitled to, or cannot be granted rights of a special character. The doctrine of human rights has been put forward as a substitute for the concept of minority rights, with the strong implication that minorities whose members enjoy individual equality of treatment cannot legitimately demand facilities for the maintenance of their ethnic particularism.

(Inis Claude, National Minorities)

Standing outside Richmond Elementary School waiting to pick up his granddaughter—Amaya—after her 1st day in kindergarten caused Carl to think back to the time he did the same thing 25 years ago on his son's 1st day in kindergarten. Parents then as now were milling about chatting with each other, waiting for the school bell to ring. The chatting was very friendly, mostly about the expected comments they would receive from the children about their 1st day at school or about their anxiety over their child's 1st day at school. Typical comments were

> "I wonder how Chang got along with the teacher and other kids."
> "I watched the clock most of the day, wondering if the school was going to call me because Marilyn was having difficulty."
> "Ramon's English still needs a good deal of work and I can't have difficulty helping him."
> "I hope Emily tells me more than she didn't like the food."

This grouping of parents would provide an excellent Norman Rockwell magazine cover entitled "Precious and Anxious Moments in American School Life." Ironically, although the chatter among this group of parents was pretty much the same as it was years ago when Carl stood outside the same school waiting on his son, there was a noticeable difference.

A difference that was rarely captured in Norman Rockwell's picturesque scenes of American life was not that of the parents milling about chatting, or the anxiousness of the people who were chattering; the difference was the racial and ethnic backgrounds of the parents who were chatting. More than six different racial/ethic groups were represented, including at least one biracial couple.

Richmond, like so many other U.S. schools in the 21st century, has racial and ethnic diversity, along with several other forms of diversity. Gone (or at least going) is the presence of primarily Black and White parents that Carl had experienced years ago. However, it should be noted that at that time, Carl appreciated the civil and friendly coming together of Black and White parents, primarily because such an act of the simple mixing of these two racial groups was a positive testimony to the results from bitterly contested civil rights struggles. However, what soon became apparent and resented by Carl and other Black parents was that parent-school engagement was structured according to an assimilationist majority-minority model in which minority students and their homes and culture were seen as deficit and needing to fit into the White mainstream. In other words, social justice, that is, equity and cultural recognition, were not achieved.

Today, many schools and classrooms across the United States reflect a wide array of student diversity. This diversity is different from what it has previously been in U.S. schools. European birthrates are decreasing: Ninety-three out of every 100 children are now being born in Asia, Africa, and Latin America. These data represent a major change since the beginning of the 20th century when one-third of the world's population was born in Europe. Currently European descendants are only one-tenth of the world's population. This population shift underscores the change in the patterns of U.S. immigration. During the 1st decade of the 20th century, 97% of new arrivals came from Europe. Presently 85% come from Asia and Latin America. The result of this change in demographics is that in 1960 the United States was 10% people of color; it now has become 30% people of color (Cortes, 1999).

Cortes contends that these population demographic changes are ethnically tipping the balance between racial and ethnic groups in schools and communities. He notes that by the end of 1998, Anglos had become a numerical minority in 243 counties, with 42 making that transition within the past 5 years. Cortes argues that this darkening of the United States has led to three evolving patterns of schools and locales:

- In a myriad of schools and communities, students of color have become the majority.
- Anglos comprise neither of the two major ethnic groups in many bicultural schools and communities.
- Multicultural schools and communities exist in which no single group forms a numerical majority. (p. 3)

Classrooms may have five to six, and sometimes more, students of different racial/ethnic groups. Here is a typical picture of many classrooms in the United States: There are 30 students (approximately 15 girls and 15 boys); 16 are White, 5 are African American, 6 are Latino (3 Mexican Americans, 2 Puerto Ricans, and 1 Cuban American), 1 is American Indian, and 2 are second-generation Asian American. Two of the African American students, 2 Latino students, and 3 White students come from families that live below the poverty line, while another 3 White students are from upper-income homes. About two-thirds are from homes that identify as Christian; 3 are Islamic, 2 are Buddhist, 1 is Jewish, and the remaining students are from homes that are nonreligious. Adding to this, an increasing number of students are the offspring of biracial parents.

These distinctions for the most part are not readily visible, because most of the students are wearing jeans and sweaters or sweatshirts. However, two of the girls do wear headscarves. The students' families vary widely: Only 4 students come from families in which the father but not the mother works outside the home, 6 are from singe-parent families (2 of which live below the poverty line), and both parents of the remaining 20 students hold or have recently held jobs at least part time. Most of the students grew up speaking English, but 3 of the Latino students speak Spanish at home and 1 White student speaks French at home.

The students' academic skills vary widely: Two students spend part of the day in a class for children with learning disabilities, another spends part of the day in a class for children with special needs, one is in a program for gifted students, and one is in a speech therapy program. Three students work with an English as a second language teacher for a part of the day.

This new racial, ethnic, bilingual, and religious diversity argues for a conversation on parent engagement that is different from the one Carl experienced 25 years ago and those in educational literature, which represent majority-minority approaches.

The argument in this chapter is for a pluralistic approach to parent-teacher/school engagement that brings the different groups together within the context of constructive pluralism (which we define below). While we acknowledge that in a number of communities, especially those in some urban and rural areas, schools are as they were years ago—predominantly or totally made up of one racial/ethnic group—our discussion has implication for those communities too. This is so because, whereas the community maybe homogenous, the world where the students of the community most likely will live and work is heterogeneous.

To present our argument we begin with a review of parent-school engagement in the education literature over the past 30 years. Here, we pay attention to how models of parent-teacher/school engagement acknowledge the majority-minority approach that structures the procedure. We pay particular attention to how educational reform has affected the discourse on parent-school engagement. Next, we present our argument for a model of constructive pluralism, after defining the term.

Models of Parent-School Engagement

The No Child Left Behind Act (NCLB) of 2001 contains multiple references to parents and the importance of involving families in many aspects of their children's education. Specifically, the act dictates that schools that receive Title 1 funding must involve parents in school improvement plans and in school decisions. Districts are to develop policies to strengthen their parent involvement programs, as well as develop a school-parent compact that outlines how the school, parents, and staff are to share responsibility for the achievement of the students. Most notably, NCLB dictates that schools are to increase their efforts to communicate with parents for a variety of reasons, including to inform them of their child's progress, the school's progress in meeting annual achievement goals, the qualifications of teachers, or the option to transfer or take advantage of free tutoring if the school is low performing or to provide information about effective parent involvement practices (Epstein, 2005).

While these mandates are made clear in the law, few specific guidelines to help districts and schools carry out the mandates are presented. Furthermore, these requirements deal more with informing parents than engaging or involving them. This is particularly significant for schools that are considered low performing, which must tell parents not only that their child's school is "in need of improvement" but also that they have the option to transfer to a different school. These schools would likely benefit greatly from an increased effort to engage parents, yet efforts to do so could be thwarted by a steady departure of parents who opted to transfer.

In general, the law lacks conviction and guidance regarding parent involvement. Without better defined guidelines to seriously engage parents, schools will likely approach parent involvement as they always have, which in most cases reflects a traditional, majority-minority approach.

Even before the push from NCLB to implement parent involvement programs, different models and frameworks of parent, child, and school relationships were presented and discussed in the education literature. Each model identifies ways for parents and schools to become partners in order to increase student achievement. The models feature many positive elements (e.g., specific types of involvement to implement, the view of parents as intellectual resources, and curriculum transformation) but generally ignore the demographic diversity of the parents and therefore miss out on opportunities to engage pluralistic groups of parents.

The following list of parent engagement models is not exhaustive. Those that are presented, however, represent the models and frameworks that are currently being explored and implemented in schools.

The School-Family-Community Partnership Model. Arguably the most widely acknowledged model is that of Epstein (2004). Her School-Family-Community Partnership model features the following six types of involvement:

- *Parenting*: Help families create home conditions to support their child's progress and learn parenting skills, and help schools to better understand families.
- *Communicating*: Carry out effective communications from school to home and from home to school.
- *Volunteering*: Organize volunteers to support the school and students.
- *Learning at home*: Engage families in helping their children with homework and other curriculum-related activities.
- *Decision making*: Encourage parent leaders and include families as participants in school decisions.
- *Collaborating with the community*: Organize services and resources from the community, and provide services to the community.

Each of these types of involvement is to be developed and nurtured by schools in order to effectively create a partnership and ultimately affect the achievement of students. Epstein recommends that schools work to enact each type of involvement by establishing a comprehensive program as well as a team of individuals, including parents, teachers, students, and administrators, who can work to develop the program.

Epstein's model of school and family partnerships is currently implemented in schools and districts across the country. The benefit of this model is that schools and districts have a framework from which they may comprehensively work to partner with families. If taken seriously, this model with its six types of involvement could bring all parents into the school, and the school into all homes.

One criticism of this model, however, is that when a partnership is established between a school and parents, it is done so under the conditions set by the school. In most cases and in most schools, these conditions represent the values and beliefs of the White majority. This means that those families who are not part of the dominant majority or do not buy into the majority-minority model must "parent," "communicate," "volunteer," "learn at home," "make decisions," and "collaborate with the community" based on the terms set forth by the school. The school itself is not expected to adapt based on the diverse needs and experiences of the families, but rather families are expected to hold up their end of the partnership by becoming involved the way these six types define involvement. Little if any attention is given to taking advantage of cross-cultural discussions where students' school and home-community life are the focus of student achievement. What we mean here is that in many multicultural/multiracial schools, cross-cultural friendships abound within school and outside school (Grant & Sleeter, 1996; Nieto, 1999). A majority-minority model of parent-teacher/school engagement ignores such opportunities.

The Math and Parent Partnership in the Southwest Model. A second model of parent engagement, although one that doesn't receive as much attention as the one discussed above, is Project MAPPS (Math and Parent Partnerships in the Southwest). Developed by Civil and Bernier (2006), this model of parent involvement views parents, particularly "minority" and working-class parents, as intellectual resources. The aim of the model is to help parents to "assume a leadership role in organizing other members of their community for the purpose of collectively learning how to help their children by cooperating with schools" (Delgado-Gaitan, 1990, p. 167). MAPPS encourages parent leadership in mathematics activities through three main components:

- Leadership development meetings for parents that intend to break the traditional balance of power found in schools. Parents who attend these meetings learn how to facilitate workshops for other parents and discuss issues related to parent recruitment.
- Mathematics Awareness Workshops (MAWS) that cover key topics in K–12 mathematics. These workshops are often facilitated by parents.
- Math for Parents (MFP) classes that are attended by parents who also are members of leadership teams.

This model is unique in that it shifts the balance of power from the schools to the parents. Parents are able to become involved in the schools in ways that reach beyond the traditional types offered by Epstein. They are active participants in the schools as well as in their children's mathematics education, and their partnership is developed on an equal plane.

One issue with this model is that it is not necessarily sustainable in its original form. Civil and Bernier (2006) report how a district chose to maintain MAWS once the project officially ended, but instead asked teachers to facilitate the workshops rather than parents. Such a change that shifts the balance of control back to the schools may suggest to parents that schools are inclined to resist an equal balance of power. Such a shift reverts back to or maintains the traditional majority-minority model of parent engagements and neglects to take advantage of cross-cultural discussions about mathematics awareness. In doing so, the diverse demographic groups we cite above may argue that their values, norms, and voice should be apart from the structure in a public space, and that equal respect (e.g., cultural recognition) is paramount.

The Curriculum Enrichment Model. A third model of parent engagement, the Curriculum Enrichment Model, aims to enrich the school's curriculum by incorporating the contributions of families by opening up the lines of communication between parents and teachers (White-Clark & Decker, 1996). Success for this model is measured by the connection established between parents and what and how their children learn. Schools that adopt this model believe that parents can make a contribution to student achievement. They argue that families' cultures and values should be represented in the curriculum, and that students will be more successful when there is continuity between the learning that takes place at home and that occurring at school. Parents are seen as experts and resources.

One of the criticized elements of the model is the option left open to schools to decide how families' culture should be included in the curriculum. For example, will the curriculum present the families' culture in the context of food, fairs, and festivals or will the curriculum present the families' cultures in the context of a transformative curriculum? Either approach would be considered curriculum enrichment; however, the first maintains the majority-minority model, whereas the second potentially moves away from a majority-minority model by transforming the curriculum to more equitably represent the cultures of all students in the school, and not just those from the dominant majority.

The Transformative Education Context Model. A final model, Transformative Education Context (Olivos, 2006), sets out to transform not only the curriculum but all aspects of education. Advocates of this model are inspired by the work of Paulo Freire. Freirian principles of dialogue and problem-posing education are two major components of the model. The use of these principles facilitates critical reflection and dialogue about education for parents. Also, the principles support parents having equal voice in the decision-making process. In addition, the Transformative Education Context Model argues that since knowledge is socially constructed, all participants should have a voice. Accordingly, curriculum knowledge is constructed out of the history and culture of the different racial and cultural groups in the school and an equal balance of power exists between parents, schools, and students.

What is gained from this approach is a community where the members work to benefit the whole community and not any one group in the community, and thereby all of the students' educational experiences are enriched. The use of Freirian dialogue and problem posing are examples of strategies that schools may use to achieve a true transformation. However, the model calls for a dramatic paradigm shift that will require schools to move away from current majority-minority ways of thinking.

Constructive Pluralism for Parent-School Engagement

We begin this section with a definition of constructive pluralism and discuss constructive pluralism as an opportunity to move beyond a dualistic model of parent-teacher/school engagement. Next we discuss the question, Why constructive pluralism? and offer four reasons: It meets demands of a global society; illuminates global, national, and local discussions on minority rights; acts as glue for alliances; and increases social capital. We end the chapter with a concluding statement.

Defining Constructive Pluralism. Constructive pluralism is a form of *pluralism* that pays particular attention to "minority and marginalized groups" in a society in that it seeks, acts for, and needs their active participation. It is *constructive* because it is created, or built, through the participation of groups with one another. It goes beyond the awareness and acceptance of diversity, contending that *diversity* is not authentic (structured) engagement among groups of people, and that it is not pluralism. Constructive pluralism requires that groups strive to see each other through the perspectives of the particular group. The development of a democratic community is not about minority groups being assimilated into mainstream culture, adopting mainstream values, and only using mainstream language. Instead, constructive pluralism strives toward cultural groups' claims for "special" rights/social justice (e.g., recognition) in cultural, educational, religious, and linguistic matters over and above those of equal citizenship.

Diana Eck, the director of the Pluralism Project at Harvard University, tells us that pluralism is not an ideology, but rather the dynamic process through which people engage with one another in and through their very deepest differences. Eck argues that pluralism is not just another word for diversity. It goes beyond mere plurality or diversity to active engagement with that plurality. She contends that diversity—religious, ethnicity, race—is an observable fact of American life today.

The makings of pluralism are surely here, but without any real engagement with one another, this might prove to be just a striking example of diversity. But the diversity alone is not pluralism. Pluralism is not a given, but must be created. Pluralism requires participation, and attunement to life and the energies of one another. In the world into which we now move, sheer diversity without this real engagement will be increasingly difficult and dangerous (Eck, 2006).

Eck makes the following observations about pluralism:

- Pluralism is the engagement, not the abdication, of differences and particularities.
- The language of pluralism is that of dialogue and encounter, give and take, criticism and self-criticism.
- Vigorous engagement, even argument, around "the common table" is vital to the very heart of a democratic society.
- Whether in the public school, the city council, or the interfaith council, commitments are not left at the door. The "common table" of civic life grows and its shape is refigured with each new group of participants, each new seat added (p. 1).

From this definition of constructive pluralism where engagement of differences, give and take, criticism, and discussions around a "common table" are critical to a democracy, we question whether models of parent-school engagement that mainly foster majority-minority structure (e.g., mainstream school + African American parents, or mainstream school + Latino parents) are adequate for present-day society. In addition, policymakers must be asked, "Are such models fair to the mainstream, that is, White students, who must live in a global world?"

Human Rights and Constructive Pluralism. Constructive pluralism takes place in a context determined by the imperative linked to respect for human rights and particularly the rights of minorities. The deference of cultural rights or the right to a cultural identity is inseparable from the general defense of human rights and fundamental liberties (United Nations Educational, Scientific, and Cultural Organization [UNESCO], 1997). That said, however, the history of *why* the majority-minority model, assimilation, and the principle of equality and nondiscrimination that dominate social policy, including education policy and practice, is so prevailing remains an important question, as is why it has been kept in the shadows of discussions in education about minority rights and pluralism. According to Preece (2001), drawing on the work of Claude (1955), "the international system created after World War II—including in the policy documents of the United Nations—was formulated largely without attention to the questions, problems, and issues of ethnocultural minorities' rights in a world dominated by the concept of the national State as the . . . unit of political organization" (Claude, 1955, p. 10). Accordingly, the only minority grievances or ideas considered worthwhile were those that dealt with majority-group discrimination (e.g., discrimination of White people against Black people), and not the cultural recognition of groups of color.

Preece (2001) notes that the Universal Declaration of Human Rights (1948)—like many if not most of the policy documents dealing with minority rights—makes no mention of special minority rights or cultural recognition, but instead endorses the principles of equality and nondiscrimination. Similarly, many states and school districts in the United States view ethnocultural diversity as an issue best solved not by constructive pluralism but instead through policies of equal respect and assimilation. This is because the focus of attention is on equal citizenship/equal treatment (that the U.S. Constitution theoretically guarantees all citizens) reached through acculturation, but not on equal respect or acknowledging the politics of cultural "recognition" (Taylor, 2007, p. 34).

Such ideas and actions, however, are becoming increasingly problematic, because groups are demanding cultural recognition instead of assimilation, and fairness along with equal respect. The civil rights movements of African Americans, women, Latinos, and gay people have promoted cultural recognition and fairness. Globalization—particularly the movement of people and technology increases in transportation, information, and communication—has given people greater access to each other, as well as the opportunity to learn about different ways of doing things. This promotion of cultural recognition and greater access through globalization has significantly added to the advocacy of demands by these groups (and others) for the illumination of their identity. Krysztofek's (2002) observation is useful here:

At present we see a new generation of human rights acquiring increasing significance. Hitherto, the order in place was founded primarily on a political rights regime, reinforced by social and economic rights, though these were not generally accepted as part of the canon. Now with the advent of the "age of identity" there have been calls for an acknowledgement of the claims of collective, community rights. (p. 291)

Krysztofek goes on to argue that "human rights—general rights (the right to life, to freedom, to own property), citizenship rights (voting, nationality, and participation in public life), rights to standards of good behavior by governments (or protection of the rule of law); and social, economic, and cultural rights—are one of the systems of rules on which the framework of the globalized world is increasingly being constructed" (p. 1). The latter have become important during the 20th and 21st century, and raise important and still controversial issues about social justice and the distribution of wealth. To add to this point, violations of human rights at the global level are a threat to world peace, and increasingly ignoring human and group rights at the national and local level is causing civil unrest.

Why Constructive Pluralism?

From the definition of constructive pluralism and the discussion of human rights, our reason for advocacy should be clearer. We believe that constructive pluralism allows for the creation of a richer society for individuals living within this society (UNESCO, 1997). But let us answer the "why" question with four responses.

Preparing Students to Meet Demands of a Global and Changing Society. First, we contextualize how these particular demands came about by briefly discussing political, economic, social, and educational changes that were taking place starting shortly after World War II. These changes provide a framework for our argument for the need for a model of parent engagement based on constructive pluralism.

Profound changes have taken place in the short 60 years since World War II when the Declaration of Human Rights (stating that everyone has the right to life, freedom of thought, equal treatment in the courts, and freedom of assembly; and no one shall be subject to torture, slavery, or forced labor) came into existence. The changes did not creep up on us; they were becoming visible during the 1960s (e.g., in the Civil Rights Act of 1964 and the Voting Rights Act of 1965), and we even saw evidence of them in 1957 when the Soviet Union lunched Sputnik. The launch of Sputnik immediately influenced world, national, local, and group and individual politics and economic and social conditions, including education. At that point U.S. society demanded a change to a back-to-the-basics curriculum, which included more science, reading, and math, and greater achievement from its students (Bestor, 1956; Cremin, 1961; Rickover, 1959).

Over these 60 years, political conditions have shifted from hegemony to controling minority groups, to "supremacy" of minority groups and low-income people (Gill, 2003; Lipman, 2005). Although minority groups did resist and advocate for their human and civil rights, this resistance has not been very successful, as only a small number of members within the minority groups have made progress. Lipman (2005), drawing on the work of Gill (2003), argues that "there has been a political shift from hegemony—power based on consensus—to a politics of supremacy as both a global and a national political process" (p. 317). Lipman goes on to state:

> Internationally, power is organized around a supremacist bloc composed of the G7 states, transnational capital, and a strata of privileged workers. This bloc uses the coercive pressures of transnational institutions, such as the IMF and WTO, to impose the dominance of the market on all countries and every sphere of social life. (p. 317)

Consequently, economic conditions are influenced by a freeing up of trade and capital flows, deregulation, the shrinking cost of communication and transportation, and an information technology revolution that makes it possible to digitize the boundaries between design, manufacturing, and marketing and locate these functions in different places (Gray, 2006). This has led to a move from nation-based manufacturing to global markets, causing many low-income people and people of color to accept minimum wage employment in the service industry (Lipman, 2005).

Social conditions have become complex and problematic. Whereas there are signs that racial and ethnic attitudes are improving, the American Psychological Association report *Violence and Youth: Psychology's Response* identified "prejudice and discrimination" as one of the three leading causes of violence among American youth (1993). In addition and more recently, the FBI in 2003 reported "that racial bias again represented the largest percentage of bias-motivated incidents (48.8%), followed by religion bias (19.1%), sexual orientation bias (16.7%), and ethnic bias (14.8%)" (Civil Rights Coalition for the 21st Century, 2004, p. 1).

Education conditions have also changed as the educational system is increasingly being forced into a market model. The educational system is moving away from the traditional concept of education as a publicly provided social good that gives attention to the "whole" individual. Instead, education is more about how to prepare a workforce to function in our technological society. The focus is also on how education/schooling in our country lags far behind the world outside of schools (Grant & Grant, 2008).

These political, economic, social, and education conditions argue for an education that will help to engender a new humanism that contains an essential ethical component and promotes knowledge of and respect for the culture and spiritual values of different groups of people. This new humanism could also serve as a much needed *counter weight* to a globalization that would otherwise be seen only in economical or technological terms (quoted in Azad, 2004, p. 6).

Parent-school engagement, therefore, should not ignore, but take into account, the problems and issues mentioned above as they pertain to and affect all groups in general and all groups individually. In other words, all (e.g., students) will need to acquire knowledge, skills, and attitudes that transcend conventional/traditional intellectual paradigms that accentuate one lens (e.g., nation-state or ethnic identity) over another (Olson, Evans, & Shoenberg, 2007). Schools are the fundamental institution in society (beside the home) where such learning in a democratic society should take place.

Most educators will argue that the primary purpose of schools is to educate, and that it has long been understood—although there is increasing resistance from neoliberals—that education consists of more than the development of academic skills and the accumulation of knowledge. In addition, most educators contend that schools have a further duty and responsibility to teach respect for the rights of all members of society and that one of the central purposes of schools in a democratic society is to encourage the critical and independent thinking necessary for citizens' effective participation. The construction of conversations for parent-school engagement using a constructive pluralism approach will better prepare schools to fulfill their duty and meet their responsibility to prepare students to effectively participate in society.

Constructive pluralism is the active engagement with diversity (of people and ideas). It moves beyond accepting tolerance and differences; it advocates nurturing, meetings, and exchanges that reveal common understanding, which ultimately lead to real commitments and real differences (Eck, 2006). Eck's remarks in an essay on pluralism, although pointed at religious pluralism, have strong implementation for our work on advocating for a framework that guides conservation on constructive pluralism and parent-school engagement. In these remarks she identifies places and spaces where conversation on pluralism should take place. Eck asks:

> Where are those public spaces, those "tables" where people of various religious traditions and none meet in American society? They are certainly in neighborhoods and community organizations, schools and colleges, legislatures, and courts, zoning boards and planning commission, interfaith councils and interfaith coalitions, chaplaincies and hospitals. In every one of these areas of public life, Americans are now facing new questions, new challenges, and new tensions in appropriating a more complex sense of who "we" now are. (p. 5)

In other words, Eck advocates for pluralism to be the "glue" wherever diverse people gather, and, we would add, where conceptual and ideological ideas need to be engaged in order to address the "new questions, new challenges, and new tensions."

Illuminating Global, National, and Local Discussions on Minority Rights. Constructive pluralism helps to illuminate the discussions that are taking place in the international community and increasingly in the United States about "minority rights." In the United States *minority rights* and *human rights* are not frequently used terms. These terms are more a part of the international discourse on inequality and inequity, especially in policy documents of the United Nations (e.g., UNESCO). Nevertheless, debates about "English only," the wearing of head-scarves, children of minorities, noncitizens, and immigration are all debates about minority rights and human rights. A global perspective on minority rights—that is, the rights of racial/ethnic, religious, and linguistic minorities and indigenous people—is central to international human rights law, and the debates over such rights are one of the major problems and issues of contemporary politics.

Questions concerning these rights are seen as prevailing questions that have engendered attention since (as we noted above) the end of World War II. Advocates of minority rights and constructive pluralism argue that, although progress has been achieved in dealing with majority-minority discrimination, subsuming the problems of minorities under the broader problem of ensuring basic individual rights to all human beings, without reference to membership in ethnic groups, is unacceptable. In addition, assumptions that members of minorities do not need, are not entitled to, or cannot be granted rights of a special character are based upon narrow Eurocentric ways of seeing the world.

Human rights do not impose one cultural standard (Ayton-Shenker, 1995). In addition, at this time of "new questions, new challenges, and new tensions," Ayton-Shenker's observation that if a group is recognized and its history and culture is supported by the larger pluralistic community (e.g., Whites, African Americans, Latinos, Asian Americans) its members are far more likely to join in and add to the total group knowledge and understanding that has significance in a global society. Ayton-Shenker (1995) additionally contends that a balanced interaction of cultures is needed and for this we must promote a social and cultural pluralism with a juridical status that incorporates all cultures, and, we would add, especially those cultural groups living in the school district, in attendance at the school or both.

Advocates of constructive pluralism argue that the state (school district) role includes ensuring and promoting access to the history and contributions of the cultural groups in the school district as well as having policy and guidelines in place that ensure that (minority) groups are not omitted or shortchanged in the instructional process. Such actions, advocates believe, will be positively significant for the entire community, as they will help to build positive relations across cultural groups and encourage people to become increasingly aware of and concerned about the importance of cultural and human rights. Unfortunately, however, globalization and migration flows continue to suppress identities or make them obsolete as a result of contact with other cultures, hence making it necessary to defend each individual's own rights. Developing a model of parent engagement in the schools that is based on constructive pluralism would be one way to counteract this suppression of cultural identities.

Forming Alliances Among Bicultural Groups. The third response to the question, Why constructive pluralism? is in part a statement for schools where no single group forms a numerical majority. Using a constructive pluralism approach to parent-school engagement at such schools would encourage the establishment of an alliance among minority groups that would serve them and the larger society.

During the civil rights movements alliances were formed between minority groups, for example, African Americans and Latinos. This alliance has suffered, as tensions between Blacks and Latinos have developed over the rise in the Latino population, competition over employment opportunities, immigration policies, bilingual education, political representation, and the overall uncoupling of Latinos' interests from Blacks' political and economic issues (Ertll, 2007; Vaca, 2004). Yet many in both communities are still suffering; they have not received the fruits of the civil rights movement. Latinos and African Americans both face high unemployment rates, high dropout rates in schools, systemic poverty, gang violence, a disproportionate number of members in prison, and continual discrimination.

In the *San Diego Union-Tribune*, Ertll (2007) writes about the need for alliance between Latino, and Blacks. He addresses both the difficulties and importance of alliance and offers suggestions for improving alliances between African Americans and Latinos that are consistent with a constructive pluralism approach and for parents of African Americans and Latinos who attend the same school. Ertll's suggestions include the following:

- Doing more to point out the history of positive relations between African Americans and Latinos, such as the important role Mexicans played in the Underground Railroad during slavery and Cesar Chavez marching with Martin Luther King Jr.
- Being sensitive about the words and claims that group makes to one another. Ertll noted that during the pro–immigrant rights marches in 2006 some Latino leaders argued that the immigrant rights movement was the new civil rights movement, and this infuriated many African Americans. He contends that groups should reach out to one another as they are advocating for issues particular to their group in order to show a wider representation.

- Stopping bickering with each other and address one another in a respectful and thoughtful manner. Additionally, he argues that groups should help each other achieve this dream first by studying and respecting each other's history and culture and then by working together in common cause.

Finally, Ertll states, "We cannot continue to blame each other, much less prey on each other. And we should not compete for the title of the country's most victimized minority group. That is a losing game" (paragraph 13) .

Increasing Social Capital. The need for increasing the social capital of bicultural communities figures significantly in their empowerment. Indeed, "one of the most striking findings to come from social science in recent years reports an apparent erosion within the United States, normally the most civic of nations, in the propensity of individuals to engage in community affairs, to trust one another, and to associate together on a regular basis" (Hall, 2002, p. 21). In fact, some are arguing that in the United States there is a decline in social capital (Levine, 2007; Pharr & Putnam, 2000).

Definitions of *social capital* include "the collective value of informal neighborhood ties in the modern metropolis" (Jacob, 1961, p. 23). Bourdieu (1986) defines social capital as "the aggregate of the actual or potential resources which are linked to possession of a durable network of more or less institutionalized relationships of mutual acquaintance and recognition" (pp. 248–249). In other words, social capital is membership in a group. The World Bank (2003) describes social capital as "a set of horizontal associations between people, consisting of social networks and associated norms that have an effect on community productivity and well-being" (p. 1). Krishna (2003) adds that "social capital facilitates coordination and cooperation" (p. 3). James S. Coleman (1988), meanwhile, locates social capital within the context of education and argues that it facilitates individual or collective action, generated by networks of relationships, reciprocity, trust, and social norms.

These definitions have a connection to our use of the term. We are using social capital to mean the social good—private and public—for democracy that comes out of civic engagement or citizens participating in a social network. These social networks include unions, religious institutions, political parties, block clubs, knitting clubs, and for our purposes parent-teacher/school engagement organizations. The purpose of a parent-teacher/school network built upon the premise of constructive pluralism would be to mobilize energies to build a successful school community for all students (Levine, 2007; Pharr & Putnam, 2000). The sense of community that we are advocating is the conception of community mainly defined by McMillian and Chavis (1986): a feeling that members have of belonging, a feeling that members matter to one another and to the group. They are not color-blind to one another, but affirm each other's history and cultural values and possess a shared faith that members' (i.e., groups') needs will be met through their commitment to be together.

Increasing evidence shows that *social* cohesion in a democracy is *critical* for societies to prosper economically, for *development* to be sustainable, and for citizens to have a flourishing life (Levine, 2007; Putman, 2002). *Social capital*, it is argued, is not just the sum of the *institutions* that underpin a *society*, but is the glue that holds them together (Coleman, 1988). With the decline in community involvement in the United States and its significance to democracy (Delgado-Gaitan, 1990; Olivos, 2006), parent-teacher/school engagement that uses constructive pluralism as an approach will contribute greatly to the welfare of the school community. The social capital fashioned within a constructive pluralism approach will foster and support a bonding network that will connect the diverse groups of parents, students, and staff in the school who have a similar aim (e.g., educational reform) and sustain reciprocity across the groups. In addition, a constructive pluralism approach will help to sustain bridging networks that support bringing diverse groups together around issues of educational improvement in the local school, and will help to sustain a generalized reciprocity of ideas and values across the group.

Framing Bicultural Parent Engagement in Constructive Pluralism

A parent-school-engagement approach framed in constructive pluralism is essential for school today and significant to U.S. democracy. Discussions about engagement, we must point out, are also about "power interest." This is because engagements are conditioned and contextualized through the production and use of knowledge (e.g., a state's history and policy) and "regimes of truths"—each society has its regime of truth, its "general politics" of truth (e.g., educational reform) which it accepts and makes function as true (Foucault, 1994, p. 67). Knowledge and the regimes of truth are an active interpretative, an interested affair that is usually controlled by people with more power, money, and status than other people (Zimmerman, 2003, p. 3). Here, we are arguing that the "majority" model of parent-school engagement has the power interest and employs the regimes of truths of those who hold power.

Those in power—and this is what majority-minority models of school engagement support—shape the agenda for school meetings; determine school policy, including funding allocations; and determine what gets to count as "true."

Constructive pluralism, we contend, will offer marginalized and oppressed people as a group (alliance) an opportunity to use their voices to contest ideas and claims put forth by power elites.

A constructive pluralism approach to parent engagement, we understand, will be difficult, and we agree with the observations (noted above) made by Ertll. However, when diverse groups come together around the table the diversity of perspectives offered multiplies the opportunities to question and reconceive traditional ways of conducting school business. Moreover, wide-ranging debates, which constructive pluralism advocates, promise to strengthen the work done within any particular tradition. Debates over models of engagement (mentioned above) allow group members to develop standards of rigorous argumentation, but debates between traditions force group members to confront the problematic character of their most basic assumptions—allowing each way of perceiving parent-school engagement by group members to gain a reflective understanding of itself in comparison with other ways of seeing parent-school engagement. And since those foundational assumptions often embody one's (i.e., groups') most critical mistakes, an approach to constructive pluralism characterized by cross-paradigm discussion promises especially fruitful insights (Margonis, 1996).

The influence of globalization, especially the movement of people, has increased the challenges that confront schools and increases the need for forums that support social capital, especially the norms of reciprocity (e.g., bonding networks and building networks), which we believe will be better met by a constructive pluralism approach to parent engagement. Cortes (1999) has written about these challenges, and we use his ideas liberally to inform our suggestions. Cortes identifies the a number of features of school life that we believe a constructive pluralism approach to parent-school engagement would help. We outline these below.

- *Record Keeping:* Changing student demographics are challenging the current system of racial categorization. How will schools keeps records, prepare reports, and conduct analysis of academic achievement and other school-related activities that will satisfy parents and other institutions? Broad-based parent support would be helpful when engaging with other societal agencies.
- *Evolving Identities:* Increasing numbers of students (e.g., especially those of biracial marriages) refuse to identity with belonging to a single racial groups. Also, students who are new arrivals wish to keep connections with family and friends in their home country. Because of the marvels of transportation and communication, students today, unlike the young people who arrived at Ellis Island years ago, have the technical mechanisms to do both. They would paraphrase Gloria Esteban, who

stated, "The United States is my country; Cuba es mi tierra [Cuba is my soul]." How school administrators address the emergence and assertion of new student groups that develop out of this evolving orientation toward race, ethnicity, culture, and language will be better informed by a constructive pluralism approach to parent-school engagement.

- *Pluralism:* As schools plan curriculum and instructional activities, the evolving identities of students (described above) have major implications for educational policies and practices. Will schools continue to promote activities and practices that mainly foster assimilation and acculturation approaches even as students resist, or will they accept the students' dedication to becoming good American citizens while maintaining their ethnic and racial culture, and in some cases their global connections? Parents of these students acting with a constructive pluralism approach will be in a better position to help work out such challenges.

- *Intergroup Relations:* As we noted above, students of color—Latinos, African Americans, Asian Americans, new arrivals—are increasingly making up the school population as the White population of students decreases. The demographic changes challenge administrators to move beyond the dualistic majority-minority paradigm. The challenge—change and transition—we believe will be more caringly facilitated by a constructive pluralism approach that supports bonding and bridging networks.

These increasing and changing student demographics, often accompanied by financial cutbacks, are bringing with them the need for schools to make decisions around human and technical resources (e.g., language teacher, school social worker, school nurse, computer lab, and new textbooks), and services the school provides (e.g., whole-day kindergarten, services of a speech pathologist, and school breakfast program). How school administrators and teachers make decisions about school activities and services will be better informed by a constructive pluralism approach where parents are engaged in the decision making. In other words, by way of constructive pluralism parents would not receive word of a decision made by the school in which they did not participate or about which they have little knowledge, but instead would have the opportunity to participate in the decision making.

Finally, we repeat from Claude's (1955) statement, shown at the beginning of the chapter: "The general tendency of the postwar movements for the promotion of human rights has been to subsume the problem of . . . minorities under the broader problem of ensuring basic individual rights to all human beings, without reference to membership in ethnic groups. [And] . . . the doctrine of human rights has been put forward as a substitute for the concept of minority rights" (p. 211).

Although, and rightly so, the statement was an act of progress, it nevertheless failed to deal with social justice—equality and cultural recognition—for groups of color. Presently globalization, especially the movement of people, and social justice *demands* better than that which took place 60 years ago. Constructive pluralism as an approach within the United States offers a way to meet the demands of a democratic society in ways that will best serve all groups in society.

Discussion Questions

- Describe a local community where pockets of the population are homogenous but where students and adults in the community at large live and work in heterogeneous settings.
- How is the ethnic diversity of school communities (multicultural, multilingual, religious) an intellectual resource? What are the implications of such an intellectual resource for school-parent-engagement activities/ program/services?
- What are the power-relation tensions between majority-minority communities that are suggested by each of the four models of parent engagement?
- What should a parent-teacher-school engagement look like within the context of constructive pluralism?
- What are the existing conditions of a school community that promote constructive pluralism and parent engagement? How is vigorous engagement facilitated in the "common table"?
- Why constructive pluralism for the local, national, global society? How can it serve as glue for alliances for human rights and social justice? How can it serve for closing the achievement gap within and outside the geography of our school communities?
- How can constructive pluralism address intergroup relations and the evolving identities of our school communities, regions, and nation?

Suggested Readings

Anyon, J. (2005). *Radical possibilities: Public policy, urban education, and a new social movement.* New York: Routledge.

Apple, M., & Beane, J. (Eds.) (2007). *Democratic schools: Lessons in powerful education* (2nd ed.). Portsmouth, NH: Heinemann.

Au, W. (Ed.). (2009). *Rethinking multicultural education: Teaching for racial and cultural justice.* Milwaukee, WI: Rethinking Schools.

Biesta, G. (207). Education and the democratic person: Towards political conception of democratic education. *Teachers College Record, 109*(3), 740–769.

Bonilla-Silva, E. (2006). *Racism without racists: Color-blind racism and the persistence of racial inequality in the United States.* Lanham, MD: Rowman & Littlefield.

Boulding, E. (1988). *Building a global civic culture: Education for an interdependent world.* New York: Teachers College Press.

Parker, W. (2003). *Teaching democracy: Unity and diversity in public life.* New York: Teachers College Press.

Renner, A. (2009). Teaching community, praxis, and courage. A foundation pedagogy of hope and humanization. *Educational Studies, 45*(1), 59–79.

Zou, Y., & Trueba, H. (Eds.). (1998). *Ethnic identity and power: Cultural contexts of political action in school and society.* Albany: State University of New York Press.

References

American Psychological Association. (1993). *Violence and youth: Psychology's response (Vol. 1: Summary Report of the American Psychological Association Commission on Violence and Youth).* Washington, DC: Author.

Ayton-Shenker, D. (1995). *The challenge of human rights and cultural diversity, United Nation background note.* Retrieved from www.un.org/rights/dpi1627epoliticascience .dal.ca/course_info/syllabi_docs/summer07/poli3303.pdf

Azad, J. L. (2004). *Globalization and its impact on education.* Retrieved from cie.du.ac.in/ Globalization%20and%20Its%20Impact%20on%20Education%.

Bestor, A. E. (1956). *The restoration of learning.* New York: Knopf.

Bourdieu, P. (1986). The forms of capital. In J. G. Richards (Ed.), *Handbook of theory and research for the sociology of education* (pp. 241–258). New York: Greenwood Press.

Civil, M., & Bernier, E. (2006). Exploring images of parental participation in mathematics education: Challenges and possibilities. *Mathematical Thinking and Learning, 8*(3), 309–330.

Civil Rights Coalition for the 21st Century. (2004). *Cause for concern.* Retrieved from http:// www.civilrights.org/publications/reports/cause_for_concern_2004

Claude, I. (1955). *National minorities: An international problem.* Cambridge, MA: Harvard University Press.

Coleman, J. (1988). Social capital in the creation of human capital. *American Journal of Sociology, 94* [Supplement], S95-S-120.

Cortes, C. (1999). The accelerating change of American diversity: The new multiculturalism packs a 1-2-3 punch for public schools. *American Association of School Administrators, The School Administrator.* Retrieved from http://www.aasa.org/publications/sa artcledetail.cfm?ItemNumber=3

Cremin, L. (1961). *Transformation of the school: Progressivism in American education, 1876–1957.* New York: Alfred A. Knopf.

Delgado-Gaitan, C. (1990). *Literacy for empowerment: The role of parents in children's education.* New York: Falmer Press.

Eck, D. L. (2006). *From diversity to pluralism. Pluralism Project at Harvard.* Retrieved from http://www.pluralism.org/pluralism/essays/from_diversity_to_pluralism.php

Epstein, J. (2004). School, family, and community partnerships link the plan. *Principal, 69*(6), 19–23.

Epstein, J. (2005). Attainable goals? The spirit and letter of the No Child Left Behind Act on parental involvement. *Sociology of Education, 78*(2), 179–183.

Ertll, R. J. (2007, October 12). Why African-Americans and Latinos must get along. *The San Diego Union.* Retrieved from http://www.signonsandiego.com/uniontrib/20071012/news_lz1e12ertll.html

Foucault, M. (1994) *Technologies of the self.* In P. Rabinow (Ed.), *Michel Foucault, Ethics: The essential works of Foucault, 1954–1984* (Vol. 1, pp. 223–251). Harmondsworth, UK: Penguin.

Grant C. A., & Grant, A. (2008). Schooling and globalization: What do we tell our kids and clients? What are we being told? *Journal of Ethnic and Cultural Diversity in Social Work, 16*(3&4), 213–225.

Grant, C. A., & Sleeter, C. E. (1996). *After the school bell rings.* London: Falmer Press.

Gray, J. (2006). Global delusions. *New York Review of Books, 53*(7), 20–23.

Hall, P. A. (2002). Great Britain: The role of government and the distribution of social capital. In Robert D. Putnam (Ed.), *Democracies in flux* (pp. 21–58). New York: Oxford University Press.

Jacob, J. (1961). *The death and life of great American cities.* New York: Random House.

Krishna, A. (2003). *Social capital, community driven development and empowerment: A short note on concepts and operation.* Retrieved from http://lnweb18.worldbank.org/ESSD/sdvext.nsf/68ByDocName/AnirudhKrishna/$FILE/A+PDF.pdf

Krzysztofek, K. (2002). Global governance, global culture, and multiculturalism. *Canadian Journal of Communication , 27*(2), 291.

Levine, P. (2007). *The future of democracy: Developing the next generation of American citizens.* Medford, MA: Tufts University Press.

Lipman, P. (2005). Eduation ethnography and the politics of globalization, war, and resistance. *Anthropology and Education Quarterly, 36*(4), 315–328.

Margonis, F. (1996). Introduction, philosophical pluralism: The promise of fragmentation. *Philosophy of Education Society.* Retrieved from http://www.ed.uiuc.edu/EPS/PES-Yearbook/96_docs/margonis_intro.html

McMillan, D. W., & Chavis, D. M. (1986). Sense of community: A definition and theory. *American Journal of Community Psychology, 14*(1), 6–23.

Nieto, S. (1999). *The light in their eyes: Creating multicultural learning communities.* New York: Teachers College Press.

Olivos, E. M. (2006). *The power of parents: A critical perspective of bicultural parent involvement in public schools.* New York: Peter Lang.

Olson, C. L., Evan, R., & Shoenberg, R. F. (2007). *At home in the world: Bridging the gap between internationalization and multicultural education.* Washington, DC: American Council on Education.

Pharr, S. J., & Putnam, R. D. (2000). *Disaffected democracies: What's troubling the trilateral countries?* Princeton, NJ: Princeton University Press.

Preece, J. J. (2001) Minority rights: Between diversity and community. *German Yearbook of International Law, 44,* 237–240.

Putnam, R. D. (2002). *Democracies in flux.* New York: Oxford University Press.

Rickover, H. (1959). *Education and freedom.* Boston: E. P. Dutton.

Taylor, C. (2007). *Critical vision.* Retrieved from http://wwwcriticalvision.blogspot.com/2007/05/charles-taylor-on-multiculturalism-and.html

United Nations Educational, Scientific, and Cultural Organization (UNESCO). (1997). *Universal declaration of the human genome and human rights.* Retrieved from http://portal.unesco.org/en/ev.php-URL_ID=13177&URL_DO=DO_TOPIC&URL_SECTION=201.html

Vaca, N. C. (2004). *The presumed alliance: The unspoken conflict between Latinos and Blacks and Whites and what it means for America.* New York: Rayo/HaperCollins.

White-Clark, R., & Decker, L. (1996). *The hard to reach parent: Old challenges, new insights.* Fairfax, VA: National Community Education Association.

World Bank. (2003). *Social capital.* Retrieved from http://www.iccr-inteational.org/foresight/docs/monitoring/Social%20Developments/ Social%20Capital%20Indicators.pdf

Zimmerman, M. E. (2003). Architectural ethic, multiculturalism, and globalization. *Professional Ethics, 2*(4), 1–14.

Part III

Operationalizing Transformative Parent Engagement

8

A Parent Advocate's Vision of a 21st-Century Model for Bicultural Parent Engagement

Mary Johnson

For all too long, educational researchers have provided limited pictures of who we are as parents of color from working-class communities (Comer, 1995; Epstein, 2002). While they speak of "partnerships," their models of parent involvement work only to legitimize the voice and the power of school officials, and to stifle our rights and due process as parents. Comer and Haynes (1991), for example, claimed to advocate for an "ecological model" of parent involvement and to "involve parents at all levels of school life" only to later add a disclaimer that we (parents) must "not supersede or challenge the authority of principals and their staffs" (p. 1). This approach to parent involvement is insincere, misleading, and based on an asymmetrical and coercive power relationship between homes and schools (Cummins, 2001). Therefore, there is an urgent need to create new models of parent involvement in schools that will authentically respect the rights *and* power of parents of color from working-class urban neighborhoods (Olivos, 2006).

As parents and community members of children of color in the public school system, we need to think about how we need to be involved. This chapter describes how one group of parents from South Los Angeles County has created a distinct approach to parent involvement—an approach that has proved powerful for working-class parents of color who often have no voice in the decisions that most affect their children's learning experiences. It documents a bottom-up (rather than top-down) model of accountability that has been effective in getting urban parents of color involved in advocating for their children's and communities' best interests.

Advocating for one's children's educational interests is a time-consuming and demanding task, but a necessary one. As a mother whose children all attended urban schools in South Los Angeles County, I understand that there are many pressing needs and challenges in our neighborhoods. I see the daily distractions and the influences of urban life on low-income children of color that can divert them from their educational obligations. I also see, however, the richness of our neighborhoods in their social networks, diverse languages, diversity of population, and rich multicultural history of our communities. Unfortunately, however, public schools in U.S. urban areas often mirror only the challenges and not the strengths of these communities. They highlight what is wrong with our communities, not what is right. They view our communities as deficient, disadvantaged, and in need of curing (Payne, 2005), without taking into consideration that schools are here to serve our communities and sometimes it is the school system that needs to be fixed as well.

Researchers have documented the challenges often faced by children who attend urban school districts in their academic careers: uncertified teachers, lack of teaching materials (e.g., textbooks), crumbling facilities, low expectations of children of color by school personnel, educator and administrator indifference, violence, crime, and racial and ethnic tension (Espinosa, 2009). The parents and community members of these urban areas, however, don't need researchers telling us what we already know. What we need are action research tools to document these conditions and the organizing strategies in order to change them (Shirley, 1997). Documenting the urban school experience is what I and hundreds of other parents have been doing for the past 10 years as parent and community advocates of South Los Angeles and as members of Parent U-Turn, a nonprofit organization I and some of my fellow parents founded in 1999.

Parent Curriculum Project

A brief history of Parent U-Turn takes us back to 1997, and the University of California, Los Angeles (UCLA) Parent Curriculum Project (PCP). PCP was a UCLA-led initiative that I and some of my neighbors from Lynwood (CA) participated in. It was a series of 13-week seminars modeled after UCLA's subject-matter projects for teachers.

PCP is a professional development program for parents eager to ensure that all students have equal access to educational opportunities. PCP aims to build the knowledge and leadership of parents, to increase their involvement in schools, and to create a neutral and supportive environment in which parents can reflect on education, schooling, and reform. Parents develop leadership skills in communication and mediation to assist other parents in connecting with counselors and teachers so that all parents can help navigate their children through the school system (Johnson & Muñoz, 2010).

Under the direction of Dr. Angela Hasan, director of PCP, I developed skills that I always knew I had: leadership skills to engage people, collaboration skills, and communication skills. In addition to developing my personal skills , however, I learned to interact with school authorities using the tools, methods, and documents that are only valued in the school system: written letters to school officials, attendance at school-sanctioned meetings, and use of acronyms and school lingo and jargon. Furthermore, I learned to uncover what the state academic standards were, what quality instruction looks like, and how to monitor and assess teaching and learning in the classroom.

The PCP parent trainings were much different from any other "parent education" workshop I had attended. The PCP program viewed us parents as assets to our children's education, as knowledgeable individuals who have something to offer to the schools. This was in contrast to those parent programs that are frequently offered by school districts and schools that assume the reason children of color do poorly in school due to (parents' and communities') inadequacies. Therefore, rather than teach us "parenting skills" or how to "work with our children" at home, PCP helped us develop research and advocacy skills that we could use to improve the school experiences of our children.

We learned, for example, how to do a visible inspection of our children's classrooms. We also learned that a math classroom should have students' current work posted around the room as well as math equation posters and other math tools that engage students. Additionally, we learned that teachers should be using state content standards to develop their lesson plans and how to compare our children's California State Standards Test scores and the California High School Exit Exam scores against others students' data in California. This last exercise helped us parents begin to look at how our children were doing in our neighborhood schools in comparison with what students in more affluent communities were accomplishing.

Empowering Parent Advocates

After participating in the UCLA PCP, two other parents and I founded Parent U-Turn (PUT) in 1999. This name is a play on words, attempting to express the following challenge: "Parents: It's your turn. It's your turn to be a teacher, your turn to be a researcher, your turn to be an education advocate and activist. It's your turn to take back your community."

PUT is an autonomous, multicultural, and nonprofit parent organization consisting of approximately 200 parents from South Los Angeles County cities and dedicated to improving the educational opportunities of urban students in Los Angeles schools and communities. PUT membership consists of single parents, married parents, foster parents, and grandparents of all races and nationalities. The primary goal of PUT is to address the ways that parents can best assist their schools in creating a successful learning environment for their children (Johnson & Muñoz, 2010).

As its current chairperson, I like to describe PUT as a professional development program for working-class parents and parents of color. Our members come from diverse racial, ethnic, and social backgrounds. They also come from different positions in society: Some of the members are immigrants, and others are residents of the surrounding communities of Los Angeles County; some are proficient in English and many have a home language other than English; and some feel comfortable approaching teachers and administrators to ask questions and seek answers, whereas others are in the process of acquiring their voice. In other words, there are no requirements to be a participant in PUT and the program is open to all parents and community members. One thing we do have in common, however, is that we all want to advocate for our children and for our community. We view ourselves as active, political advocates for our neighborhoods and our schools. This type of work requires us to break the low expectations school personnel have of working-class parents of color and to assume our roles as the legitimate researchers and advocates for our children.

The parents of PUT have worked with UCLA researchers and local school districts in Southeast Los Angeles for over a decade to identify school conditions that have proved to be barriers to student achievement. This work has entailed, among other things, creating surveys, conducting focus groups, attending board meetings, holding public demonstrations, and writing news stories. All this has been done with the purpose of documenting the problematic conditions under which our children are expected to learn and their teachers are expected to work. Conversely, the ultimate goal of these endeavors is to improve those conditions in our urban schools.

This type of action research, educational work, and advocacy has required parents of color from urban communities to assume roles not traditionally expected of them. And, since 1997, I have personally seen the parents I have worked with in my community acquiring voice and agency by moving from traditional parent involvement roles to ones of greater advocacy. These are roles that parents are capable of and ready to assume, even though their potential is often not recognized by nationally recognized experts whose models imply that working-class parents of color need to be coerced or bribed, through the use of categorical state and federal programs, into participating at their children's schools or "trained" on how to be better parents and partners (Epstein, 2002; Espinosa, 2009).

This transformation of parents of color from school spectators to active education participants has been made possible by sharing common concerns and the collaborative conditions found in PUT. The nonprofit organization is also driven by the assumption that working-class parents of color are more than capable of undertaking leadership roles not only in their schools but in their communities as well. The skills of engaging with schools are developed in PUT as parent participants, who may still be becoming familiar with the culture of the U.S. public school system, take greater leadership roles in the organization in roles such as translators, directors of specific tasks or projects, organizers, recruiters, or workshop leaders. The leadership the parents assume in the organization often transfers into the schools context, as well as parents taking on new roles in their form of involvement. They go from being fund-raisers for parent-teacher organizations (PTO) or being classroom parent volunteers to being members of the advisory board to the superintendent, textbook adoption committees, staff interview committees, and project mangers and site coordinators for the UCLA Parent Curriculum Project (PCP).

The roles that parents of color have taken follow the path I have taken as a parent advocate. Once a participant in the UCLA PCP, I eventually ended up serving as executive director of the entire project. In my role as executive director, I wanted to make a difference in the participants' lives, since I was all too familiar with their experiences. I understand, through firsthand experiences, not only the hardships the parents and their children go through in their daily lives in our communities but also the resistance they (we) face in dealing with school bureaucrats who view us as obstacles and undermine our potential to create change. Moreover, there are many educators who do not want parents of color to be socially conscious and empowered. They prefer having compliant, docile parents who will follow the dictates of the school without questions or suspicions (Olivos, 2006).

The empowerment of working-class parents of color often makes school authorities, including classroom teachers, uncomfortable, as is the case in our work. After one particular series of trainings sponsored by PUT in one urban school, for example, newly empowered parents began to go to school-sponsored meetings not as compliant audience members, but as informed parents asking tough questions about quality teaching and adequate resources. They went to parent-teacher conferences and asked to see teachers' lesson plans and rubric assessments to justify failing or low student grades. In other words, these parents began acting like "high status" parents (Shannon, 1996). These actions in this particular case did not sit well with the educators at this particular school.

Teachers began to report to the school administrators that the parents were being "harsh" with them because they were asking specific educational questions. The principal eventually got so upset about what the parents were learning that she called the UCLA PCP for an emergency meeting. Her feeling was that if she had known that UCLA and PUT were going to be training parents on their educational rights, she would not have approved the program in the first place.

These are the attitudes parents of color often face when they try to become advocates for their children. As long as we are humble in our demeanor, meek in our requests, and obedient in our relationship with school "experts," we are accepted in the schools. When we ask hard questions, demonstrate frustration, and make demands for basic educational rights, we are often rebuffed, repressed, and resisted by school personnel.

Action-Based Approaches to Recasting "Parent Involvement"

I began this chapter by reflecting on my personal experiences and growth as a parent advocate, first through the PCP, and later through PUT. In this final section of the chapter, I would like to discuss further my ideas of what parent involvement for working-class parents of color should be. Therefore, the goal in this last section of the chapter is to improve on Epstein's (1992, 2002) model of parent involvement by modifying her model and adding my perspective on parent engagement that includes *all* parents in our ethnically and linguistically diverse school communities for the 21st century.

It has been my experience as a parent of color living in a multicultural and urban working-class area of the United States that Epstein's model, which is often cited by school officials as the definitive word in parent involvement, is not fully appropriate or comprehensive for our needs. It also fails to take into consideration our potential and draws on the assumption that the school must always be the one to bring us in, to entertain us, and to provide for us. In other words, this model disempowers parents of color from the potential we have to create change in our schools.

The model of parent engagement that I advocate to be implemented comes from my work with PUT and the Los Angeles Unified School District Parent Collaborative. I worked with fellow members of these groups to create seven different types of action-based approaches that we feel are necessary to move urban working-class parents and communities of color from audience members to active participants. The model presented in this chapter is the first document created by PUT parents regarding what is needed to become advocates for our children. In our estimation, these seven types of approaches will help empower parents of color to make informed decisions about the education, safety, and health of their children in urban and underperforming schools. This was the first time in my school district that urban parents had come together to conceptualize and write a document to engage parents on how to navigate the system in an effort to improve student achievement.

When recasting Joyce Epstein's six areas of parent involvement, we used her model as an initial guide and added what we felt she left out and created what we, as parents of color, believe all parents need in order to successfully navigate our children's career opportunities from preschool to beyond high school and into college. The seven types of action-based approaches are assumed to be directed by parents, especially from urban working-class communities.

TYPE I: Access to Information and Data Collection. Parents need to be informed, to have access to timely and accurate information in order to best support their children's academic success. This includes the following:

- Parents using, analyzing, and collecting data about their schools.
- Parents understanding data and using data that drive responsive reforms.
- Parents becoming empowered to investigate and document conditions in their schools by becoming researchers in their own communities.
- Parent access to information about the resources and rights to support their children.

In Epstein's six areas of parent involvement, she does not mention anything regarding data collection. We now live in a data-driven society and failure to acknowledge the need of data for parents to reflect on school conditions places parents of color at a disadvantage. Type I involvement in our model is also aligned with the intention of No Child Left Behind, section 1118, and the California School Accountability Report Card. This element is also driven by the principle that an informed parent is a powerful agent for social change.

TYPE II: Parents in Decision-Making Roles. Parents need to provide leadership in schools by being equal partners at the table with teachers and administrators in multiple ways. For example, they need to be actively involved in setting policies and in making key school decisions along with school leaders. In such a process, they advocate and work for the schools to have adequate resources to carry out their missions and obligations. In addition, parents provide training and evaluation of school effectiveness and structures. Finally, parent involvement in decision making seeks to incorporate ongoing voice and input from families and the community. Parents in decision-making roles should include the following:

- Genuine parent participation in local advisory committees.
- Effective advocacy and educational involvement as a direct result of understanding how systems are structured (e.g., how decisions and power are distributed between schools, staff, parents, and students).

- Providing parents with knowledge, skills, and opportunities to actively engage them in all levels of the decision-making process—classroom, school district, county, state, and federal levels.
- Consistent representation of parents on the school decision-making teams.

While Epstein (2002) addresses decision-making in her fifth type of parent involvement, in our estimation, her view of decision making is too general. Her fifth type (decision making) lacks content or suggestions on what it should look like in practice. In other words, it is left too open to interpretation, thus exclusively in the hands of educators who often are the ones who define what parent involvement is. In other words, this lack of clarity leaves too much up to school authorities to decide what this decision-making should look like.

TYPE III: Parents as Student Advocates. Parents need to be active advocates for their children by knowing how to navigate and negotiate the school system. We need to support the creation of an environment where parents have access to information and educational and social support systems to be effective advocates in monitoring and directing the education of our children. This includes the following:

- Parents need to know what children need in their social and academic development, how to obtain resources, and how to implement a plan of action.
- Parents need to understand the power map of educational positions and responsibilities, the details of their functions within the structures of the educational system.
- Parents need to understand what and how to be able to communicate in an educational setting, often needing to use terms spoken by educational professionals.

Our Type III of parent involvement is often not addressed in other parent involvement models such as those by Epstein (1992) and Comer (1995). We argue that parents from working-class communities need to know how to engage professional educators if they are going to be public participants in their children's education. Only when parents know the rules of engagement, particularly the language of education, can they hold the system accountable.

In our effort to support working-class parents and increase their understanding of the public school system, PUT published *The Parent Survival Guide* in 2005. Its goal was to assist parents in navigating the school system, grades K–16. *The Parent Survival Guide*, sponsored by Congresswoman Linda Sanchez and written by urban parents who have struggled themselves in navigating the school system, is a map that parents of color can use to understand the ins and outs of the public school structure. For example, *The Parent Survival Guide* breaks down the different offices of a school district and their individual responsibilities. This is of importance because most parents complain about how schools frequently send them from one office to another.

The Parent Survival Guide also covers such topics as college preparation, scholarships and grants available for undocumented immigrants and African American students, the ABC's for student success, services available under special education, and information about how to work within the school structure. The guide also assists immigrant families and parents of color in finding support for their college-bound children with scholarship information (such as the name of organization, requirements, contact information).

And finally, a very important feature about this guide is its accessibility to working-class parents of color. *The Parent Survival Guide* is published in both English and Spanish and is written in a manner that avoids jargon and inaccessible educational terminology.

TYPE IV: Parents as Leaders at Home and in the School Community. Parents need opportunities to build leadership and advocacy skills to enhance student-parent-community partnerships. For example, schools can provide parental training that will serve family and community needs by providing resources and information for obtaining educational and health and social services. These parent leadership skills to serve school-community include the following:

- Parents' skills in intergenerational and cross-cultural communication strategies, with a special emphasis for immigrant families.
- Twenty-first-century parenting skills that focus on prevention, such as how to develop boundaries, parent-child communication, identification of risk factors (e.g., drugs and gang involvement).
- Parents' skills in understanding the college requirement and financial aid process.
- Leadership skills for conducting meetings, facilitation, public speaking, conflict resolution, and cross-cultural training.
- Communication skills for being more effective in navigating their children through K–12 to college.
- Skills for collaborating with schools to receive ongoing support and technical assistance to equip parents for effective school-community participation.

While Epstein (1992) does discuss parent roles, they are limited in content and context. In our summation, there is no room in Epstein's model to broaden the content to go beyond homework to address urban parents' needs. Parents in urban schools, however, are in need of proactive community and social resources to deal with gang influences, drug problems, and criminal activities that go beyond basic parenting skills.

TYPE V: Effective Two-Way Communication. Communication in multicultural and multilingual communities accepts and promotes languages that parents speak in their home. Communication between home and school not only must be a regular, two-way occurrence, it also has to be relevant and meaningful. These multicultural and multilingual ways of communicating with parents must include, but not be limited to, email, newsletters, personal contact, letters/fliers, and the school marquee. Parent liaison roles in multicultural schools must also help bridge open communication between school and home and help create effective home-school relationships. This includes the cultural awareness for school personnel to effectively work with parents of diverse cultural, linguistic, and economic backgrounds and experiences. In many urban and multicultural communities, the parent liaison role is the key to fostering relationships with parents and open communication between schools and communities. There is, however, no relationship more important than that between parents and teachers and that is the idea behind the partnership with institutions of higher education, such as the Urban Parent Teacher Education Collaborative.

The Urban Parent Teacher Education Collaborative (UPTEC) is a pioneering model for other universities. By creating a space for a university professor and a grassroots parent organizer to team-teach a class for preservice teachers, institutions in California like Pepperdine University are beginning to recognize parents as experts in the area of how and what is needed to educate children in urban schools. The UPTEC allows future teachers to have contact with urban parents before they come into our school communities. In workshops, preservice teachers are given strategies for interacting with parents in order to learn how to build a working relationship with them. PUT members and teachers, for example, practice role reversals that allow both teachers and parents to acquire a better understanding and respect for the importance of each other's roles.

The UPTEC model of teacher education seeks to build a clinical laboratory for prospective teachers to acquire skills in working with parent communities. The desired attributes include the following:

- Increase and sustain teachers' knowledge, skills, and positive attitudes toward families through their participation in a community-dialogue forum with urban parents.

- Moving beyond classroom-based teaching methods that offer teachers direct field experiences working with families.
- Develop effective practices that prepare teachers to work with families and communities in culturally appropriate ways.
- Establish a context for teachers to learn about the sociocultural dimensions of urban communities.
- Increase working relationships between novice residence teachers with families and students that break down perceptions of stereotypes and improve student achievement.

TYPE VI: Acquiring District-Level Support. School district support structures must be provided to build parent involvement and skills capacity (as outlined in PUT's Types I–V) that are well defined and where meaningful participation such as dialogue, empowerment, and action are critical components of educational reform. District-level support structures must be fully funded and led by parent councils that will:

- Provide parents with training and capacity building opportunities to effectively engage in school reform at the local and district levels.
- Provide parents with information and resources to meet the social and academic needs of the whole child.
- Provide parents with all necessary skills to support students and school programs.

We acknowledge that Epstein's six types of parent involvement do engage the issue of parent participation at the district level, including the establishment of "independent advocacy groups" that will serve to lobby for school reform and improvements (National Network of Partnership Schools, 2006). Yet the focus of PUT's district-level support is in developing parental capacity to engage schools/districts with information and developed skills.

TYPE VII: Creating a Friendly School Atmosphere. Schools need to create and maintain a school environment that creates belongingness. This begins by posting welcome signs throughout the school in the many languages of the school community, including English. The staff of each school will provide mandatory customer service every year for the entire school. Parents will be asked to fill out a survey on services rendered.

A friendly school atmosphere is a characteristic left out of Epstein's six types of parent involvement that were adopted by the state of California. The number one complaint in urban schools from parents is that school staffs are often rude and unfriendly. This is the major reason parents give for not participating or volunteering at local schools. For PUT the schools are part of the community and parents are the core of the community in ensuring friendly and supportive services for its children.

In actualizing a friendly school atmosphere parents need to be involved with the school in decision-making committees. PUT used the federal parental involvement requirements under the No Child Left Behind law to back up its demands for friendly school atmosphere change. It is a process of engagement with the school, its administrators, teachers, and support staff personnel that requires both collaboration and trust.

PUT as a Model of 21st-Century Parent Engagement

Placing PUT's seven types of parent involvement into practice is hard work. Beginning in November 2005, one neighborhood district signed an agreement with PUT creating new systems of parent involvement. For example, parents now sit on panels that interview applicants for teaching jobs. The school district trains parents on understanding test scores and other school data. Schools hold elections for parents who sit on decision-making panels. Now parents are sitting on the textbook committee. They are sitting in on interviews. Parents are feeling welcomed at the school.

Since its founding, PUT has collaborated with a number of organizations throughout Los Angeles to promote the interests of parents and children of color in the region by advancing the notion that these communities have a deep interest in and desire for education, particularly in advocating when they feel their children have been wronged. For example, PUT has worked with UCLA's Institute of Democracy, Education, and Access to promote parental leadership skills and broaden parents' knowledge of school structures. As a demonstration of their commitment, parents from Southeast Los Angeles cities rode chartered buses every week, for 7 weeks, to attend these leadership classes. At the classes, UCLA professors acted as mentors to parents on different subjects, helping them to develop research methods and skills that would empower them to be their own historians of their neighborhoods and communities. In addition, parents learned how to read school data and documents related to the policies that govern schools.

It is a great feeling when you know that your mentors are learning from the students. Back in 1997, parents were thought of only as research projects or subjects. These same parents are now consulting on the same research projects as experts. Our relationships have broadened from students to colleagues working on projects as equals in giving input and strategies on social justice issues. It feels good to be able to give back to people who have shared their knowledge and time and to help urban parents bring bottom-up accountability into our schools.

And finally, the problems found in South Los Angeles are not exclusive to our part of the country. Working-class, bicultural parents are facing the same dilemmas around the country. School populations are changing, yet practices to include this growing bicultural parent population into school affairs are not. This makes the case study presented here even more important. A vision for 21st-century parent engagement can draw from PUT's methods and goals. They can be used as a framework for engaging historically disenfranchised parent communities.

Discussion Questions

1. How are PUT's seven types of parent involvement different from Epstein's six types of parent involvement?
2. What role are parents expected to play in actualizing PUT's seven types of parent involvement?
3. Why are the majority of school/school districts hesitant to train bicultural parents in the complex ways of navigating the educational system?
4. What are the skills that are essential for bicultural/multicultural parents to develop in order to navigate the preschool-to-university educational system?
5. What are the skills that are essential for teachers to develop in order to be equipped and have proactive relationships with parents as they work to develop the social and academic skills of their students?

Suggested Readings

Jordan J. I. (Ed.). (2002). *African American teachers and their culturally specific classroom practices.* New York: Palgrave.

Nieto, S. (2008). *Affirming diversity: The sociopolitical context of multicultural education* (5th ed.). New York: Longman.

Ritblatt, S. N., Beatty, J., Cronan, T., & Ochoa, A. (2002). Relationships among perceptions of parent involvement, time allocation, and demographic characteristics: Implications for policy formulation. *Journal of Community Psychology, 30*(50), 519–549.

Spring, J. (1999). *Deculturalization and the struggle for equality: A brief history of the education of dominated cultures in the United States.* Boston: McGraw-Hill.

Valdés, G. (1996). *Con respeto: Bridging the distances between culturally diverse families and schools.* New York: Teachers College.

Wink, J. (2000). *Critical pedagogy: Notes from the real world.* New York: Longman.

References

Comer, J. P. (1995). *School power: Implications of an intervention project.* New York: Free Press.

Comer, J. P., & Haynes, N. M. (1991). Parent involvement in schools: An ecological approach. [Special issue]. *The Elementary School Journal, 91*(3), 271–277.

Cummins, J. (2001). *Negotiating identities: Education for empowerment in a diverse society.* Ontario, CA: California Association for Bilingual Education (CABE).

Epstein, J. (1992). School and family partnerships. In M. Alkin (Ed.), *Encyclopedia of educational research* (6th ed., pp. 1139–1151). New York: Macmillan.

Epstein, J. L. (2002). *School, family, and community partnerships: Your handbook for action* (2nd ed.). Thousand Oaks, CA: Corwin Press.

Espinosa, L. M. (2009). *Getting it right for young children from diverse backgrounds: Applying research to improve practice.* Boston: Pearson.

Johnson, M., & Muñoz, V. (2010). *California guide for public schools. Los Angeles: Parent U-Turn.* Retrieved from http://www.californiaparents.net/ContactUs.html

National Network of Partnership Schools. (2006). *Six types of involvement: Keys to successful partnerships.* Retrieved from http://www.csos.jhu.edu/P2000/nnps_model/school/sixtypes.htm

Olivos, E. M. (2006). *The power of parents: A critical perspective of bicultural parent involvement in the public schools.* New York: Peter Lang.

Payne, R. (2005). *A framework for understanding poverty.* Highlands, TX: Aha Process, Inc.

Shannon, S. (1996). Minority parental involvement: A Mexican mother's experience and a teacher's interpretation. *Education and Urban Society, 29*(1), 71–84.

Shirley, D. (1997). *Community organizing for urban school reform.* Austin, TX: University of Texas Press.

9

Bicultural Parents as Transformative Change Agents Through Action Research in Schools and in the Community

Martha Montero-Sieburth

In 2007, Sam Redding, the well-known editor of the *School Community Journal* and parent advocate, published an editorial entitled "Rallying the Troops." This was in response to the call to action made by Heather Weiss, Joyce Epstein, Kathleen Hoover-Dempsey, Anne Henderson, and William Jeynes in the study and practice of school-home relations and family-school-community partnerships at the 2005 annual meeting of the American Educational Research Association (AERA) in Montreal. Like many other parent advocates, Redding felt that given the meager funding that supported parental involvement, and the lack of evaluations, there was an even greater need to demonstrate the effectiveness of research on parental involvement during this age of scientific rigor and demand for empirical evidence. Thus he referred to the questions posed by these scholars at the meeting as a means not only to center a research agenda, but also to put into action an organized movement. The questions were the following:

1. Can we change parenting behaviors? If so, which ones should we change?
2. How do we understand the transformation of schools to make parental involvement integral?

3. How can teachers and schools be supported in encouraging parental involvement? What is needed in preservice preparation of teachers? In-service professional development?
4. How do we educate "community-organizing parents" in ways to improve families, schools, and communities?

I agree that a movement in parental involvement is critical particularly at this time of massive demographic changes, migration, globalization, and transnationalism, and the questions posed are both laudable and essential in setting a research agenda. However, I find that their content conveys much of the same issues that have been the basis of the research on family, community, and parental involvement during the past 30 years and that the paradigms that underlie these questions have not shifted in their intent or meaning. In fact, I contend that the issue of parental involvement has been eschewed in favor of a one-size-fits-all paradigm and without understanding the role of bicultural parents. Bicultural parents have not been a central focus of much of this research except when it has been conducted at the grassroots level or through enterprising university outreach community projects.

Parent-Driven Action Research

I would like to consider what bicultural parents might emphasize if they were to construct the questions posed previously. In that vein, I reframe these questions accordingly. In response to question 1 about changing parenting behaviors, there are several issues. First, it assumes that there is a right or wrong answer about the types of parenting that produces achievement outcomes. Second, it also assumes that one can ideally choose from a variety of behaviors that correspond to education. Embedded in this question is a fundamental paradigm difference, which although not openly stated, relates to the relationships of power that exist between parents who have access to power and those who do not. While one can clearly see the need for some parents to change, the more relevant issues here are *for what reasons* and *why?*

Bicultural parents are often adapting to new environments, cultures, and societies and are constantly experiencing change without their even knowing what such change is about. They often do not know what they need to do or how to respond to the educational demands being made of them by schools. Moreover, not all parents are at the same place, and bicultural parents may respond quite differently, depending on their time in the United States; whether they are immigrant or U.S. born; whether they are schooled and literate; and whether they have had exposure to schooling, have completed their education, and speak English. Some bicultural parents may react from existing at a survival level ("Tell me what I need to know about schools and what I should do"). Others may respond from being at an exploratory level ("How do I present myself, what skills and knowledge must I have before the principal or the teacher?"). And, still others, who might already be settled and well integrated into U.S. culture, may respond with assertiveness, knowing what their rights are ("I know what I have to do to get results and have my rights respected").

Thus, the idea of capturing what needs to be specifically changed in parents assumes the existence of a static culture that is readily detected and can be altered. Such thinking is not in line with the current research on bicultural parents, which shows that they are often in the process of re-creating their own cultures (Villanueva, 2005). Take, for example, the case where a bicultural parent in our action research projects finds out that her daughter, age 13, has been given a condom at school by the nurse without any previous discussion or conversations with her. As the parent commented, "When did I lose control over my child's life? How is it that others are doing the job that belongs to me as a mother?" And "what can I, or must I, do to regain my child and keep to the values of our family together?"

Obviously this parent's dilemma tells us more about what the school and the nurse need to understand about the social and cultural communication between this parent and her child. But more important, this incident highlights unaddressed questions: Should we change these parenting behaviors? If the answer is "yes," then the follow-up questions become, On what basis? And, why? I argue that understanding what the parenting behaviors of bicultural parents are and how these are manifested in U.S. society are the necessary initial steps to engage parents and involve them in schools.

Question 2 emphasizes "the transformation of schools to make parental involvement integral." Instead, bicultural parents, I believe, would ask, "How do we understand the transformation of parents, especially bicultural parents, in making and helping schools become integral?" By shifting the emphasis to parents, a rationale for conducting action research *with and by them* can be made.

Question 3's emphasis on teachers and schools being supported to encourage parental involvement would also need to be turned around to ask, "How can parents, especially bicultural parents, be supported to encourage teachers and schools to engage with them?" Similarly, the second part of the question, which asks, "What is needed in pre- and in-service professional development of teachers to help them become more knowledgeable about how to involve parents?" implies that there is a direct cause and effect between parents and professional teacher development. It may be more the case that teachers in the pipeline or already teaching can learn more about bicultural parents by being exposed to them within the communities where they live and not necessarily within university contexts where they are often considered in abstract ways.

Being able to follow parents in their homes, focusing on their teaching of children, and how they speak and work with their children, may reveal more about what needs to be learned than what a university classroom can convey.[1] The question to be asked is, "How and when are the voices of bicultural parents acknowledged and listened to within university settings?"

In signaling what might be the perspectives of bicultural parents, my intent is to show that the ways parents configure their views may be quite different from the ways academics address parental involvement, despite their use of an extensive corpus of research literature. Academics may know certain things about parental involvement, but there is much that is not known about how bicultural parents respond to education. Their presence in the research literature is simply not visible, and while this may have less to do with a lack of interest, I believe it has more to do with the fact that bicultural parents are seen as being at the periphery and not at the center of parental involvement models even though they have some of the largest numbers of children attending schools.

Unfortunately, the prevalent paradigm of "one size fits all" assumes that all parents can learn how to parent, become engaged in schools, and use available power structures from mainstream middle-class European White parents. Under this paradigm, which operates in a unimodal lockstep process, bicultural parents are undistinguishable from all other parents. Hence, the ways they communicate, help, or provide support to their children as well as the way in which they obtain access to the power structures of middle-class European White parents is often ignored. Knowing how to deal with deeply entrenched political domains, such as parent-teacher organizations, the local school site councils, and making decisions, are expected processes.

Operating under such assumptions often leads other parents to expect that these parents should operate within a "normalized" notion of parenting and if they do not respond in certain expected ways, bicultural parents become stereotyped as not caring about the education of their children. Parental involvement under these premises becomes considered from the perspective of what has to change in bicultural parents before they are considered engaged or active in schools.

In an attempt to break out of this mold and uncover the underlying paradigms that are represented and the perspectives that bicultural and bilingual parents actually have with regard to education, I undertook several action research projects over a 6-year period with parents to share with them the research methods and thinking that is often attributed mostly to academics. As a result, the parents experienced their own knowledge and skills in their process of contributing and transforming schools as future change agents.

Because much of the general literature on parental involvement is covered in other chapters, in the next section I highlight some of the literature as it pertains to bicultural parents.

The Research Behind Parent Involvement

Parental involvement programs, according to Shepard and Rose (1995), have been in existence for the past 100 years in the United States. They have evolved from a 1960s deficit home intervention model approach to a language and socialization difference model seen during the 1970s and early 1980s, and in the 1980s to 1990s until the present, we have shifted to the more current empowerment and participatory models (as evidenced in this volume). The former orientations were based on home interventions to change parental behavior, while the latter are based on a focus of choice and decision making whereby parents ably use resources, engage in dialogue, and effectively problem-solve. Such shifts have been dictated by educational policies on the one hand, and on the other, by community-based parent group initiatives and the need to understand shifting demographics.

In this field, the research of Redding, Langdon, Meyer, and Shelley (2004) has provided multiple perspectives and interpretations of parental involvement. Henderson and Mapp (2002) have synthesized the field, and Jeynes (2002) has linked parental involvement and achievement outcomes to social capital domains. The research of Joyce Epstein and her colleagues (2002, 2004) has resulted in the elaboration of different stages for parental involvement and engagement, now universally adopted, which have sample practices, challenges, redefinitions, and expected results, which include (1) Parenting, (2) Communicating, (3) Volunteering, (4) Learning at Home, (5) Decision Making, and (6) Collaborating with the Community.

Kathleen V. Hoover-Dempsey and Howard M. Sandler's research (1995, 1997) has also made the psychological aspects of parent-child relationships known through their identification of (a) the parents' role construct, which includes their belief about involvement; (b) the sense of parent's self-efficacy; and (c) the types and kinds of school invitations parents receive as affecting parental involvement. Erin McNamara Horvat, Elliot Weininger, and Annette Lareau's (2003) research has uncovered social-class differences and the ways that parents respond to problematic issues in schools, with middle-class parents reacting collectively, using contacts with professionals to mobilize information, authority needed to contest issues, and expertise, while working-class and poor parents do not use access to such networks. Violand-Sanchez, Sutton, and Ware (1991) have posited ways in which home-school cooperation can be fostered by language-minority families as partners in education.

Studies by Henderson and Mapp (2002) as well as Ascher (2002) and Baker and Soden (1988) have shown that direct curriculum related outreach and developing a climate of trust enhances the participation and engagement of parents in schools. In addition, William Jeynes's (2002) studies reveal that parental involvement is most significant in contributing to minority-student learning in communities where there are limited reservoirs of social capital outside the school and reduced expectations for children's success. Many of the results of these studies and their effectiveness have affected programs such as Success for All; Wings and Roots; Coalition for Essential Schools; Accelerated Programs; and James Comer's psychological family, education, and community model.

Yet the majority of these studies, many of which have been applied to families from diverse socioeconomic and ethnic backgrounds in preschool, middle school, and high school, characterize the role that parents should have toward the school and academic achievement, without distinguishing the effects of home environments on student learning and school-based initiatives. On this point, Pomerantz, Moorman, and Litwack Scott (2007) argue that such distinctions need to be made, because each may have different effects on children's schooling. Parental involvement research, they point out, reports on the naturally occurring involvement of parents, using parents', teachers', and children's reports that are reflected longitudinally through children's grades. They also address interventions aimed at promoting parents' involvement in children's schooling through reading contracts, academic activities, and so on.

Such research highlights two models: (a) a skills development model, in which parents' involvement improves academic achievement based on making available skill-related resources (language capabilities, phonological awareness, metacognitive skills) and (b) a motivational development model, in which parents provide intrinsic reasons such as valuing schooling, fostering personal enjoyment, and providing for academic competence to their children (Pomerantz et al., 2007). While both skill and motivational development may work hand in hand in helping children achieve, by actively engaging parents in providing resources, motivating children to engage and enjoy learning, and providing skills that prepare children to learn, they indicate that it is the motivation of parents, internalized by children, that helps them value schooling in positive ways (Pomerantz et al., 2007). Furthermore as Pomerantz et al. stipulate, it is *how* parents are involved, the *who* of parents' involvement, and the *why* of parents' involvement that identifies the quality of parents' involvement rather than the extent of their involvement.

Pomerantz et al. conclude that the involvement of parents is beneficial to children of all ethnic backgrounds and the more exposed children are to academic endeavors such as reading, the better their reading skills become in later grades. Moreover, parent involvement may be beneficial for children when it is autonomy supportive, where children solve problems on their own, when it is process focused, and where the emphasis is on the pleasure of effort and learning. Parent involvement in this is way is characterized by positive effects or connectedness, and is accompanied by positive rather than negative beliefs about children's potential.

In addition to Pomerantz et al.'s research, Gutman and Eccles (1999) and Eccles and Harold (1996) indicate that parent involvement may be more beneficial among families of children at risk, of children growing up in poor uneducated families, than for European American children, since it enhances their already difficult experiences in environments that detract from their academic experiences.

Yet as extensive as this research corpus is, several issues need to be singled out. The research has often represented the perspectives of dominant, mainstream European Whites on underrepresented groups' models of parental involvement. The ways that bicultural parents cope with ever changing home and school modalities, their home parenting behaviors, the influence of community-based organizations on their parenting roles, or the expectations they share as newcomers or established members of a community have often been unexplored.

While much of the research stipulates that parental involvement may be the single most important indicator of student achievement in school (Darder & Upshur, 1992; Epstein, 1988, 2002, 2004; Fan & Chen, 2001; Hoover-Dempsey & Sandler, 1995, 1997; Pomerantz, Grolnick, & Price, 2005; Wheelock, 1990), studies conducted by Mattingly, Radmila, McKenzie, Rodriguez, and Kayzar (2002), which concur with Pomerantz et al.'s (2007) findings, show no evidence of a causal relationship between parent involvement and student achievement. Mattingly et al., for example, argue that the effects of such interventions have not been clear, nor have they shown the benefits of such programs. Such interventions have not undergone rigorous evaluations of parent involvement programs and the research has been insufficient to draw firm conclusions about the effects of interventions.

The research that has emerged from linkages between university faculty and bicultural communities is becoming regionally and even nationally recognized for its impact in creating political spaces for dialogue and collaboration. Examples include the Parent Leadership Development Program at the University of San Diego; the Parent Curriculum Project of UCLA (see Chapter 8, Johnson's chapter, in this book for more information about this project); and later UCLA's Institute for Democracy, Education and Access in Los Angeles; Latino Youth Incorporated in Chicago; Calvary Bilingual Multicultural Learning Center in Washington, DC; Concilio of Latino Service Organizations in Dallas; and Padres Unidos in Denver. However, their projection as national programs or models for affecting parental involvement, except for James Comer's (2004) family and community model, is unknown.

Even the most recent legislation, No Child Left Behind, touts parental involvement as the basis for school partnerships and for maintaining the continuities between home and school. According to John Rogers (2006), parental involvement is mentioned more than 100 times in the current No Child Left Behind legislation and its policies on test accountability and choice were expected to spur parental involvement that would lead to poor parents demanding greater expectations of their schools. Yet as Rogers shows, these options have not been realized, because there is no understanding of the lack of resources and tools for collective action of poor parents. Through grassroots efforts such as Parent-U-Turn, Rogers demonstrates that parents can create public power that helps them focus on shared inquiry and the kind of collective action that demands action and accountability (see Johnson, Chapter 8, in this volume).

The shift in focus of parental involvement from European American mainstream parents to bicultural and Latino parents has taken place as a result of institutes such as the Harvard Family Research Project (Weiss, Kreider, Lopez, & Chatman, 2005); organizations such as the National Council of La Raza; as well as community-based organizations throughout the Midwest, South, and West, where through their own grassroots initiatives, there has been an intentional focus on bicultural Latino parent issues. In this regard, Jorge Ostering and Armandina Garza (2004) of the National Council of La Raza have advocated using Latino community-based organizations as a source of leadership that can strengthen the involvement of Latino parents in schools. Like Epstein, Armandina Garza has identified six different types of Latino parent engagement opportunities that community-based organizations and schools can engender.

In reviewing both the Epstein and Garza models in Table 9.1, different operating paradigms are evident. These include (1) Parents as Leaders, with shared power between school and parents; (2) Parents as Collaborators; (3) Parents as Teachers; (4) Parents as Supporters; (5) Parents as Parents; and (6) Parents as Contributors to School.

Table 9.1 Comparison Between Epstein's and Garza's Paradigms

Epstein's Six-Step Model of Parental Engagement	Armandina Garza's Model of Latino Parent Engagement
Parenting	Parents as Leaders
Communicating	Parents as Collaborators
Volunteering	Parents as Teachers
Learning at Home	Parents as Supporters
Decision Making	Parents as Parents
Collaborating with the Community	Parents as Contributors to School

In addition to these organizations, several scholars have researched bicultural families and parental involvement as growing numbers of students obtain access to education (Gibson, 2002). Barri Tinkler (2002) conducted a massive review of the literature on Latino parent involvement in K–12 education; Janet Chrispeel and Margarita Gonzalez's (2004) research shows that educational programs do in fact increase Latino parents' practices at home, and Linda Holman (1997) identifies in her studies ways to work effectively with Latino immigrant families. Robin Waterman (2008), for her part, has shown that the pervasive deficit views, in the case of Mexican parents, hinder parents and school staff from effectively supporting student achievement. Thus, it appears that what are needed are more collaborative forms of working between bicultural parents and school officials.

For their part, Latino scholars have focused on the cultural and economic factors that influence Latino parents' perceptions of involvement. Salinas-Sosa's (1997) research shows that early on engagement activities for collaboration of Latino parents are effective; Irene Villanueva's (2005, 2006) studies argue that family and cultural awareness research as well as their incorporation in the curriculum has challenged many of the stereotypes about Latinos' lack of interest in the education of their children. Research by Carrasquillo and London (1993), Delgado-Gaitán and Trueba (1991), and Valdes (1996) have identified learning opportunities provided by schooling. Delgado-Gaitan's (2004) research has demonstrated how Latino folkways of doing things and Latino parents' critical reflections of their *consejos* (advice) become critical social markers. She explains that physical resources, emotional climate, and interpersonal interactions all serve to support Latino parents in their socializing of children to education.

Valdes's (1996) research on Latino parents' child-rearing practices shows that such parents are different from White, middle-class parents. Zarate's research (2007) also has yielded different perceptions about parental involvement from Latino parents regarding *educación*, or life participation.[2] She found that *educación* was more frequently mentioned by parents than was academic involvement, and while homework assistance was acknowledged as significant, these parents reported their lack of curriculum knowledge as a limitation. These parents also mentioned that the policies and the reception they experienced in school was more problematic than language issues—a point that Alejandro Portes and Lingxin Xao (2004) identify as contributing to nonbelonging, particularly for Mexicans in schools, who do not see any other alternative but to drop out of school.

The research has shown that bicultural parents encounter difficulties in obtaining access to schools, not speaking English, not having transportation to school, lacking the knowledge of how schools function and are organized, and assuming a locus parentis role for schools derived from their countries of origin. Yet much more research is needed, particularly in terms of the way that bicultural parents teach their children at home, the education of the first and second generation, pre-emigration levels of education and class status, and attainment of social and cultural capital (Scribner, Young, & Pedraza, 1999). Equally important is research on the migration processes of the first generation, the types of family patterns that they bring from their countries of origin, the types of changes they experience, and how these families become restructured once in the United States (Curiel, 1991; Feliciano, 2006). We do not know how offspring of bicultural families may need to adapt to even more different patterns than those of their parents, and in this sense, the notion of families in change needs to also be studied in relation to parental involvement (Landale & Oropesa, 2007; Swidler, 2001).

Research Questions Guiding the Action Research Projects

While bicultural parents are addressed in the chapter, I focused specifically on Latino immigrant and residentially settled parents for these studies. The action research for each of the four projects (to be detailed later in this chapter) used the following research questions:

1. What do Latino parents understand of U.S. schooling and the ways that curriculum, assessment, and teaching are organized at their children's schools? Additionally, what are their roles as parents vis-à-vis these schools' practices?
2. How can parents gather data about what is going on in their schools and how can they use such data for clarifying issues and making decisions using the skills of ethnographers in observing, recording field notes, audiotaping, collecting material culture, interviewing key school personnel, memoing, and writing reports?
3. Later, as the research in these projects unfolded, this last question was added to frame the research: What can parents learn from using this type of research approach that enables them to understand their roles in school, their agency and ability to become empowered to transform their schools? And what are burning issues that parents bring to their need for agency?

Preparing Parents to Conduct Action Research

In my community work as a university researcher engaged with diverse ethnic groups throughout the greater Boston metropolitan area, for the past 25 years, I wanted to use the skills and knowledge of a qualitative researcher and ethnographer to identify how parents participating in community-based organizations could become "researchers" of the schools their children attend.

Just as an anthropologist studies the culture of a community, I believe parents could learn the essentials of ethnographic research by negotiating entry, collecting material culture, conducting observation, recording field notes, audiotaping, interviewing, memoing, visiting schools, and writing reports to understand how schools and curriculum are organized, and how school policies and practices persist. With some training, such parents could become aware of their own abilities and competencies, become empowered by the use of data, and eventually come to see themselves as change agents, able to identify and decipher the kinds of organization, teaching, and leadership that take place in schools. I also believe that by using their homegrown experiences, these parents could confront their fear of obtaining access to schools without viewing them as totally foreign or distant. They could overcome the limitations they experience in schools when they undertake the traditional walk-through, where they conduct rapid analysis without the knowledge and skills of researchers and with untrained eyes that often result in facile negative observations and highly biased reports.

Given this rationale, I assembled a series of focus group meetings at different community sites with high concentrations of Latino/bicultural parents to conduct action research projects that would "train parents," the term in vogue at the time of this research, in engaging them further in the education of their children. Each project session consisted of either the research sequence which I had planned, or the presentation of topics or burning issues which had emerged from the discussions with parents. For the former, I conducted a needs assessment of the readiness of parents for the research sequence, and for the latter, I queried parents on the topics they most wanted and needed to help their children. The topics that emerged varied from presentations on carpal tunnel syndrome, which many of them suffered from factory work with repetitive tasks, to understanding the creativity of children, to helping their children "without papers" gain entry into a university, to knowing about the research on bilingual education and second-language learning to help them determine placement options for their children.

The research agenda was negotiated several times over, since the participation of parents varied from one focus group meeting to another, and the training on topics was conducted in the language of participants' preference, Spanish or English or a combination of both. By being able to train parents in the use of ethnographic methods and, at the same time, focusing on the timely issues they identified, their knowledge base and skills could be expanded and they could control the amount and quality of data they needed for making decisions. Through such training, I was able to uncover their motivation for learning, identify some of their basic primary needs, and recognize the nascent leadership that was evident in the way they organized within each group.

Parent Engagement at Work

As shown in Table 9.2, I engaged with four sets of parents, training them in action research and conducting action research. The first action research group I engaged in was with a diverse group of parents from working- and middle-class backgrounds from Central America and Puerto Rico at a community-based organization. The second action research group was another diverse group of parents. It was composed of a high concentration of Central and South American newcomers and 15- to 20-year residents of working- and middle-class backgrounds. This group met after mass. The third action research project was conducted with a group of parents, undergoing an organization process as a parent group, and was mostly made up of newcomer and seasoned Dominican residents concerned with the bilingual schooling of their children. The prominent leader of the group had been politically involved in the Dominican Republic, where he continued to maintain strong transnational connections. The group had working- and middle-class parents who had completed their university studies in the Dominican Republic. The final action research group was mostly made up of Central American and South American parents from working- to middle-class backgrounds. Their involvement was initiated by the incoming Latina principal of their school.

Action Research Group I: January 1999 to December 2000. Training and research was conducted in one of the key community agencies working with Latino parents. These parents had completed a 4 to 6 week parent curriculum course that had focused on self-esteem, the role of communities and schools, and parent responsibility. The director of the community-based organization felt that these parents were ready for further training and after meeting with them and recruiting those who could invest the six sessions for the initial sequence, it was evident they could undertake the tasks involved. While the parents were not paid for their participation, they did receive child care during the time they were in sessions. However, there were times when the number of children being cared for was greater than the number of parents participating, and some of the Dominican mothers changed diapers as well as fed their children while the sessions were in progress.

The group of 10 parents of Puerto Rican, Dominican, and Guatemalan backgrounds, in which 2 were males and the rest females, were taught to map the community, schools, and classroom through didactic methods, record field notes, and conduct interviews. Of these, the Puerto Rican parents had lived from childhood to adulthood in the United States and used English more than Spanish. The Dominican parents already had been 10 years in the States and the newcomers were the Guatemalan parents. Both these groups used Spanish extensively and English haltingly. The most educated were also the Puerto Rican parents, who had gone to university. They were followed by the Guatemalan parents, who had

Table 9.2 Parent Involvement Action Research Projects

Action Research Groups	Participant Backgrounds	Numbers Participating	Outcomes	School Visits or Actions
I. Community-Based Group	Central and South Americans	Initially 30, subsequently 10 during sessions	Interviews, observations, fieldwork	Two school visits with two parents
II. After-Mass Group	Central American	Initially 40, subsequently 12 during sessions	Resume writing, health issues, educational training	Job seeking, four parents with jobs
III. Dominican Parent Group	Dominicans	Initially 20, subsequently 12 during sessions	*Topical issues:* bilingual education, rights and law	Galvanizing parent group
IV. Latino Parent School Group	Central Americans, South Americans	Initially 35, subsequently 20 during training and preparation for protest sessions	Observations, interviews at PTO meetings *Topical issues:* rights, bilingual education	PTO participation, volunteer groups, protests, meeting with consultants, union leaders

graduated from high school and had 1 year of technical training. The Dominican parents were the least educated and had less than a high school diploma, yet of the five women, two continued to take courses to enhance their training and eventually received community college credits.

Infighting between the Central American and Dominican women frequently occurred, and class differences were often cited as the reason for creating "chismes," gossip or "bochinches," which mostly took place outside the training sessions but were shared via telephone or in person. For the Guatemalan parents, the idea of Dominican mothers diapering or feeding their children while the training session was being conducted showed "they had no education." The Dominican women, on the other hand, referred to the perceived submission of the Guatemalan women as "not being sufficient as a woman."

Spanish was initially used with all the 10 parents, but as the training continued, it was the Puerto Rican parents who spoke English who preferred information in English. These were the parents who visited the schools and completed the training cycle. In referring to education, some of the parents shared the following comments: "I believe that my child has the right to be in school"; "In taking these classes, my children know that I am protecting their interests"; and "My biggest worry is that my child be interested in school, that when he reaches adolescence, he does not leave school. I need to learn how I am going to help my son so that he is more interested in being in school than leaving the school. I see so many adolescents on the street, who don't go to school and it is because the parents don't show any interest or because the teachers do not inject any interest in the students so that they keep going to school. There are so many factors which influence a child to leave school. That is why I want to study and learn about what I can do to prevent this situation." The Guatemalan parent whose child was thought of as being advantaged in 3rd grade asked for more materials to read to her child, yet the teacher explained that she could not take the time to spend with her after school to share materials because she would run against teacher union regulations about after-school limitations.

In addition, after completing the sequence and showing evidence of their understanding through written memos and conducting two school visits at one of the local elementary schools, these parents identified several issues that they were unaware were taking place at the school. They created their own interview questions and asked the administrators and teachers to explain how they taught bicultural children. In interviewing the principal, they recognized that his stated support for bilingual education was different from the data they gathered during the observations and interviews with teachers. Teachers were told by the principal to hide any of the Spanish textbooks, and to only use English textbooks in classes. A teacher, who defied the principal and used the Spanish textbooks, was afraid the other teachers would "rat on her" and hence was extremely careful about carrying out such subversive actions.

In mapping her observations, one of the parents noted that few Spanish words were ever written on the activity chart for parents, nor were there substantive books in the library that were written in Spanish except for translated versions of Mickey Mouse and Donald Duck. These two parents not only noted the lack of Spanish signs, or information for parents in Spanish, but during the interview with the principal and after reading and memoing their notes, detected his aversion to bilingual education and recognized that he had maintained a hypocritical stance with the bicultural parents. He said one thing publicly, but professed another agenda, which he imposed upon the teachers.

Thus at the end of this action research, although 10 parents participated in all the training, these 2 remained constant. They eventually became invested in parent training themselves. One became a parent organizer at one of the local community organizations and the other a strong advocate in the local school site council. The aftermath of the training was that although the training was attractive for the parents, the administrator of the community-based organization left. A new administrator, previously a military officer, was hired and his agenda was completely different.

During his tenure there was hardly any community outreach and he was in the position for less than a year after discontented parents complained and the community organization was closed and resurrected with a different orientation by the new manager several years later. As a result, the parent training, which could have set into motion a multiplier effect, was reduced to the agendas held by the new administration. Rather than work with the model that had been generated and was homegrown and successful, models that came from out of state, with different orientations, were adopted. The momentum that had been put into motion by the former administrator was simply ignored and the process of action research with parental input moving it forward was administratively dismissed.

This action research project helped to demonstrate the importance of continuity and the need to keep abreast of the political maneuvering that often takes place as community-based organizations become successful and attract funding. To the demise of this program must be added also the demise of the training and the lack of cooperation between the community-based organization and parent outreach.

Action Research Group II: February 2001–May 2001. From the experience of the first action research group, a second group was formed from an after-mass group at one of the local Catholic churches in order to follow up on keeping the training going for parents. Initially, 40 parents showed up at the first and second meeting, but these numbers dwindled to 12 parents from Colombia, El Salvador, Peru, and Mexico who participated, once the project was cleared and each week's topic was reviewed by the priest. Of the total 10 sessions held, 4 were about ethnographic research and the remaining 6 focused on particular interests of the parents.

These parents were mostly immigrants, with some having arrived less than 6 weeks previously and others having lived in this highly Latino-concentrated area for as many as 10–15 or 20 years. Women participated more than men, but two or three men came to the sessions, mostly because their wives insisted on bringing them. Two of the men had parallel households in their native countries, with a wife and one set of children there and another wife and children in the United States. The educational levels of these participants ranged extensively, with three having university degrees, six having completed high school, two having completed 3rd grade, and one clearly illiterate parent who asked us to write down his answers.

Instead of the research sequence offered in its totality, parents in this group selected a combination of some research and topics to be addressed. They were trained to observe and interview during the initial sessions, and the rest of the sessions focused on topics such as the nature of bilingual education, what the research says about bilingual placements, what to do with creative children, and advancement in one's career. Several revealed that they were lawyers in their own countries, but had to start at the bottom to find a job; they wanted to know what a curriculum looked like, and thus some of the most attractive sessions were on curriculum vitae development and the massage sessions that they requested for their hands, which suffered from carpal tunnel syndrome from repetitive tasks in the factories.

Because of their extended workloads, they could meet only on Sundays, so each month we had one major meeting lasting for several hours. For many of these parents, the balance between work and home and their support of their children was an issue. Several parents worked two and three jobs, not knowing how their children used their afternoons once they arrived home from school. They regarded money as a means to better their lives, but found that work distanced them from their children and did not allow them to share the values they were raised with. One of the Colombian mothers emotionally expressed:

> From what I understand in these classes, I break my back working for my children in two jobs, and because I am not here, when they need me, I may be shortening their opportunities. I need to weigh what this means in the long run.

Other parents expressed statements such as the following:

> How can your children go to the university that is in line with your economic situation? What I expect of schools here, which I do not see, is that they teach the children how to behave well with others and with their parents, and to teach them not to use drugs.

Regarding their reason for participating, some stated: "As a parent you have to live all the experiences and be well informed to know how to help our children. That is why we are here."

Some echoed their frustration with schools and their inability to intervene. One Colombian mother in tears discussed her communication with a teacher:

> My husband is trying to finish his high school here with tremendous effort. He was a high school teacher in our country. We try to help our daughter who is in 8th grade and we check her report card each month. She was doing well, and I know that parents sometimes do not care, she was

getting C's, but then she received an F. We see her work every day and my husband helps her on weekends. When we called the teacher, she said our daughter was lazy. When we questioned her further, she said the problem was that our daughter is lazy.

During the training, we uncovered that the role of the priest was quite important in these parents' lives and in defining their educational vision. During the negotiating of entry, our training had to vie with the city's police department's presentation of drug use among youth. The priest circulated fliers admonishing parents to come to these meetings, and close to 60 parents appeared. Using fear tactics, the police asked parents to detect drug use in their children by checking the dilation of their eyes, their behavior, and the friends they associated with. Many parents left concerned and our initiative was off to a difficult start, since our presentations were not crisis oriented, but rather action oriented. We found ourselves competing not only with the police department, but also with other community-based organizations that procured their funding based on the numbers of persons they attracted to their office and would be able to count. Much like Latin American markets, members of these community organizations would be at mass distributing leaflets and offering prizes to those parents who would visit their offices.

In addition to these obstacles in obtaining access to bicultural parents, we were curtailed by the fact that in order to meet with the parents after mass, requests for their participation had to be made at each of the information-sharing sections of each mass. I found myself confessing more often in order to obtain the agreement of this priest. It became painfully obvious that he controlled the knowledge of the parishioners. He scrutinized our presentations for censorship of any references to sex, abortion, or leftist thinking. At one of the masses, this priest admonished the bicultural parents to remove their children from bilingual education programs and to place them in English-speaking programs. From the pulpit, he said, "Your children will fare better if they learn English, which is the language of America, and leave their Spanish behind." Yet as many parents reported, they believed it would be in their children's best interest to continue in bilingual programs of their mother tongue, but felt they did not want to incur the wrath of the priest. Left in a quandary and in deference to the priest, many took their children out of the bilingual programs and placed them in English-speaking programs.

Not only did these actions hurt our process, but they provided us with an understanding of the power some priests have over the community. We encountered further difficulties in meeting the parents in the basement of the church after each mass. To reduce costs, the priest turned off the heat during the winter months in the basement, so we had our sessions with coats on. However, for bingo games and kermises and for the occasions when parents prepared food and the funds obtained were donated to the church, the basement was heated.

From these obstructions to action research, it became clear that having a neutral space was essential for these parents to be themselves and to act freely of their own accord. Furthermore, we became painfully aware of the power that a priest can yield in dictating educational choices and the types of commitments parents must have to his agenda. Realizing that the 800 to 1,000 parents who showed up for mass each Sunday contributed their tithe to the church, given their low-paid salaries, and some of the parents painted the priest's home during the summer months in exchange for information about housing and possible jobs, while receiving spiritual sustenance, made us reflect on the role of the church, liberation theology, and liberatory education, which had been disseminated during the 1970s throughout all Latin America and which was the Catholic Church's response to the poor.

I realized that parents in these situations need a great deal of support, some of which has to do with providing family biliteracy programs, women's leadership and development, and emancipatory models of learning. Many of these parents were willing and able learners who needed the opportunities to progress in their education in order to support the education of their children. I attempted to link their stated needs to the delivery of our university programs, with the hope that eventually, based on a competency learning model, educational programs could be brought from the university to the community and this would further their education. Yet the dean of the college who could provide this, and who was a Latino who understood these issues, was replaced by another dean by the provost and was returned to a teaching position.

Action Research Group III: December 2001 to 2002. The action research of the third group grew out of the concerns of 20 parents, mostly of Dominican backgrounds, whom we met in a meeting about the elimination of bilingual education in their schools. This ongoing parent group was being reorganized by one of the Dominican leaders in order to become a nonprofit organization.

Spurned by one of the school administrator's elimination of the program, these parents met with a lawyer to protest how bilingual education in this community was being replaced by English immersion. The lawyer contacted us and our team was brought into this community setting.

A total of 20 Dominican parents, which later decreased to 12, met as a community group to assess what they could do and how they should strategize. The research sequence that we presented appeared to be appropriate, since they could obtain information that many of them did not know. Many felt they did not have access to the schools, since new laws had taken place, the admittance of parents into the schools was being curtailed, and criminal offender record information checkups based on personnel reviews were introduced. Two of the six sessions focused on ethnographic research and the other sessions were based on helping parents understand the research findings for bilingual education in relation to English immersion, the ways that they could form committees and target issues, and finally the roles they could play as a nonprofit organization in advocating for the use of Spanish in learning for their children.

While these parents were highly vocal and politically astute, they felt sheer frustration at not being able to overturn the roadblocks the school administration presented. After several sessions, it became apparent that without strong leaders in this parent group, who would take up the initiative of all of the parents, they would be silenced; and this was in fact what occurred. The parents were not able to change what became the superintendent's decision to eliminate bilingual classes, even through meetings and special requests. They even legally filed a lawsuit against the decision, but in the end, they had no choice but to abide by the terms set up for the schools (Olivos & Ochoa, 2008). These parents felt defeated.

Clearly the political agendas of a new superintendent with support from multiple stakeholders made it difficult for a not fully organized parent group to stand on its own, and even with legal help, and knowledge of bilingual education, their momentum for action was lost in the lack of greater leadership than the one single parent who led the group. Building a political agenda with backing and leadership was evident learning yielded by this research.

Action Research Group IV: September 2005–December 2005. The fourth group of 20 Latino parents from Guatemala, Venezuela, Mexico, Puerto Rico, and Colombia were constituted from the stated need parents expressed to participate more actively in their children's school. Having been in the community for as many as 15 years and without much support, these parents were galvanized by the new Latina principal who came to their school. Some of the parents wanted to volunteer and be valuable in the school. When the librarian of the school made a display for Thanksgiving that depicted the Pilgrims and Indians in a village setting, one of the bicultural parents asked me as the trainer, "Shouldn't we be part of that scene? Aren't we the new Pilgrims?"

The education of these parents ranged widely, with some having completed 3rd grade, others primary school, and a few secondary school, and at least three had university degrees. They were from working- to middle- and upper-class backgrounds, with two of the members being married to doctors and lawyers.

Under the guidance of a new principal, of Spanish background, these parents, many of whom had been in this school district and had felt alienated and marginalized, were invited to participate in leadership training from September to December 2005. The new principal felt that this would allow parents to understand their role in the school, where close to 47% of the student body was Latino. At the same time, the principal offered parents the opportunity to learn English as a second language for those parents who did not speak English, and Spanish to those non-Spanish-speaking teachers who were interested in communicating with parents. While these parents actively engaged in the training session and developed skills that were useful, the principal's initiatives at offering Spanish classes created a volatile situation for several of the parents, who felt that Spanish was being imposed upon the children and tax monies were being used to support Spanish, and the statement was made, "We are in America, and English is the language of America." The end result was the suspension of the principal and her eventual resignation. The accusations leveled at her was that she gave preferential treatment to the bicultural parents and did not consider the Anglo parents, even though she had planned to offer the same leadership program to Anglo parents in the second semester.

While this training did not result in the advancement of Latino parents in terms of their being able to overturn the suspension of the principal, it did allow for two of the bicultural parents to eventually become part of the school's PTO, where they served for several years.

The promise of action research in this case was totally confronted by the entrenchment found in a community that hired from within and had for the first time hired from outside, yet the values and conformity expressed was that of a community that did not want change, although it was surrounded historically and ethnically by changing social and economic demographics. The context was saturated with fear about the incoming immigrant groups, and Latin Americans, who had now rented homes and whose children were attending schools, and were viewed as a threat. Given these feelings, any change would be disruptive, and as we continued to work with the bicultural parents, we confronted this fear, when several parents were told, "Go back to where you belong," and "You have no rights here."

Learning from the Parent-Driven Action Research Initiatives

From these four action research–driven projects with bicultural parents, issues became apparent from the findings that are worth consideration and that articulate some of the tensions and possibilities for future collective action research.

Parent Issues. First, in terms of the bicultural parents' own preparation for understanding what was at stake in the education of their children in all these projects, it is clear that Latino/bicultural parents often do not have the type or kind of information that is essential for making educational decisions, and obtaining that information is not easily made possible by contextual or prevailing political agendas. Hence, how to gain substantive information and how to overcome the fear of knowledge are two major hurdles to overcome for this collective action to move forward.

Second, bicultural parents often react to educational concerns they encounter out of crisis, often requiring them to rely on one-to-one problem-solving from others, and not strategy-building opportunities that enhance their abilities to manage and make decisions. Training in management, decision making, and leadership are as important for these parents as is English learning and family biliteracy.

Third, the access to the social and cultural capital that other parents may have is something that bicultural parents may not necessarily seek, because it may not be evident, but at the same time, the dominant mainstream culture may not value the social and cultural capital of bicultural parents. For example, changing the way that the volunteer parents react to helping bicultural parents into the school by not allowing them access needs to be openly confronted as a control of social and cultural capital. Thus, bicultural parents need to know what goes on in the schools and how they have rights.

Fourth, bicultural parents often allow fear to set in, especially given the obstacles and barriers they have in not speaking English or obtaining access to the power centers of the PTO. Yet if their latent but nascent leadership skills are tapped and developed, they do not have to underestimate their own power in taking responsibility and making decisions.

In summary, focusing on bicultural parents means being willing to see them in differentiated contexts with a variety of educational issues that they need to confront. In these action research projects, parent participation varied widely, with few parents being consistently present at each of the training sessions. For many of them, the time spent in training was time away from their spouses and children. Given their heavy workloads of close to 60 or 70 hours a week, many either felt too tired to attend all the sessions or were pressured by family demands. Hence, gathering of critical information about what was meaningful to them was made on the run. Figuring out and identifying their habits and preferences as well as how to translate their concrete experiences into doable research practices took a great deal of listening. The degree to which they have access to schooling seems to determine their commitment and constancy in engagement; thus projects of this sort need to be worked out in the community and with the schools and universities.

Understanding the context in which these parents situate themselves and their stages of incorporation in U.S. society is also critical. It is important to know what bicultural parents need, whether it is basic survival, gaining specific information, or learning about their rights in the education of their children. Figuring out where they are, what they need, and how to identify sources of knowledge are some of the critical issues that were learned from this study. In addition, the transitions that have taken place in Latino families and the structures they adopt as they live in the United States need to be understood. Some Latino families are sibling-headed families; other family constellations involve parents having two sets of families, one in the home country, and another in the United States. Thus action research of this type also needs to accommodate for such changes and to understand how to work with parents undergoing such transitions.

In addition, action research of this type needs to be accompanied by family literacy programs, whereby parents are supported in their learning by being able to read and write and to use the power of the word (McCaleb, 1997). Access to English-speaking programs is part of the empowerment, especially for first-generation bicultural parents, and for second-generation children, it is the maintenance of the mother tongue that is critical. Furthermore, models such as those provided by Epstein, while generic and universally used, may not be applicable to bicultural parents' own parental involvement processes. Note the differences that exist between Epstein's six-step model and that created by Armandina Garza presented in this chapter. Most likely these bicultural parents would create a more flexible, culturally oriented, and context-specific model.

Action Research Issues. In terms of conducting action research, several issues are significant. First, it is clear that action research as a collaborative endeavor begins in a community where there is a degree of sustainability for its development. That is, there must be, as Paulo Freire often said, spaces where the opportunity to converge, think out loud, and initiate change can be conducive to action. Impenetrable spaces or spaces with divergent agendas about the agency of bicultural parents, where they are considered to be passive and simply followers but not leaders, cannot provide the grounding for action research to succeed; thus neutral spaces, not churches or political forums, are needed, but buildings or areas where parents find the freedom to express themselves openly.

Second, as a researcher, for me it becomes inevitable to dissect the degree to which politics intervenes in education. Yet each of these cases appears to challenge the entrenched politics and agendas that exist for the minoritization[3] of bicultural parents, whether through new administrations in community centers oriented to parents, or priest-directed behaviors of parents, or principal-led interventions in the teaching of Spanish, or requesting an equitable education for children in a school district by using one's mother tongue. Naming the political processes and concretizing issues with parents that deem attention and action are perhaps some of the ways that such entrenchment can be opened up and diminished.

Third, overcoming these barriers requires more than changing the assumptions by which these parents are considered to be involved and engaged in the education of their children. It also requires deconstructing the belief that all parents, in sending their children to school, are aware of how schools in the United States function, how they are organized, how the curriculum is shaped, how parents are to participate, and how the current standards of education have become translated into learning outcomes and products that parents can readily access. For many bicultural parents, knowing about the education of their children becomes not only a personal and critical issue, but also a public matter in which they are held accountable. Thus one of the key purposes of this research is to gain an understanding of what bicultural parents consider education to be and what their notion of schooling is, what an ideal school is, and what the school their children attend represents. Only by unpacking these notions can the assumptions about what they want in education be known.

Fourth, community-based organizations can also play a significant role, but only if their trajectory involves helping these parents by integrating them into the actual training of other parents, and into institutionalizing their roles within the same organizations. Two of the graduates of the first community organization project in this study now lead their own schools, but were able to do so only after they were able to experience for themselves what it means to become a leader.

Bicultural parents become differentially involved in schools based on their levels of education, access, and use of first and second languages; social and cultural capital knowledge; generational and country of origin; and host family patterns and political consciousness. There is a prevailing monocultural model of parental involvement that is not necessarily effective for the variety of needs expressed by these parents. Instead, a contextually bound set of options is necessary that highlights how parents actually organize themselves around educational issues; how they are able to have access to knowledge and power, particularly when English is not their mother tongue and they may be illiterate; where there may be trade-offs between economic survival and education; and where knowing the concrete issues of schooling and educating their children may not be sufficient. Such options will enable bicultural parents to acquire the social and cultural capital to be part of the PTO, use research to expand their knowledge, and find ways to express their political opinions in order to successfully navigate the educational system of the United States.

Discussion Questions

1. How can parent empowerment become a reality in today's schools, given what you understand to be the embedded structures that exist from reading this chapter?
2. What would you do to bring the voices of parents into schools and how would you proceed in guaranteeing their presence in a more direct and assertive fashion?

3. What have you learned about action research of parents that you might want to develop in your own situation and could you spell out how you would go about developing such a research agenda?
4. What can you take away from this reading that makes you comprehend the role of bicultural parents in schools today?

Notes

1. During the early 1990s, Harvard Medical School experimented with a model of community interventions where future doctors were trained in the communities they served by the families of the patients they were learning to diagnose and create case studies. This model of community outreach in learning was quite successful in transmitting what the hospital teaching could not convey and in contextualizing the teaching of medicine.

2. The concept of *educación* has been discussed by several scholars as being the lifelong learning that takes place in Latino communities. That is, to be educated means that you acquire not only formal knowledge of the school but also the social norms and behaviors of the society you live in and such learning is acquired from the combination of family, schooling, and community contexts. In that regard, this is a comprehensive concept of learning.

3. The concept of minoritization refers to maintaining groups whose status is viewed as a minority in relation to majority groups in an inferior and devaluated status.

Suggested Readings

Delgado-Gaitán, C. (2001). *The power of community: Mobilizing for family and schooling.* Lanham, MD: Rowan & Littlefield.

Eccles, J. S., & Harold, R. D. (1996). Family involvement in children's and adolescent's schooling. In A. Booth and J. F. Dunn (Eds.), *Family-school links: How do they affect educational outcomes?* (pp. 3–33). Mahwah, NJ: Lawrence Erlbaum.

Hoover-Dempsey, K. V., & Sandler, H. M. (1995). Parental involvement in children's education: Why does it make a difference? *Teachers College Record, 97*, 310–331.

Lareau, A., & Horvat, E. M. (1999). Moments of social inclusion and exclusion: Race, class and cultural capital in family-school relationships. *Sociology of Education, 72*(1), 37–53.

Zarate, M. E. (2007). *Understanding latino parental involvement in education: Perceptions, expectations, and recommendations.* Los Angeles: Tomas Rivera Policy Institute.

References

Ascher, C. (2002). *Improving the school-home connection for low income urban parents.* New York: ERIC Clearinghouse on Urban Education. (ED293973

Baker, A. J., & Soden, L. M. (1988, September). *The challenges of parent involvement research.* New York: ERIC Clearinghouse on Urban Education. (ED419030)

Carrasquillo, A. L., & London, C. B. G. (1993). *Parent and schools. A source book.* New York: Garland.

Chrispeels, J., & Gonzalez, M. (2004). Do educational programs increase parents' practices at home? Factors influencing Latino parent involvement. *Harvard Family Research Project.* Retrieved from http://www.hfrp.org/family-involvement/publications-resources/do-educational-programs-increase-parents-practices-at-home-factors-influencing-latino-parent-involvement

Comer, J. U. P. (2004). *Leave no child behind: Preparing today's youth for tomorrow's world.* New Haven, CT: Yale University Press.

Curiel, H. (1991). Strengthening family and school bonds in promoting Hispanic children's school performance. In Marta Sotomayor (Ed.), *Empowering Hispanic families: A critical issue for the 90's* (pp. 75–95). Milwaukee, WI: Family Service America.

Darder, A., & Upshur, C. (1992). *What do Latino children need to succeed in school? A study of four Boston public schools.* Boston: Mauricio Gaston Institute for Latino Community Development and Public Policy.

Delgado-Gaitan, C. (2004). *Involving Latino families in the schools.* Thousand Oaks, CA: Corwin Press.

Delgado-Gaitan, C., & Trueba, H. E. (1991). *Crossing cultural borders: Education for immigrant families in America.* London: Falmer.

Eccles, J. S., & Harold, R. D. (1996). Family involvement in children's and adolescent's schooling. In A. Booth & J. F. Dunn (Eds.), *Family-school links: How do they affect educational outcomes?* (pp. 3–33). Mahwah, NJ: Lawrence Erlbaum.

Epstein, J. L. (1988). How do we improve programs for parental involvement? *Principal, 66,* 6–9.

Epstein, J. L. (2002). *School, family, and community partnerships: Your handbook for action* (2nd ed.). Thousand Oaks, CA: Corwin.

Epstein, J. L. (2004). Meeting NCLB requirements for family involvement. *Middle Ground, 8*(1), 14–17.

Fan, X., & Chen, M. (2001). Parental involvement and students' academic achievement: A meta-analysis. *Educational Psychology Review, 13,* 1–22.

Feliciano, C. (2006). *Another way to assess the second generation: Look at the parents.* Washington, DC: Migration Information Source. Retrieved from http://www.migrationinformation.org/ Feature/print.cfm?ID=36

Gibson, M. A. (2002). *The new Latino diaspora and educational policy: Education in the new Latino diaspora: Policy and the politics of identity.* Westport, CT: Ablex Publishing.

Gutman, L. M., & Eccles, J. S. (1999). Financial strain, parenting behaviors, and adolescents' achievement: Testing model equivalence between African American and European American single- and two-parent families. *Child Development, 70,* 1464–1476.

Henderson, A., & Mapp, K. (2002). *A new wave of evidence: The impact of school, family, and community connection on student achievement.* Austin, TX: Southwest Educational Development Laboratory.

Hoover-Dempsey, K. V., & Sandler, H. M. (1995). Parental involvement in children's education: Why does it make a difference? *Teachers College Record, 97,* 310–331.

Hoover-Dempsey, K. V., & Sandler, H. M. (1997). Why do parents become involved in their children's education? *Review of Education Research, 67,* 3–42.

Holman, L. J. (1997, April). Working effectively with Hispanic immigrant families. *Phi Delta Kappan, 78*(8), 647–649.

Horvat, E. M., Weininger, E. B., & Lareau, A. (2003). From social ties to social capital: Class differences in the relations between schools and parent networks. *American Educational Research Journal, 40*(2), 319–351.

Jeynes, W. H. (2002). A meta-analysis: The effects of parental involvement on minority children's academic achievement. *Education and Urban Society, 35*(2), 202–218.

Landale, N. S., & Oropesa, R. S. (2007). Hispanic families: Stability and change. *Annual Review of Sociology 33,* 381–405.

Mattingly, D. J., Radmila, P., McKenzie, T. L., Rodriguez, J. L., & Kayzar, B. (2002). Evaluating evaluations: The case of parent involvement programs. *Review of Education Research, 72*(4), 549–576.

McCaleb, S. P. (1997). *Building communities of learners: A collaboration among teachers, students, families, and community.* New York: St. Martin's Press.

Olivos, E. M., & Ochoa, A. M. (2008). Reframing due process and institutional inertia: A case study of an urban school district. *Equity and Excellence in Education, 41*(3), 1–14.

Osterling, J. P., & Garza, A. (2004). Strengthening Latino parental involvement: Forming community based organizations/school partnerships. *Journal of Research and Practice, 2*(1), 270–284.

Pomerantz, E. M., Grolnick, W. S., & Price, C. E. (2005). The role of parents in how children approach school: A dynamic process perspective. In A. J. Elliot & C. S. Dweck (Eds.), *The handbook of competence and motivation* (pp. 259–278). New York: Guildford.

Pomerantz, E. M., Moorman, E., & Litwack Scott, D. (2007). The how, whom, and why of parents' involvement in children's academic lives: More is not always better. *Review of Educational Research, 77*(3), 373–410.

Portes, A., & Xao, L. (2004). The schooling of children of immigrants: Contextual effects on the educational attainment of the second generation. *National Academy of Sciences, PNAS, 10*(33). Retrieved from www.pnas.org/cgi/doe/10.1073/pnas0403418101

Redding, S. (2007, Fall/Winter). Rallying the troops. *School Community Journal, 15*(1), 7–13.

Redding, S., Langdon, J., Meyer, H. J., & Shelley, P. (2004, April). *The effects of comprehensive parent engagement on student learning outcomes.* Paper presented at the annual meeting of the American Educational Research Association, San Diego, CA.

Rogers, J. (2006). Forces of accountability? The power of poor parents in NCLB. In S. Chrismer, S. T. Hodge, & D. Saintil (Eds.), *Assessing NCLB: Perspectives and prescriptions. Harvard Educational Reviews, 76*(4), 611–641.

Salinas-Sosa. A. (1997). Involving Hispanic parents in educational activities through collaborative relationships. *Bilingual Research Journal, 21*(2), 103–111.

Scribner, J. D., Young, M. D., & Pedraza, A. (1999). Building collaborative relationships with parents. In P. Reyes, J. D. Scribner, & A. P. Scribner (Eds.), *Lessons from high performing Hispanic schools: Creating learning communities* (pp. 36–60). New York: Teachers College Press.

Shepard, R., & Rose, H. (1995). The power of parents: An empowerment model for increasing parental involvement. *Education, 115*(3), 373–377.

Swidler, A. (2001). *Talk of love: How culture matters.* Chicago: University of Chicago Press.

Tinkler, B. (2002). *A review of literature on Hispanic/Latino parent involvement in K–12 education.* Denver, CO: University of Denver, Assets for Colorado Youth.

Valdes, G. (1996). *Con respeto: Bridging the distances between culturally diverse families and schools.* New York: Teachers College Press.

Villanueva, I. (2005, April). *Incorporating students and families in the curriculum: Challenges, constraints, and transformation.* Paper presented at the American Educational Research Association Meeting in Montreal, Quebec, Canada.

Villanueva, I. (2006, April). *The voices of Chicano families: Cultural awareness versus acculturation and assimilation.* Paper presented at the American Educational Research Association Meeting, San Francisco, CA.

Violand-Sanchez, E., Sutton, C. P., & Ware, H. W. (1991). *Fostering home-school cooperation: Involving language minority families as partners in education.* Washington, DC: National Clearing House for Bilingual Education.

Waterman, R. A. (2008). Strength behind the sociolinguistic wall: The dreams, commitments, and capacities of Mexican mothers. *Journal of Latinos and Education, 7*(2), 144–162.

Weiss, H. B., Kredier, H., Lopez, M. E., & Chatman, C. M. (2005). *Preparing educators to involve families.* Thousand Oaks, CA: Sage.

Wheelock, A. E. (1990). *The status of Latino students in Massachusetts public schools: Direction for policy research in the 1990s.* Boston: Mauricio Gaston Institute for Latino Community Development and Public Policy.

Zarate, M. E. (2007). *Understanding Latino parental involvement in education: Perceptions, expectations, and recommendations.* Los Angeles: Tomas Rivera Policy Institute.

10

Becoming Civic: The Active Engagement of Latino Immigrant Parents in Public Schools

Veronica Terriquez and John Rogers

Alex Ramirez, the leader of Los Padres, an organizing network in California, encourages immigrant parents to participate in educational reform to improve their children's schools, develop skills for civic participation, and gain political power. Parents often join Los Padres because they are frustrated with the poor quality of local public schools. Los Padres helps parents analyze official school reports, survey neighbors about school conditions, and inform district officials about their concerns. Many of these immigrant parents previously have had limited involvement in U.S. civic institutions. Yet they attend school board meetings, participate on committees overseeing the education of English learners, and serve on school site councils with the power to shape policies and budgets. Ramirez explains that his organization seeks to "give access to those parents to the decision making process in education." While Los Padres includes naturalized citizens, legal residents, and undocumented immigrants, all members participate in the electoral process. Parents meet with and vet potential candidates for the school board. They participate in phone banks and canvass door to door in their local precincts. Ramirez notes, "You don't have to be a citizen to be active and make change in your community."

The work of Los Padres highlights the important role of public schools in the civic engagement and civic development of immigrant parents. While not all immigrant parents are as politically engaged as members of Los Padres, many participate in a variety of school-based civic activities. Immigrant parents attend school events, dialogue with other members of the community, volunteer in classrooms, plan school activities, and serve on decision-making bodies. These patterns of civic participation are not universal; some public schools provide a more welcoming and supportive environment for immigrant civic engagement than other schools. Yet when schools create opportunities for meaningful civic participation, they support both democracy and school improvement. Such opportunities can potentially enable immigrant parents to support their own children's education, provide valuable services to the school as a whole, contribute the knowledge and insight necessary for culturally responsive pedagogy and policy, and develop skills for effective political participation.

The civic engagement and civic development of immigrant parents is an important, yet often forgotten, goal of public schools. Much of the current rationale for parent participation focuses narrowly on school reform. Certainly, parent engagement can contribute to educational improvement (for example, by fostering greater commitment to school goals). But just as certainly, parent participation in school-based civic activities can play a role in revitalizing democratic life. Further, the civic engagement of immigrant parents in their children's public schools can promote immigrant integration. That is, such participation can incorporate the interests and concerns of immigrants into policy decisions in a way that enhances public life, expands economic opportunity, and benefits both immigrants and the receiving society (Pastor, 2008).

With few exceptions, there has been little empirical work on immigrant civic engagement in such parents' children's schools. Our chapter focuses on Latino immigrant parents. Latino immigrants comprise a significant or increasing proportion of parents of public school children in many parts of the United States, and understanding their experience can provide insights into patterns of school-based civic participation in communities with established or growing Latino populations. We explore the following: How does the school-based civic participation of Latino immigrant parents compare to that of nonimmigrant parents? Is there a difference in the rates of participation between recent immigrants and those who have lived in the United States longer? What is the significance of Latino immigrants participating in school decision making and efforts to improve children's schools? How do community-based groups like Los Padres enable more robust forms of civic engagement? This chapter draws upon a set of empirical studies in California to offer some initial responses to these questions.

Our findings suggest that, notwithstanding some of the challenges to meaningful and democratic participation of nonmainstream parents addressed in other chapters of this book, many Latino immigrants participate civically in their children's schools. We find that this engagement increases over time for immigrants.

We note that Latino immigrants participate in school decision making and in efforts to improve local schools. Further, we find that school-based civic engagement can be particularly robust when immigrants are members of and supported by grassroots community organizations.

The chapter proceeds in five sections. Section 1 addresses the civic goals of public schooling and talks about why these civic goals matter for immigrant parents. Section 2 draws on survey data to explore the parental participation of recent immigrants, more established immigrants, and U.S.-born citizens in school organizations and activities. Section 3 draws on a survey of Latino immigrants who belong to a labor union to focus attention on the participation of immigrants in school decision making and efforts to improve local schools. Section 4 illuminates how support from grassroots community organizations can bridge immigrant parents' interest in their children's schools to robust forms of civic engagement that potentially enhance the power of immigrant communities inside and outside schools. Finally, section 5 considers the implications of these findings for federal and state policies.

The Civic Goals of Public Schooling

Civic engagement refers to a broad set of public activities through which community members seek to shape their collective lives. Steven Macedo (2005) identifies five forms of civic engagement: (1) learning about the political system and the issues of the day; (2) addressing collective problems through voluntary service, joint action, and decision making; (3) mobilizing political pressure through such means as lobbying elected officials, writing persuasive letters, attending public meetings, or protesting; (4) participating in electoral campaigns; and (5) voting. Public schools are potential sites for parents to participate in many of these civic activities. Further, public schools can prompt these forms of civic activity by raising issues such as resource distribution and identity formation that touch parents' most deeply felt concerns about the future of their children and their community.

The civic engagement of parents in and through public schools addresses the long-standing, but never fully realized, vision of public schooling for democracy. This vision was at the center of the 19th-century common school movement, which held that a self-governing state required the development of an informed and engaged citizenry. As Horace Mann (1848) noted, "It may be an easy thing to make a Republic, but it is a laborious thing to make Republicans" (para. 17). While Mann focused most attention on the civic education of the young, his republican ideology shaped the participation of adult citizens, who often were called upon to mobilize community resources and oversee the daily operations of the emerging public school system. In the mid- to late 19th century, this school system was characterized by radical decentralization of educational governance. As David Tyack (2003) points out, so many parents served as school board members within the framework of local control that they represented the "largest body of public officials in the world" (p. 130).

Significantly, the democratic purpose of common schooling was circumscribed by prevailing ideologies of nativism and White supremacy. Notwithstanding the common school movement's rhetorical commitment to inclusiveness and opportunity, almost all 19th-century school board members were U.S.-born White males. When greater numbers of immigrants began serving on school boards at the turn of the 20th century, a countermovement emerged to centralize and professionalize educational governance. Paradoxically, the administrative progressives effectively reasserted the power of U.S.-born White elites while articulating a commitment to democratic education (Spring, 1994). Hence, American educational history has produced both a robust ideal of public schooling for democracy and many examples of exclusionary practice.

In recent decades, policymakers have called for the civic engagement of parents in public schools in ways that extend and reshape the rhetoric of the common schools movement. For example, in its 1998 Omnibus School Reform Act, the California's legislature reasoned, "It is essential to our democratic form of government that parents and guardians of school age children attending public schools and other citizens participate in improving public education institutions" (California Education Code Sec. 51100).[1] Yet while lawmakers support an array of civic engagement strategies for parents, their primary goal shifted from advancing democracy to advancing school improvement. The 2001 No Child Left Behind Act (NCLB) envisioned parents leading trainings for other parents, participating in the development of school improvement plans, and sitting on decision-making bodies (NCLB 1118 and Non-Regulatory Guidance). Notably, little of this vision was enacted in most public schools because of weak legislative language (*should* rather than *must*) and a lack of policy oversight (Rogers, 2006). Yet today policymakers continue to evoke a rhetorical commitment to parental civic engagement because they recognize that in the public's mind, parent participation is linked inextricably to the central goals of public schooling.

While the common school movement and current NCLB policies address the importance of parental participation generally, two arguments can be made about why parental civic engagement matters, particularly for immigrant parents. First, as newcomers to American political life, immigrants need opportunities to develop an understanding of how the political system works and how they can act efficaciously within it. More than any other public institution, schools provide immigrant parents with a site to meet and work with other community members around issues of personal and communal concern. Second, immigrants need to develop strategies for advancing their interests within extremely unequal political structures. The growing political inequality in the United States, wherein the "privileged participate more than others and are increasingly well organized to press their demands on government . . . [while others] speak with a whisper that is lost on the ears of inattentive government officials," means that it is important to attend to opportunities that politically marginalized groups have to exercise their voice (American Political Science Association's Task Force on Inequality and American Democracy, 2004, p. 1). The local character of educational governance means that there is likely more space at school sites for meaningful civic participation than in sites with more centralized control. Further, schools represent a particularly compelling site for immigrant civic activity, given the high percentage of immigrant parents with children in public schools.

Parent Involvement in School Activities

As alluded to in past research and other chapters in this volume, immigrant parents, including Latino immigrant parents, encounter barriers to actively engaging in their children's schools. Some parents may be unfamiliar with the U.S. school system or may lack the confidence to participate in school activities (Valdes, 1996). Full-time employment in one or more jobs also lowers Latino immigrants' participation in their children's schools (Terriquez, 2007). In some cases, school personnel make parents feel unwelcome, communicate negative views of immigrant families, or discourage the active participation of parents, especially if they seek to challenge school policies or practices (Arias & Morillo-Campbell, 2008; Auerbach, 2002; Olivos, 2006; Quiocho & Daoud, 2006; Ramirez, 2003).

In spite of barriers and challenges, Latino immigrants manage to become civically engaged in school-related activities. Extensive research on immigrant incorporation generally reveals that, over time, immigrants learn to participate in local institutions and play an active role in redefining their local communities (Alba & Nee, 2003). In fact, some research has shown that after living in the United States a decade or more, immigrants begin to resemble their native-born counterparts on some social or economic indicators (Antecol & Bedard, 2006; Borjas, 1985; Leclere, Jensen, & Biddlecom, 1994; Ramakrishnan & Espenshade, 2001).

In this section, we explore participation in various school-related activities among parents in Los Angeles County, California, to demonstrate how schools provide immigrants with an avenue for civic participation, especially those who have lived in the United States for a while. Latino immigrants who mostly come from Mexico and Central America constitute almost one-quarter of the county's population of nearly 10 million residents (U.S. Census Bureau, 2006), and approximately one-half of parents of public school students (see *Los Angeles Family and Neighborhood Survey, 2001* [author tabulations], in Peterson, Sastry, Pebly,

Ghosh-Dastidar, Williamson, & Lara-Cinisomo, 2004). While both the size and concentration of Latino immigrants are exceptionally high, the Los Angeles case can provide some insights into Latino immigrant civic engagement in other urban centers with growing Latino immigrant populations.

Our analysis relies on data from the 2001 Los Angeles Family and Neighborhood Survey (L.A. FANS), which provides information for a representative sample of English- and Spanish-speaking Los Angeles County parents (Sastry, Ghosh-Dastidar, Adams, & Pebley, 2003).[2] The survey includes questions for mothers or other primary caregivers about their engagement in the school of a randomly selected child and sibling (when present).[3] Since information regarding school participation was collected primarily from mothers and other female caregivers, 98% of our sample consists of women.[4] While the L.A. FANS data allow us to make claims about general patterns of Latino immigrant civic engagement in schools, they neither account for the breadth or depth of parental participation nor provide insights into the tensions between bicultural parents and schools that are discussed in other chapters in this volume.

In our analysis of immigrant parents' school-based civic engagement, we draw on a sample of 1,025 Latino immigrants, and a comparison group of 598 U.S.-born citizens. Of the U.S. born, 48% are White, 16% are African American, 3% are Asian American, and 33% are Latino. We chose to compare Latino immigrants to all U.S.-born parents, as opposed to just U.S.-born Latinos, in order to assess immigrants' civic engagement relative to a broadly defined population of native-born residents. We focus on three forms of parental civic engagement in children's public schools: (1) participation in a parent-teacher association (PTA) meeting or other parent meeting, (2) attendance at a school event in which the child participated, (3) and volunteering in the classroom or library. These forms of school involvement provide parents with potential opportunities to meet other parents, learn more about school programming and school politics, and contribute to the school community. These activities also may afford parents opportunities to voice their opinions.

Because of the nature of the data we analyze, our findings speak to how immigrant parents participate rather than assessing whether schools encourage such participation. Just as immigrant economic progress does not mean we have seen the end of workplace discrimination, immigrant parents' school-based civic engagement should not be understood as evidence that all or even most public schools provide immigrant parents with a welcoming and supportive environment. Rather, our analysis focuses on the civic agency of immigrant parents.

Table 10.1 provides descriptive statistics for parent engagement in school-based civic activities. Results show that 27% of recent immigrant Latino parents participate in PTA and other parent meetings.

Table 10.1 Descriptive Statistics for Parent Civic Engagement in Schools (Los Angeles County, L.A. FANS 2001)

	Immigrants in U.S. ≤ 10 yrs	Immigrants in U.S. > 10 yrs	U.S.-Born
PTA or other Parent Meeting	27%	47%	37%
Attend School Event	36%	64%	70%
Volunteer	16%	29%	33%
Sample Size *(unweighted)*	183	842	598

Descriptive statistics are weighted.

The participation of recent immigrant parents in such meetings, although comparatively low, is still notable, considering that recent arrivals must deal with the challenges of settling in their new country and becoming familiar with local institutions (Alba & Nee, 2003; Portes & Rumbaut, 2006). Our results suggest that school meetings can potentially serve as a space for recent arrivals to become incorporated into the school community and other social networks.

Perhaps surprisingly, descriptive statistics indicate immigrants who have lived in the United States over a decade are more likely than U.S.-born parents to have attended a PTA or other parent meeting. Forty-seven percent of immigrants who have lived in the United States over 10 years reported attending a parent meeting compared with 37% of U.S.-born parents. Latino immigrant parents and U.S.-born parents may attend different types of parent meetings.[5] For example, the PTA, a national organization, has historically attracted middle-class White parents.[6] In some school communities, immigrant parents may therefore be drawn to parent meetings targeting immigrants or parents of English learners, rather than to PTA meetings. Additionally, since Latino immigrants tend to send their children to poorly resourced schools (Oakes, Valladares, Renée, Fanelli, Medina, & Rogers, 2007), some are also likely to attend meetings that aim to address problems or issues that arise in schools. Regardless of the type of meeting attended by parents, it is important to recognize the high level of participation among immigrants who have lived in the United States over a decade. Meetings provide immigrants with the opportunity to meet other parents and to gain exposure to what is going on at the school site. Depending on the nature of the meeting and the openness of school staff, parents may be able to work with other stakeholders to address school problems or issues, contribute to planning of school programs, voice concerns, and learn about school operations. At the same time, it is important to recognize that in some settings, school personnel expect immigrant parents to passively participate in meetings, and may discourage their leadership and activism.

Parents can also participate civically in schools by attending school events or by volunteering at the school site. Although results indicate that recent immigrants engage in these activities at relatively low levels (with 36% attending a school event and only 16% volunteering) their involvement increases dramatically after they have lived in the United States for over a decade. For these immigrants, the percentage participating in a school event increases to 64%, while the percentage volunteering increases to 29%. Immigrants who have lived in the United States for over a decade are still, however, slightly less likely than U.S.-born parents to attend a school event or volunteer. Specifically, 70% of nonimmigrant parents reported attending a school event, and 33% reported volunteering.

These descriptive statistics reporting overall patterns of Latino immigrant civic engagement in children's schools do not tell the whole story. Parents' immigrant background and length of residency in the United Sates are not the only explanations for the above patterns. In particular, the socioeconomic background of immigrants affects their integration in their new country (Alba & Nee, 2004; Portes & Rumbaut, 2006) and shapes the information, skills, social confidence, and other resources that they draw upon in order to interact with school personnel and participate in school-related activities (Lareau, 2000, 2003). Parents' socioeconomic status can also shape the ways in which school personnel respond to parents and the extent to which they welcome their participation (Reay, 1998).

L.A. FANS data demonstrate dramatic differences in socioeconomic background between Latino immigrants and nonimmigrants in Los Angeles County. Both recent immigrants and those who have lived in the United States over a decade are notably less educated and have lower incomes than the native-born parent population. While 67–70% of immigrants lack a high school degree or equivalent, only 15% of U.S.-born parents do not have a high school degree. At the same time, 4–7% of immigrants hold a college degree or more, while over one-fifth of the U.S.-born population hold a college degree or more. Inequalities in income are also striking. The mean family income for recent Latino immigrants is $24,000 and $33,000 for those who have lived in the United States for over a decade. Meanwhile, the mean family income for the U.S. born is notably higher, at $69,000.[7]

We examined differences in the civic engagement of immigrants and the U.S. born, after adjusting for education and income inequalities. We conducted logistic regression analysis to estimate parents' likelihood of attending a PTA or other parent meeting, volunteering at the school, or attending a school event. Table 10.2 shows the probability of participating in school-based civic activities for parents with a high school diploma and a family income of $30,000, comparing recent Latino immigrant parents, Latino immigrant parents who have lived in the United States more than 10 years, and U.S.-born parents of all racial/ethnic backgrounds.[8]

Accounting for the lower socioeconomic status of Latino immigrant parents relative to the U.S.-born parents further underscores the importance of schools in providing opportunities for civic engagement for Latino immigrants. Our findings show that recent immigrants are slightly less likely to participate in PTA or other parent meetings than U.S.-born parents. The difference—a probability of .17 compared with a probability of .21, respectively—is not statistically significant. This means that that there is not enough evidence to demonstrate that recent immigrants are less likely to attend parent meetings than the U.S. born, after accounting for inequalities in education and family income. At the same time, the probability of participating in a parent meeting for long-term Latino immigrants is .46, notably higher than the probability for U.S.-born parents. Although the role of parent respondents in meetings is unknown, the relatively high participation of immigrant parents demonstrates the potential of school-based parent meetings to serve as a space for immigrants to make meaningful contributions to their school communities and become active in political processes relating to children's education.

Regression results for volunteering and attending a school event also show some important trends. While the probabilities for attending a school event and volunteering are comparatively low for recent immigrants, little difference exists

Table 10.2 Descriptive Statistics for Parent Socioeconomic Status (Los Angeles County, L.A. FANS 2001)

Educational Attainment	Immigrants in U.S. ≤10 Years	Immigrants in U.S. >10 Years	U.S. Born
Less than High School	67%	70%	15%
High School or Equivalent	19%	16%	26%
Some College	7%	10%	36%
College Degree or More	7%	4%	22%
Mean Family Income	$24,134	$32,731	$69,307
(standard deviation)	$1,710	$1,394	$3,064
Sample Size (unweighted)	183	842	598

Descriptive statistics are weighted. Percentages may not sum to 100% because of rounding error.

in the likelihood of attending a school event and volunteering between long-term immigrants and U.S.-born parents with similar education and income backgrounds. The probability of attending a school event is around .75 for both long-term immigrants and the U.S. born, while the probability for volunteering at the school site equals .26 and .18, respectively.[9]

Research generally shows that Latino immigrants are less likely than the U.S. born to participate in civic activities (Segura, Pachon, & Woods, 2005). This is not the case with civic participation that occurs within schools. The participation of immigrants in parent meetings, school events, and volunteer activities highlights the important space schools occupy for the civic development of immigrants. As our analysis shows, recent immigrants may be less civically involved in school-related activities, but their lower rates of participation are only temporary. Despite challenges that they may encounter in participating in the children's school process, immigrants who have lived in the United States over a decade manage to engage in school-related civic activities at the same rate or even higher than U.S.-born parents.

Engagement in Decision-Making Bodies and School Improvement

As discussed in other chapters in this volume, parent engagement extends beyond traditional forms of school involvement. In this section, we examine Latino immigrant parent participation in school decision-making bodies and in efforts to improve local schools. Public schools provide several avenues for parents to participate in school decision-making bodies, such as school site councils, Title I committees, and bilingual advisory committees that approve plans for school programming and spending. Some schools also offer other formal and informal committees in which parents themselves run programs or provide advice to school personnel. Additionally, parents may influence school programs through participation in grassroots, nonprofit, or church-based organizations that provide parents opportunities to voice their concerns and, at times, take collective action to improve local schools.

To document Latino immigrant parent participation in school decision-making bodies and efforts to improve local schools, we use data gathered in 2007 from a randomly selected sample of the Los Angeles County membership of the Service Employees International Union (SEIU) Local 1877. Local 1877 represents janitors and other low-wage service workers and is known for engaging members in activist causes (Milkman, 2006). The survey sample of 344 Latino immigrants—135 fathers and 209 mothers—consists of 49% Mexicans, 29% Salvadorans, 16% Guatemalans, and 6% others. Eighty percent have less than a high school degree.

We recognize that because of a history of union activism, parents who belong to Local 1877 are likely to have had significant opportunities to participate in workplace organizing efforts and political campaigns when compared with other Latino immigrants in Los Angeles. Because of their workplace civic experience, parent union members may feel more comfortable participating in school decision-making bodies and efforts to address problems in local schools. At the same time, most union members work full time, limiting their availability to participate in school-related activities. Despite differences between our sample of immigrant parents and the general population of Latino immigrant parents, we find that reporting on their engagement in school-related civic activities is valuable and demonstrates the importance of schools in providing a space for immigrant parents to collectively problem-solve at the local level and address the specific needs of their own communities. Moreover, our findings highlight the potential of schools to serve as a place for parents to develop and exercise community leadership.

Our data show that schools provide opportunities for a notable proportion of Latino immigrant parents to contribute to decision-making processes, at least within our sample. Approximately 28% of survey respondents indicated that they had attended a Title I, school site council, or other advisory committee meeting where parents help make decisions about their school. Our exploratory interviews with survey respondents indicate that some parents were, in fact, members of the school site council and regularly contributed to school decisions. One mother reported attending workshops on school funding and then later informally training other school site council parent members on how to make decisions about the school budget. Other parents stated that they participated in more informal, ad hoc meetings, where the principal or other school personnel met with a group of parents to make decisions about school events or obtain feedback regarding school programs. These examples offer testimony of the importance of school-based committees in creating opportunities for immigrant parents to voice their concerns and work with others to contribute to the school community.

Our data also indicate that a notable percentage of parents, 31%, attended a meeting outside school where people had talked about the need to improve the local public schools. Our survey data do not provide specific information about topics discussed and issues addressed at meetings, yet they do suggest that Latino immigrant parents participate in social networks concerned with taking an active role in improving educational opportunities for their children. Engagement in such networks is particularly important, considering that 68% of respondents' children, like the children of a significant proportion of Latino immigrants, attend schools that have been designated as Program Improvement schools. Program Improvement schools are those that have not met adequately yearly progress on test scores and other measures as specified by the 2001 No Child Left Behind Act. While the burden for improving local schools should not be on parents, it is important to note that immigrant parents are engaged in meetings where the issues of improving local schools are raised.

Although our data are not gathered from a representative sample of Latino immigrant parents, our findings suggest that a notable proportion of such parents may be involved in meetings where parents contribute to school decisions or discuss school improvement. These findings evidence the role that schools can play in immigrant integration. In participating in school decision making or efforts to improve schools, parents learn about political processes that they potentially can use in other arenas of their lives. Moreover, they engage in collective problem-solving and work toward making public institutions more accountable.

Community Organizations and Robust School-Based Civic Engagement

Jannelle Wong (2006) argues that, given the declining role of political parties, community-based organizations have become the major force for promoting civic engagement and incorporating new immigrants into American civic life. In this section, we discuss how Latino immigrant parents, through their affiliation with community organizations, focus on improving local schools, learn about the political system and current issues, address collective problems, mobilize political pressure, and participate in electoral campaigns.

To outline the politically powerful civic engagement of Latino immigrants in school-related issues, we use data gathered from representatives of 11 community organizations in California that work directly with Latino immigrants and other parents, and are affiliated with educational reform networks. As shown in Table 10.3, our sample includes four professional advocacy or service organizations, five parent-led organizations focused on educational reform, and three broad-based organizations that organize communities to address an array of social issues. The scope and size of these organizations varies widely. The smallest of these groups include fewer than 100 core participants in a particular community, while the largest has several hundred thousand across California. Four of the organizations focus their work in a particular neighborhood, three work across a school district or county, and five groups are statewide.

Table 10.3 Community Organizations Working with Latino Immigrant Parents

	Organization type	Scope of work	Core participants
1	Advocacy or Service	District- or County-wide	100–500
2	Multi-Issue Organizing	Statewide	10,000–100,000
3	Advocacy or Service	Statewide	1,000–5,000
4	Parent Ed/Organizing	Neighborhood	100–500
5	Parent Ed/Organizing	District- or County-wide	100–500
6	Multi-Issue Organizing	Neighborhood	50–100
7	Parent Ed/Organizing	Neighborhood	0–50
8	Advocacy or Service	Statewide	100–500
9	Parent Ed/Organizing	Statewide	1,000–5,000
10	Multi-Issue Organizing	Statewide	100,000–500,000
11	Parent Ed/Organizing	Neighborhood	50–100

All the community organizations engage Latino immigrant parents in learning about the politics of public schooling and how to address educational issues that affect their own communities. The grassroots organizations develop the civic capacities of Latino immigrant parents through an array of parent education structures. Four of the organizations hold parent institutes that provide weekly workshops for up to 15 weeks. The workshops generally combine instruction in how the educational system works, with leadership training aimed at enabling parents to work in groups, win allies, and communicate with the media. Workshops sometimes bring together groups of parents who otherwise do not interact with one another. For example, in many of the organizations immigrant Latino parents learn side by side with African Americans who often are long-term residents of the neighborhood.

Two of the statewide organizations hold daylong trainings that bring parents together from across different regions to study particular policy issues. The importance of gathering and using data is emphasized in several organizations. Three organizations encourage groups of parents to research an educational issue that they want to address, and then develop a "change plan" to improve their school or district. All the neighborhood-based organizations train parents in how to obtain access to and make sense of official state data about the quality of local schools.

Grassroots organizations create links between larger constituencies of parents and formal decision-making bodies. Leaders of organizations provide information or training for parents on how to effectively participate in school governance meetings and school board meetings at the district. In all but one organization, immigrant parent members serve on school and district governance or advisory councils, and meet with district or state officials. Individual immigrant parent members therefore have the opportunity to represent the interests of a larger group of parents who belong to the community-based organization.

Grassroots organizations also engage Latino immigrant parents in conducting community outreach and exerting political pressure around educational issues. One multi-issue organizing group instructs its members on how to meet neighbors door to door to discuss the community's educational problems. Two of the organizations regularly convene public forums so that parents can voice their issues and increase community support for campaigns. One group frames the forums as "People's Hearings"—in which parent members "testify" about experiences they or their children have had in local schools.

Organizations engage Latino immigrant parents in other strategies to communicate their knowledge and interests to key stakeholders. Through public demonstrations, Latino immigrant parents work with others to share testimonies, solicit signatures, distribute leaflets, and engage in other such activities. Parents also collectively meet with local elected officials to discuss issues and request resolutions to problems. Three organizations sponsor "lobby days," during which members travel to the state capital to pressure elected representatives to demand specific changes in the school system.

Considering that many Latino immigrant parents lack U.S. citizenship, the most striking form of civic participation for Latino immigrant parents is their engagement in the electoral process. In three organizations, undocumented parents have played significant roles in efforts to increase the turnout of voters. Parents from one neighborhood organization have registered 1,000 new voters over the past few elections. The organization's director argues, "Many of those who are encouraging citizens to register are immigrants who can't vote themselves. This makes them more committed to the value of voting." Parents from her organization also go door to door during election campaigns to inform voters about candidates in the school board races. This effort has led to an increased voter turnout in their target precincts in each of the past five election cycles. Another organization engages immigrant parents in calling registered voters on the day of school board elections. One parent explained that she had come to make calls because "I can't vote, but I have four future voters at home."

Grassroots support of Latino immigrants' civic engagement in education-related issues can lead to their involvement in a broader set of civic issues over time. In other words, civic engagement in education-related arenas becomes an avenue for broader community participation. The director of a multi-issue organizing group notes, "People come in because they feel a need and urgency around an [educational] issue and then they don't stop there. . . . They come in through that door and they get involved in any number of ways in local government and planning." Some organizations explicitly encourage parents to work across different issues by linking parents to civic organizations focused on public safety or housing.

Federal and State Policy Implications

Throughout this chapter we have argued that public schools provide Latino immigrant parents with important opportunities for civic engagement. As we have shown, Latino immigrants, especially those who have lived in the United States for more than a decade, actively engage in parent meetings, school events, and volunteer activities. Latino immigrants participate in school decision making and in efforts to improve their children's schools. And when supported by grassroots organizations, they mobilize other community members around education issues and hold elected officials accountable. The civic engagement of Latino immigrant parents in and around public schools can be explained, at least in part, by the importance that these parents place on education as a means for a better life for their children.

Latino immigrant parents often participate in their children's public schools despite barriers and challenges to parental involvement that have been noted by other researchers and highlighted in other chapters in this volume. While the engagement of immigrant parents in the face of these challenges is noteworthy, it is clear that more robust civic participation could emerge with greater support from schools. School officials can enhance participation by making parents feel welcome and crafting programs that accommodate parents' needs. For example, schools should provide adequate translation services and organize parental activities around parents' work schedules. Further, schools can broaden and deepen parental participation by taking seriously the role of parents in shaping school events, activities, and policies. Schools officials should ensure all parents access to formal decision-making structures as well as to the information that is necessary to make informed decisions.

The salutary effects of immigrant parental participation on public schools and civic life generally call for policies that make opportunities for such participation commonplace in all public schools. In concluding, we identify three broad policy areas aimed at achieving this goal.

First, federal and state policies should ensure all parents have the right to participate meaningfully in their children's public school. The No Child Left Behind Act's Section 1118 on Parental Involvement establishes a broad and helpful foundation for such a right. It specifies the role of parents in developing parental involvement policies and in making data-based decisions. Section 1118 also notes the importance of providing parents materials in their home language. Yet the No Child Left Behind Act does not create a system to oversee and enforce these rights (Rogers, 2006). New policies are needed that transform the lofty rhetoric of Section 1118 into substantive protections for parents that prompt states and districts to guarantee parental involvement opportunities in all schools and require schools to report on these opportunities.

Second, the federal government needs to create protections that ensure that *all* parents, regardless of immigration status, can participate fully in their children's schools. *Plyler v. Doe* (1982) protects the constitutional rights of undocumented children to attend public schools. Yet the actions of the Immigration and Customs Enforcement (ICE) agency often make it difficult for undocumented parents to ensure that their children can take advantage of this right. In some communities, the climate of fear created by ICE raids over the past few years has undermined the ability of undocumented parents to bring their children to school and participate in school activities and events. In the near term, parents of public school children need assurances of "safe passage" to and from their children's schools. In the longer term, the civic engagement of undocumented parents demands meaningful immigration reform.

Third, state governments should provide grants to community-based organizations to support immigrant parent participation in public schools. A model for such legislation comes from Texas. In 1995, the Texas legislature created the Investment Capital Fund Grant Program calling on schools to partner with a "nonprofit community-based organization that has demonstrated capacity to train, develop, and organize parents and community leaders" (Investment Capital Fund, 1995, Sec. 7.024 [5]). Community organizations that do not report directly to school or district officials can provide immigrant parents with independent (and trustworthy) information on school quality. Further, as noted above, grassroots community organizations can play a vital role in immigrant civic development and immigrant integration (Wong, 2006).

To date, the desire to create a better life for their children has prompted many immigrant parents to become civic agents. Policy initiatives across the three areas outlined above promise even more substantial civic participation of immigrant parents in public schools. Such participation is certainly in the interest of immigrant parents, their children, and their children's schools. It also energizes and enriches our common civic life.

Discussion Questions

1. What is civic engagement? How can parents become civically engaged in their children's schools?
2. In what ways can schools provide meaningful opportunities for democratic civic engagement? In other words, how can schools serve as a place for parents to develop and exercise community leadership? As places for immigrant parents to address community-wide concerns? To learn about political processes?
3. How can school-based civic engagement contribute to the social and political integration of immigrant parents?
4. How can community-based groups support robust forms of parental civic engagement?
5. What are challenges and barriers to realizing robust parent civic engagement in schools?
6. What types of federal, state, and local policies promote or hinder the civic participation of immigrants in public schools? How can education agencies and schools assess the extent to which policies and practices promote civic engagement?

Notes

1. It is commonplace for California to invoke the democratic purposes of parental engagement in official statements. For example, the California Department of Education's Parents Rights website includes the following statement: "In a democracy parents and guardians are encouraged and welcomed to become involved in the formal education of their children enrolled in public schools."

2. L.A. FANS is based on a multistage, clustered sample design. Data were collected from households in 65 neighborhoods (census tracts) in Los Angeles County, with an oversampling of households in poor and very poor neighborhoods. When sampling weights are used, results provide information for a representative sample of mothers and other primary caregivers of data. Populations who do not speak English or Spanish are not included in this survey.

3. Some parents are represented twice in the data because L.A. FANS provides detailed information for up to two children in a household. However, sampling weights for primary caregivers make appropriate adjustments for individuals who appear twice in the data (see Sastry et al., 2003).

4. In accordance with the survey design, interviewers automatically designated biological and adoptive mothers as the primary caregivers of children when present and capable of answering the survey questionnaire. When mothers were unavailable, interviewers surveyed the child's actual primary caregiver.

5. Data do not allow us to determine the types of parent meetings attended by survey respondents.

6. The participation of Latino immigrants in the PTA may depend on local leadership and the school-site focus of the organization.

7. Family income is top-coded in the L.A. FANS; therefore figures do not adequately reflect true differences in mean family income.

8. Separate analyses not presented here compared immigrants who had lived in the United States 10–20 years and over 20 years. Results showed no difference between these two groups in the probabilities of participating in school-based civic activities.

9. Differences in the probabilities of attending a school event and volunteering between long-term immigrants and the U.S. born are not statistically significant.

Suggested Readings

Oakes, J., & Rogers, J. (2006). *Learning power: Organizing for education and justice.* New York: Teachers College Press.

Rogers, J. (2006). Forces of accountability? The power of poor parents in No Child Left Behind. *Harvard Educational Review, 76*(4), 611–41.

Rogers, J., Sanders, M., Terriquez, V., & Velez, V. (2008). Civic lessons: Public schools and the civic development of undocumented students and parents. *Northwestern Journal of Law and Social Policy, 3*(2), 201–18.

Rogers, J., & Terriquez, V. (2009). More justice: The role of organized labor in education reform. *Educational Policy, 23*(1), 216–241.

Warren, M. R. (2005). Communities and schools: A new view of urban education reform. *Harvard Educational Review, 75*(2), 133–173.

References

Alba, R. D., & Nee, V. (2004). *Remaking the American mainstream: Assimilation and contemporary immigration.* Cambridge, MA: Harvard University Press.

American Political Science Association. Task Force on Inequality and American Democracy. (2004). American democracy in an age of rising inequality. *Perspectives on Politics, 2*(4), 651–666.

Antecol, H., & Bedard, K. (2006). Unhealthy assimilation: Why do immigrants converge to American health status levels? *Demography, 43*(2), 337–360.

Arias, M. B., & Morillo-Campbell, M. (2008). *Promoting ELL parental involvement: Challenges in contested Times.* Tempe, AZ: Education Policy Research Unit.

Auerbach, S. (2002). Why do they give the good classes to some and not to others? Latino parent narratives of struggle in a college access program. *Teachers College Record, 104*(7), 1369–1392.

Borjas, G. J. (1985). Assimilation, changes in cohort quality, and the earnings of immigrants. *Journal of Labor Economics, 3*(4), 463–489.

California Education Code, §51100 (a). (1998). Retrieved http://www.leginfo.ca.gov/cgi -bin/displaycode?section=edc&group=51001-52000&file=51100-51102

Investment Capital Fund Grant Program, Tex. Education Code Ann. §7.024. (1995).

Lareau, A. (2000). *Home advantage: Social class and parental intervention in elementary education.* Lanham, MD: Rowman & Littlefield.

Lareau, A. (2003). *Unequal childhoods: Class, race, and family life.* Berkeley: University of California Press.

Leclere, F. B., Jensen, L., & Biddlecom, A. E. (1994). Health-care utilization, family context, and adaptation among immigrants to the United States. *Journal of Health and Social Behavior, 35*(4), 370–384.

Macedo, S. (2005). *Democracy at risk: How political choices undermine citizen participation, and what we can do about it.* Washington, DC: Brookings Institution Press.

Mann, H. (1848). *Twelfth annual report of Horace Mann as secretary of Massachusetts State Board of Education.* Retrieved from http://eca.state.gov/education/engteaching/pubs/ AmLnC/br16.htm

Milkman, R. (2006). *L.A. story: Immigrant workers and the future of the U.S. labor movement.* New York: Russell Sage Foundation.

No Child Left Behind Act of 2001. (2002). Pub. L. No. 107–110, 115 Stat. 1425 (2002).

Oakes, J., Valladares, S., Renée, M., Fanelli, S., Medina, D., & Rogers, J. (2007). *Latino educational opportunity report.* Los Angeles: University of California, Los Angeles.

Olivos, E. M. (2006). *The power of parents: A critical perspective of bicultural parent involvement in public schools.* New York: Peter Lang.

Pastor, M. (2008). *Immigrant integration and our regional future.* Los Angeles: UCLA Downtown Labor Center.

Peterson, C. E., Sastry, N., Pebly, A. R., Ghosh-Dastidar, B., Williamson, S., & Lara-Cinisomo, S. (2004). *The Los Angeles family and neighborhood survey, 2001.* [Working paper]. Santa Monica, CA: Rand Labor and Population.

Plyler v. Doe. (1982). 457 202 (U.S. Supreme Court 1982).

Portes, A., & Rumbaut, R. (2006). *Immigrant America: A portrait.* Berkeley: University of California Press.

Quiocho, A. M. L., & Daoud, A. M. (2006). Dispelling myths about Latino parent participation in schools. *Educational Forum, 70*(33), 255–267.

Ramakrishnan, K. S., & Espenshade, T. J. (2001). Immigrant incorporation and political participation in the United States. *International Migration Review, 35*(3), 870–909.

Ramirez, A. Y. F. (2003). Dismay and disappointment: Parental involvement of Latino immigrant parents. *Urban Review, 35*(2), 93–110.

Reay, D. (1998). *Class work: Mothers' involvement in their children's primary schooling.* London: UCL Press.

Rogers, J. (2006). Forces of accountability? The power of poor parents in No Child Left Behind. *Harvard Educational Review, 76*(4), 611–641.

Sastry, N., Ghosh-Dastidar, B., Adams, J., & Pebley, A. R. (2003). *The design of a multi-level longitudinal survey of children, families, and communities: The Los Angeles family and neighborhood survey* (Working Paper-DRU-2400/1-1-LAFANS). Santa Monica: RAND Corporation.

Segura, G., Pachon, H., & Woods, N. D. (2005). Hispanics, social capital, and civic engagement. *National Civic Review, 90*(1), 85–96.

Spring, J. (1994). *The American school, 1642–1993.* New York: McGraw-Hill.

Terriquez, V. (2007). *Predictors of parental school involvement in a Latino metropolis.* American Sociological Association Annual Meeting, New York.

Tyack, D. (2003). *Seeking common ground: Public schools in a diverse society.* Cambridge, MA: Harvard University Press.

U.S. Census Bureau. (2006). *American community survey.* Washington, DC: U.S. Department of Commerce.

Valdes, G. (1996). *Con respeto: Bridging the distances between culturally diverse families and schools: An ethnographic portrait.* New York: Teachers College Press.

Wong, J. (2006). *Democracy's promise: Immigrants and American civic institutions.* Ann Arbor: University of Michigan Press.

11

The Struggle for Democratic and Transformative Parent Engagement

Alberto M. Ochoa, Edward M. Olivos,
and Oscar Jiménez-Castellanos

There is nothing more unequal than treating unequals as equals.
(Lau v. Nichols, Supreme Court Decision, 1974)

The collection of chapters found in this volume call for alternative paradigms for viewing how parent engagement needs to be conceptualized and actualized. All call for bicultural parents and communities to be engaged in democratic schooling practices, while pointing out the limits of existing frameworks and mindsets that are necessary but insufficient for transforming school and societal structures of social inequality.

Perhaps the most challenging task for school personnel in undertaking parent engagement in the school community is establishing a balance between theory, pedagogy, politics, and personal development. We know that educators are often mandated to follow certain pedagogical policies and strategies that they must use in the classroom and school, many of which go against their own ideological principles (Olivos & Quintana de Valladolid, 2005). At the same time, they must also negotiate the unique cultural and linguistic background of every single one of their hundreds of students and parents. In addition, they must take into account the personality and spirit of each child and family.

In the past 50 years educators have seen the use of pedagogical theory and language policy that operates on the assumption that there are specific equations on how to properly educate students and parents from diverse cultural and linguistic backgrounds. What is missing here is the development of social consciousness that calls "for rigorous intellectual engagement with issues of politics, oppression, and social justice" (Cutri, 2000, p. 163). It is therefore crucial that educators and parents participate in self-reflection on their own beliefs, attitudes, and pedagogy. Furthermore, Cutri proposes a "spiritual morality" (distinct from religion) and teaching from a transpersonal level. Spiritual morality is similar to what Freire (2005) offers in his "indispensable qualities of progressive teachers": humility, lovingness, courage, tolerance, patience, and the joy of living (pp. 71–78). However, the transpersonal level gives us the driving knowledge of what we can do to promote justice, equity, and equal opportunity. Moving away from fear and into a spiritual consciousness of oneness will help, not hurt, an effective education for all children and bicultural school communities.

Social and Cultural Politics of Parental Engagement

What are social and cultural politics of parental engagement? In the context of parent engagement, Pennycook (1994) introduces the concept of cultural politics and describes it as the examination of roles and relationships and the power relations and interactions inside and outside the school that exist and that create tensions. The chapters found in this book clearly view schools as sociopolitical spaces that exist in a complex relationship with the outside world in need of being critically examined. To isolate schools from social and cultural politics ultimately leads to what Freire (2000) calls "conforming consciousness" (p. 10). In this state, individuals are passive and accept the social situations or conditions as normal, and make no effort to transform power relations. Thus, if an educator asserts that they do not have the time and effort to engage parents in understanding the social and cultural politics of the school community, we argue that they are participating in the conforming consciousness space of social irresponsibility.

We take the position that each bicultural student and parent brings into the school the experiences that he or she has gained in the outside world. However, to say that the outside society determines what takes place in the school is not entirely accurate. Schools and society are engaged in a constant interplay of influence, in which outside society affects what goes on in the school and what takes place in the school influences the outside society (Lareau & Weininger, 2003; Pennycook, 1994). When educators ignore the dynamic interaction between society and the school, they are resisting the natural phenomenon of human interaction. It takes more effort and energy to resist the social and cultural politics within the school than to move with the fluid changes and shifts of the needs of school communities.

This book calls on educators and school personnel to have a transformative consciousness. Such a person acknowledges the tensions and inequalities inherent in social and cultural politics as important. We often walk through the "ideological fog" of one's social training—a powerful hegemonic force that Freire (2005) says is "always domesticating, and when we are touched and deformed by it we become ambiguous and indecisive" (p. 10). Then, as educators begin to observe the school community and realize there are many situations that they ideologically oppose, they begin to practice Freire's indispensable virtue of "decisiveness" (p. 78). As educators understand the sociopolitical and economic conditions that create inequities or unequal access or lack of justice in schools and communities, they begin to take action, and to develop transformational consciousness. It is not until school authorities become aware of the social inequalities in bicultural school communities and their role within those conditions that they are able to carve a path of action.

To practice critical theory as an educator is to intentionally engage in dialogue with parents about social and cultural politics. Hinchey (1998) states, "Critical theory is, above all else, a way to ask questions about power" (p. 17). If the school is in constant action and reaction to the outlining society and to its power relations, educators must also be examining power relations between their students, their parents, fellow teachers, school leadership, and themselves.

Parental Empowerment Through Individual Consciousness and Social Action

In the examination of parent engagement and empowerment we contend that existing forms of parental involvement do not seek to create the conditions necessary to examine power relations and educational access and equity (Cutler, 2000; Macedo, 1991; Olivos & Ochoa, 2006a, 2006b). The empowerment of parents requires both individual consciousness and social action. Empowerment is, in the words of Peter McLaren (1998), the process through which students and parents "learn to critically appropriate knowledge existing outside of their immediate experience in order to broaden their understanding of themselves, the world, and the possibilities for transforming . . . the way we live" (p. 48).

Consequently, this volume seeks to develop empowering models of parent engagement that build upon and capitalize on parents' ability to understand their own needs and work to actualize those needs. It draws on dialogue and the networks and strengths that community people have. As a result, parents' language and culture are incorporated; community participation is collaborative; the pedagogy becomes a reciprocal interaction between students, teachers, administrators, and parents; and accountability moves toward advocacy and educational action and change that promotes democratic schooling (access, equal encouragement, due process, inclusion, civic engagement) rather than those in sole control or domination of leadership position.

Empowerment in our estimation is not to be conceptualized as an easy process, one where such a practice simply empowers a parent community and then the work is finished. Bicultural parent empowerment and advocacy requires a critical examination of ideologies and practices that impede a collaborative and authentic relationship between the public school system and bicultural communities. As a process, parent engagement through the perspective of critical pedagogy and democratic schooling (see Pearl in this volume) provides a way for educators and parents to see themselves as change agents who promote social justice and democratic values—agents who initiate actions and make a difference in schools and communities. Critical pedagogy and democratic schooling is embedded in the lived experiences and perspectives of bicultural parents and school practices and requires them to examine other experiences and conditions, as well as contradictions (Olivos, 2006). In this way, bicultural parents and school personnel move beyond reported information and opinions. They become aware that they actually exist and that they are the interpreters of their school community situation. They examine conditions in their lives and work to create strategies to change conditions that work against the quality of life of the community. Thus, this volume calls for parent engagement to be redefined using paradigms that will provide space for voice, access, inclusion, and the democratic participation of subordinate communities in the process of education.

We propose the use of critical pedagogy and action research because it breaks the binary opposition of theory and practice, the false premise that there is a divide between research and doing; it is the practice of theory for all involved (Kincheloe, 2008). Critical pedagogy disrupts the position that theory is created only at institutions of higher learning and practice is relegated only to the public schools and the two seldom encounter each other. From the perspective of critical pedagogy, theory illuminates practice and practice informs theory (Freire, 2005). Often the "right" teaching strategies will not make conflict, confrontation, or backlash go away. Through the critical pedagogy process, school community climate, power relations, knowledge production, and school policies are explored to expand understanding of practices, build new theory, and develop critical and empowered participants and learners. Since critical pedagogy begins where bicultural parents are situated, it acknowledges cultural, linguistic, social, and economic differences (Macedo & Batolome, 2001). Essential to the process of critical pedagogy in the school community are teaching and learning for democratic values and social justice; negotiating and codeveloping curriculum; creating alternative teaching and learning activities; conceiving of authentic, continuous assessment formats; engaging in critical community conversation; and maintaining the respectful treatment of peers (hooks, 1994; Pearl & Knight, 1999; Shor, 1980; Smith, 1999).

By critical community conversation we propose the use of a social justice agenda that is suggested by Bigelow, Christensen, Karp, Miner, and Peterson (1994) in their proposal of a social justice laboratory for creating more democratic school communities and society. They call for educators to confront rather than perpetuate social inequality in our society that facilitates the development of all children. Eight elements are suggested for school communities to engage in conversation to actualize democratic practices: (1) school activities grounded in the lives of students and parents; (2) critical examination of social inequality; (3) the use of multicultural, antiracist, pro-justice curriculum practices; (4) participatory and experiential engagement of participants; (5) hopeful, joyful, kind, and visionary school community climate; (6) activism as a basis in addressing school community concerns and problems; (7) academically rigorous curriculum; and (8) culturally sensitive and responsive participants.

In proposing a transformative parent engagement model we seek to capitalize on parents' ability to understand their own needs and work to actualize those needs. It is grounded in the lives of students and parents and calls for engaging in problem posing that connects them with the school community to challenge inequalities, participate in decisions affecting their lives, and work with and through people in collectively solving problems. The next section articulates five levels of parent engagement that are based on critical pedagogy and democratic value (access, equal encouragement, due process, inclusion, and civic engagement).

Tools of the Transformative Education Context Model

In earlier work (Olivos & Ochoa, 2006a, 2006b) we proposed the Transformative Education Context Model of parent engagement that provides parents and parent advocates with tools to confront the social injustices currently taking place in the public education setting for low-income youth, specifically bicultural students and school communities. The model intends that bicultural parents begin unmasking and understanding the contradictions that are found in the current educational, economic, and political system by developing a social consciousness along with their fellow parents and communities (Freire, 2000). The conceptual framework found in Table 11.1 illustrates our goal.

Table 11.1 Transformational Parental Engagement Model

Level	Theoretical & Social Focus	Parent Engagement Model	Perception of Parents as Contributors to Schools	School Community Context of Action
Open Democratic System (Transformative Education Context Model)	Conflict theory, social constructionist & interpretive that seeks transformational change toward cultural and economic democracy	Transformational education: Problem posing that seeks solutions enabling inclusion, voice, and representation in decision making	Parents as action researchers, agents of transformative change in the school and community and working for the attainment of cultural and economic democracy	Micro/Meso/ Exo/ Macro Systems Parents engage in classroom/ school/ community/ regional/state activities that are driven by action research issues that work to reduce inequality of access while working to create democratic schooling and social literacy curricula for actualizing cultural and economic democracy

Before describing the five levels of engagement, a discussion of what drives the Transformative Education Context Model is needed. In our work we use three constructs: democratic schooling, action research, and problem posing. Briefly, democratic schooling is based on the work of Pearl and Knight (1999) and the chapter found in this text on bicultural parents and democratic schooling. Pearl in his work proposes strong and deliberate democratic education, characterizing it thus:

> Strong democracy in the sense that governmental institutions such as public schools are vital to a functioning democracy but only if students learn about democracy by actually experiencing it in their schooling and only when schools accept as a major responsibility the preparation of preparing informed and responsible democratic citizens. Deliberative democracy in the sense that classrooms are viewed as places where the widest range of ideas about vital issues such as racism and justice are exchanged and those voices rarely heard or suppressed enrich the discourse. In democratic classrooms deliberation is not an academic exercise but is a serious effort to advance public good and influence policy and practice. (See Pearl, p. 104, this volume)

Furthermore, democratic schooling proposes seven fundamental principles: (1) authority that is persuasive and negotiable; (2) inclusion, where all are welcomed as equally important contributing members of a learning community; (3) knowledge development sufficient to solve the important personal and social problems and a necessary component of deliberative democracy; (4) development of democratic citizenship skills critical for effective collective action; (5) inalienable rights guaranteed all in the Bill of Rights; (6) an optimum learning environment available for all; and (7) equality that in schooling is manifest with all students equally encouraged to succeed in all of societies' legal endeavors. The seven principles are proposed for preparing active and responsible citizens. While we understand that democracy in schools will not come easily, this will not happen without strong political action at the community level and bicultural parents and their children working together to transform education.

Action research is a powerful tool for improving the practice of any organization—such as schools. It is a process that involves working with and through people to problem-solve issues and concerns. It involves formulating questions and using evaluation concepts and techniques, and employing both qualitative and quantitative methodologies (Stringer, 2007). Good action research combines learning and development of activity for the participants. Action research projects and activities enable the researcher (e.g., parent community) to become involved, to intervene in a matter of genuine concern, and to gather support for participants to act on seeking solutions to issues and problems. Action research is an opportunity for insight and understanding of learning, change, and development.

The combination of learning, research, intervention, and change causes inner and outer measurable effects on researchers and participants. The former may understand the social mechanisms involved in the enterprise and the latter may experience personal growth as a result of organizationally arranged procedures for empowerment. Kurt Lewin (1948) influenced the theory of action research through his work in social and organizational psychology. One of his main contributions is the coupling of self-managed learning and planned change. Lewin's basic change model of unfreezing, change, and refreezing is a theoretical foundation from which many processes emerge. Lewin's idea on the theory and practice of change is, *"If you want to understand a system, try to change it."* Especially for action research and educational sciences it is important to serve the dual function of objective describing and subjective directing to the possibilities of joint human efforts for change, improvement, development, adaptation, flexibility, courage, and emancipation.

Critical approaches of action research have a political intent to intervene for the sake of social justice, democracy, liberty, and emancipation. For us action research must be collaborative and entails working with bicultural parents. Kemmis and McTaggart (1988) address this posture:

> Action research is a form of collective self-reflective inquiry undertaken by participants in social situations in order to improve the rationality and justice of their own social or educational practices, as well as their understanding of those practices and the situations in which the practices are carried out. . . . The approach is only action research when it is collaborative, though it is important to realize that action research of the group is achieved through the critically examined action of individual group members. (pp. 5–6)

Finally, the third dimension that drives our parent engagement model is problem-posing education. It is a concept derived from the work of Paulo Freire (2000) that calls for developing social consciousness through a problem-posing process, with and through people, that entails dialogue, reflection, conceptualization, and action. From the perspective of John Dewey problem posing is also an inductive questioning process that structures dialogue. Both Dewey and Freire were strong advocates for active, inquiring, hands-on education that resulted in participant-centered learning and personal development. Wink (2004) states:

> Problem posing is much more than just a method or a series of methods. Problem posing ignites praxis and leads to action. Problem posing brings interactive participation and critical inquiry into the existing curriculum and expands it to reflect the curriculum of the students' lives. . . . Problem posing opens the door to ask questions and seek answers, not only of the visible curriculum, but also of the hidden curriculum. Problem posing is very interested in the hidden curriculum, which is why many are uncomfortable with it. Problem posing causes people to ask questions that many do not want to hear. (pp. 51–52)

We propose the use of problem-posing education as a process for engaging in dialogue with a school community. This process entails discussion with bicultural parent participants to become aware that they have the answers to their problems through a collegial and cooperative manner. The community advocate or facilitator serves to guide the dialogue in search of several alternatives to the problem or issue at hand and the advantages and disadvantages of the solutions proposed. Problem posing is both a short- and long-term process that examines deeply into any issue or problem, demonstrating the extent of its social and personal connections. Problem posing "focuses on power relations in the classroom, in the institution, in the formation of standard canons of knowledge, and in society at large" (Shor, 1992, p. 31). Problem posing calls for building relationships between educator, student, and parent that offer participants space for validating their life experiences, their cultures, and their personal knowledge of how their world works—as an empowering, dynamic, and participatory process.

Five Levels of Transformative Parent Engagement

We propose five levels of engagement in actualizing the Transformative Education Context Model through the use of democratic schooling principles, action research, and problem-posing education. Toward what vision? Toward parent democratic civic engagement that equips school community participants (students, parents, teachers, administrators, community stakeholders) to engage in action and reflection in order to transform unequal conditions that disempower the human condition and works for inclusion, access, equality, equal encouragement, civic responsibility, and democratic living.

The actualization of this model calls for participants to see themselves as no longer docile listeners and followers whose involvement in school activities is one of participating as an "object" driven by activities that conform to the dominant monocultural values and practices of the school community culture. Rather, the model calls for participants to view themselves as critical co-investigators involved in dialogue, reflection, and action with each other in the micro and macro spaces of their community. It calls for bicultural parents and communities to see themselves as "subjects" that create and re-create spaces to promote activities and practices that work to reduce inequality of access and oppressive practices hindering the development of the human condition. Participants as subjects are involved in community work that creates democratic schooling and social awareness for actualizing cultural and economic democracy. Toward the development of transformative parent engagement practices, the five levels of work include the following:

Level I: Connectedness
Level II: Inclusion and Belongingness
Level III: Decision Making
Level IV: Participatory Action Research
Level V: Macro Civic Engagement

Level I: Connectedness. The democratic schooling principle guiding this level of parent engagement is equal access and equality, which in schooling is manifest with all students equally encouraged to succeed in all of society's legal endeavors and where inalienable rights guaranteed in the Bill of Rights are part of the way of life of the school community. This initial level calls for schools to engage bicultural parent communities

- connecting parents to their child and in investing in their human development;
- connecting parents to participate in civic engagement activities;

- assisting parents in understanding the organizational structures of schools and how to access the core curriculum;
- providing bicultural parents with tools for becoming sociopolitically active in school community decisions ranging from accountability to school finance;
- enabling parents to connect, to share ideas and concerns, to prioritize concerns, and to explore solutions and strategies together; and
- enabling parents through leadership development training to reflect, to name concerns, and to begin to take action in improving the human condition of all children and parents in the school community.

Under this level of parent engagement, a community-based organization that works with schools to connect parents to the school community and in enabling parents to navigate the school system and obtain access to the core curriculum is the Parent Institute for Quality Education (PIQE), a nonprofit organization. PIQE (2009) is founded on the following principles: that all parents love their children and want a better future for them, that every child can learn and deserves the opportunity to attend and complete a college education, and that parents and teachers must work together to ensure the educational success of every child. PIQE engages parents in a 9-week process of dialogue and learning that reinforces and confirms the three foundational principles.

PIQE provides the information and tools that parents, especially low-income bicultural immigrants, need to become more involved in their children's education. The PIQE process have been facilitated in more than 16 languages and by community facilitators. PIQE strongly believes that parent involvement begins at home and must continue at the schools—that every child is in crisis if his or her parent/guardian is not engaged with him or her at home and in the school. PIQE's programs are a work in progress, changing and adapting to the cultural, language, and social conditions of every parent, family, and community.

With regard to this book, the Level I, Connectedness, focus is supported by Chapter 2, by Moreno, Lewis-Menchaca, and Rodriguez, who affirm that parental involvement has long been viewed as a vehicle for academic success, particularly in regard to addressing the achievement gap experienced by ethnically and linguistically diverse low-income students. They further assert that the more parents are involved in their child's schooling, the better the child will perform. In working with parents they also recommend that school personnel be cognizant of unaccounted complexities that exist with parent involvement in culturally diverse families that can create gaps and conflicts between home and school. Finally, they call for strategies for building better family-school relations between ethnically diverse families and schools and awareness of the micro-interpersonal process of how parents interact with their children and how it challenges a school's conception of parent involvement. Of importance is connecting parents to their child and investing in their human development.

Level II: Inclusion and Belongingness. The democratic schooling principle guiding this level of parent engagement is the actualization of inclusion, where all community members, especially bicultural parents, are welcomed as equally important contributing members of a learning community. This second level calls for schools to engage all parents in the school community, especially bicultural parents, in

- entering and creating a school climate where cultural, linguistic, and inclusive spaces of belongingness are part of the school's curricula;
- facilitating the demystification of the organizational structures of schooling from preschool to higher education;
- facilitating the demystification of school practices and educational and social institutional roles that directly and indirectly impact the educational access of their children; and
- building home-school-community connections that work for democratic schooling, for example, service-learning practice that allows the student-teacher-parent teacher-administrator to engage in school community projects that address educational and social inequities and power relationships inherent around issues of curriculum tracking, the achievement gap, health, water, or energy in low-income communities and communities in general.

Under this level of parent engagement, a community-based organization that works with schools to create inclusion, voice, and engagement with the school community is PICO (People Improving Communities through Organizing). PICO (2009) is based on a congregation-community model. Congregations of all denominations and faiths serve as the institutional base for community organizations that bring people together simply based on common issues like housing or education. PICO builds community organizations based on schools and community centers, which are often the only stable civic gathering places in many neighborhoods. While focusing on selected issues like education, local chapters engage people and sustain long-term campaigns to bring about systematic change in local communities.

PICO also provides intensive leadership training that facilitates people in how to use the tools of democracy to improve their communities. Community parents have learned to successfully use the levers of community engagement to bring resources and political attention to their communities. PICO has the ability to act on a comprehensive vision for their communities, cities, and regions. PICO challenges its leaders to listen to the concerns and ideas of their local school communities and work with public officials and stakeholders who are both Republicans and Democrats, conservatives and liberals, to bring needed changes to communities. PICO does public business in public through large action meetings. As a result, PICO organizations gain the reputation for being able to gather together large numbers of people over and over and to hold themselves and public officials accountable.

Two chapters in the book also point to the importance of Level II, Inclusion and Belongingness. The chapter by Lindsey and Lindsey, Chapter 3, calls for school leaders to institute a systems approach to create a climate and infrastructure that fosters, supports, and expects parent engagement in schools. The authors propose the use of *culturally proficient leadership* as a systemic approach to foster inclusion and belongingness in the construction of cultural democracy in schools. For Lindsey and Lindsey, cultural proficiency occurs in schools when leaders align their own values and behaviors and the school's policies and practices in a transformative manner to provide equitable access to learning opportunities and outcomes and for making our communities more inclusive—while using our public schools as central to that process.

Chapter 4, by Lombos Wlazlinski and Cummins, further examines what is possible for preparing teachers to incorporate the voices of bicultural parents into the curriculum. They highlight a project that connects preservice teachers with parents' culturally and linguistically diverse communities. It demonstrates the powerful nature of learning about each other by documenting the stories of families (Family Narrative Project [FNP]: Preservice Teachers and Latino Parents as Co-authors/Historias de la Vida de Familia: Estudiantes de Educacion y Familias como Co-autores). Of importance is the theoretical context of the FNP that challenges the pattern of coercive power relations that frames the experience of subordinated communities in the wider society. Their project provides an example of a medium for the inclusion of voices of bicultural parents and children (expressed and heard) that promotes a process of *empowerment,* understood as the collaborative creation of power.

Level III: Decision Making. The democratic schooling principle guiding this level of parent engagement involves authority that is persuasive and negotiable and where knowledge development is supported to solve the important educational and social problems to achieve deliberative democracy. This third level calls for schools to engage all parents in the school community, especially bicultural parents, in

- understanding power relations in the school system and the process of how school and school district decisions are made and becoming participants of the decision-making governance of the school whose focus is providing optimal learning opportunities for all students;
- engaging parent leaders in school- and district-level committees that address governance, school and district budget and finances, curriculum practices, professional development of school and district, evaluation of school programs and student achievement trends, and parental leadership development; and
- engaging in leadership development for democratic schooling (e.g., working to elect a school board or city council member from the school community).

Under this level of parent engagement, a community-based organization that works with schools and school districts in developing parent leadership in decision making is the Mexican American Legal Defense and Educational Fund (MALDEF). Since 1989, MALDEF's Parent School Partnership (PSP) program has empowered parents and community leaders throughout the nation to become change agents in their communities. The PSP program provides them with the tools necessary to become effective advocates in improving their children's educational attainment. MALDEF has as its goal reducing the high school drop-out rate, increasing college access, and establishing a network of civic-minded parents and educated youth who will help create a new generation of socially conscious Latino leadership. MALDEF is also involved in the Los Angeles Multicultural Education Collaborative (LAMEC) initiative to build community empowerment and mobilization through parent and youth leadership training centered in K–12 academic success, college access, and civic engagement.

In this book the chapters by Pearl (Chapter 6), Johnson (Chapter 8), and Shannon (Chapter 5) highlight the importance of preparing and engaging bicultural parents in decisions in the schools that have substance, meaning, and relevance to the future of bicultural children. First, Pearl provides us with principles of democratic schooling that call for civic engagement in the decision-making process of school communities. Specifically, Pearl proposes seven fundamental principles that include authority, inclusion, informed knowledge, civic engagement for collective action, rights to due process, creating optimum learning environment available to all students, and equality in schooling that is manifested with all students being equally encouraged to succeed in all of societies legal endeavors.

The intention behind schools working with bicultural communities is to engage them in action and reflection in order to transform the educational and social context into democratic living spaces. The role of bicultural parents becomes to change education from its current undemocratic nature characterized by systematic denial of encouragement to a democratic education of equal encouragement and access.

The chapter by Johnson illustrates what parents can do to become involved in the decision-making process in schools. By examining her personal experiences as a parent of color in South Los Angeles, Johnson highlights the frustrations working-class parents of color have as they attempt to advocate for their children and their community. She underscores the importance of one community organization in South Los Angeles called Parent U-Turn that offers parent workshops focusing not on improving "parenting skills" but on providing parents from urban working-class communities with the tools and skills to effectively advocate for their children.

The Shannon chapter illustrates the importance of bicultural parents becoming aware of the need to be engaged in policy and program implementation to ensure that equal access and academic rigor is provided to their children. Using the theoretical lens that Derrick Bell introduced to understand White response to integration and the involvement of parents in a biliteracy program model, she illustrates the dynamics of parent engagement in a dual language program. This program involved two parent communities that are positioned in U.S. society in dramatically asymmetric ways—socially and politically. Of importance is the question, Who drives educational policy and to benefit whom?

Level IV: Participatory Action Research. The democratic schooling principle guiding this level of parent engagement is the development of democratic citizenship skills critical for effective collective action and creating an optimum learning environment available for all students and parents. This initial level calls for schools to engage all parents in the community, especially bicultural parents, in

- providing skills to work with and through people in participatory action research (PAR);
- acquiring the tools of action research—from identifying concerns, to problem posing, to developing the methodologies for data collection, to the analysis of quantitative and qualitative data, to formulating recommendations and action plans, to empowerment evaluation;
- examining strengths and weaknesses, while mobilizing to actualize democratic schooling principles (see Pearl's chapter in this book), namely: authority, inclusion, informed knowledge, civic engagement for collective action, rights to due process, creating optimum learning environment, and equality of opportunity;
- mobilizing parent community voice and action to improve the actualization of democratic engagement for the collective we;
- making sense of information collected and uncovering relationships in classrooms, school, community, and problem-posing questions; and
- understanding dominant research methods and their effects, in order to see what is ignored by these approaches that works against the collective benefits of all students and parents.

This fourth level calls above all for parental activism guided by democratic principles that entail the construction of optimum learning environments and equality of opportunity that advocates for student and parent engagement through a service-learning and civic engagement approach. Service learning (National Youth Leadership Council, 2003) focuses on

- school-community service that has significant consequences for themselves and others;
- student and parent voices that are maximized in selecting, designing, implementing, and evaluating school-community projects;
- diversity that is valued and demonstrated by its participants, its practice, and its outcomes;
- communication and interaction with the community that are promoted and partnerships and collaborations that are encouraged; and
- the use of multiple methods that encourage critical thinking and civic engagement and is a central force in the design and fulfillment of democratic school practices.

Under this level of parent engagement, a community-based organization that worked with the school community through a participatory action research process was (the now defunct) ACORN (Association of Community Organizations for Reform Now). ACORN (2009) was a nonprofit, nonpartisan social justice organization with national headquarters in New York; New Orleans; and Washington, DC. ACORN was the nation's largest grassroots community organization of low- and moderate-income people with over 400,000 member families organized into more than 1,200 neighborhood chapters in 110 cities across the country. Since 1970, ACORN had been building community organizations that were committed to educational, social, and economic justice.

ACORN helped those who had historically been locked out become powerful players in our democratic system. Among the approaches used by ACORN was participatory action research (PAR) that involves researchers and the parent community to start with identification of major issues, concerns, and problems. PAR then proceeds to initiate investigation, data collection, reflection, and action and more continuous reflection and action. ACORN (2009) worked to ensure that all children received a quality education. ACORN advocated that if parents' hard-earned tax dollars are used to finance the public school system then they should reap the benefits. ACORN members were involved in local school communities working to implement a platform to improve the quality of public schools.

This Level IV, Action Research, approach is supported by the chapter in this book by Montero-Sieburth (Chapter 9), who documents the use of PAR in the process of training and empowering parents to actively influence conditions in their school communities. She affirms that bicultural parents using action research become aware of relationships of power that exist between parents who have access to power and those who do not. Montero-Sieburth shares in her chapter several action research projects over a 6-year period with parents. In these action research projects she identifies and shares ethnographic research methods, as well as documenting the active voices and involvement of bicultural parents in their process of contributing and transforming schools as change agents. Specifically, four action research projects are discussed in different community sites with high concentrations of Latino/bicultural parents. Using burning issues that emerged from the discussions with parents, training in ethnographic methods, the projects provide examples of how parents' knowledge and skills could be expanded to control the amount and quality of data they need for making decisions.

Level V: Macro Civic Engagement. The democratic schooling principles guiding this level of parent engagement center on parents becoming knowledgeable of civic issues that are necessary to solve important community social problems and the emphasis on the development of democratic citizenship skills that are essential for effective collective action. This fifth level calls for schools to engage all parents in the school community, especially bicultural parents, in

- positioning oneself and others for civic engagement at the micro (local) to macro (regional/state/national) levels;
- including community voices in community dialogue, in particular those often absent in policy debates;
- creating public, community, and organizational spaces for dialogue;
- working for transformative conditions in the school community that actualize democratic schooling principles, such as representation, equal encouragement, and equal access;
- working with elected officials to authentically represent and work for the community and to address its pressing needs; and
- becoming a "critical friend" in which parents assume a role that combines working with and through people in collaboration with community agencies but also with the capacity to probe and challenge insiders and outsiders to address community issues to avoid complacency (Campbell, McNamara, & Gilroy, 2004).

Under this fifth level of parent engagement, organizations that work with school communities in civic engagement include the Center for Lobbying in the Public Interest, the W. K. Kellogg Foundation, and the Casey Foundation. These three organizations/agencies support nonprofits and grassroots organizations in understanding the role of policy at all levels of government—local, state, and national and, more important, preparing community parent leaders for engagement in the policy process that includes a broad range of activities that identify, embrace, and promote needed social changes. These changes often require alterations in public perceptions and public policy. To advance change in public perceptions and public policy effectively, advocacy efforts must focus on particular arenas of policy influence.

Level V, Civic Engagement, supports creating communities, cities, and nations in which all children have an equitable and promising future and creating conditions that propel children and families to achieve success as individuals and as contributors to the larger community and society. Creating community spaces for civic engagement and to be informed of issues from different points of view is essential to democratic schooling and for advocacy in addressing inequities in the school community.

The work of Yankelovich (1998) on civic engagement offers insights into essential propositions for communities to be involved in establishing policy. Among his recommendations for action are (1) the purpose of citizen engagement is to bring policy into better alignment with public values; (2) the public must insist on a stronger voice on issues that affect their lives—such as quality of life, equal access to career jobs, multiculturalism, women's rights, lifestyle choices, and the insistence on having a stronger voice in policy formulation; (3) the need to ensure representative thinking for viewpoints with which they agree and do not agree as an indispensable skill of citizen engagement; and (4) developing the core skills of dialogue that include empathic listening, a willingness to treat all participants as equals irrespective of what their positions may be outside the dialogue setting; and the ability to force assumptions to the surface, where they can be examined openly and without prejudgment.

In this book the chapters by Grant and Potter (Chapter 7) and Terriquez and Rogers (Chapter 10) support the focus and importance of civic engagement in working to create responsible community activism for the well-being of all. Grant and Potter call for a constructive pluralistic approach to parent-teacher/school engagement that brings together and unites the different stakeholders (e.g., school staff, parents, and students) in the school community context to work for the well-being of all. More specifically, the authors argue that constructive pluralism advocates for the civic engagement of ethnically diverse parents and the school staff in order to bring about a more democratic and socially just education.

The argument for constructive pluralism is built upon the rationale that we are all affected by the demands of a global society that touch on global, national, and local discussions of civil rights, living conditions, and quality of life. The chapter concludes by presenting several features of school life that constructive pluralism can facilitate through the engagement of school staff and diverse groups of parents and communities.

The chapter by Terriquez and Rodgers more directly examines the important role of public schools in the civic engagement and civic development of immigrant parents. It draws on empirical data to show that, despite barriers to parental school participation, Latino immigrants actively participate in school-based civic activities. Parents not only become involved in parent meetings, school events, and volunteer activities, they also participate in school decision making and in efforts to improve their children's schools. They assert that when immigrant parents have the support from grassroots organizations they are able to mobilize other community members around education issues and hold elected officials accountable. Terriquez and Rodgers argue that immigrants' civic engagement in public schools can facilitate participation in civic life outside schools.

Becoming Sociopolitically Active

All those involved in social justice have long recognized the importance of social activism, of becoming sociopolitically active in our school communities. We recognize the importance of advocacy because those in power positions make decisions that directly affect the lives of youth and community members, especially low-income ethnically and linguistically diverse parents. Becoming sociopolitically active calls for being informed in order to participate in decision making, as well as working to inform others of the issues pertinent to the lives of students, parents, and educators. Forhan and Scheraga (2000) indicate:

> Becoming sociopolitically active does not happen overnight. It is an ongoing, organic process of growth and development of learning about issues, of learning how decisions are made . . . and developing skills that will enable us to participate effectively in decision making processes. (p. 196)

Given the relationship between understanding an issue and committing oneself to it, education becomes an important activity of sociopolitical awareness. In working with bicultural communities we need to be informed and we need to inform parents. In the process we will gain informed parent advocates for children and the school community.

In proposing the Transformative Education Context Model, the five levels of parental engagement, we call for connecting the school, the parent, and the community at large using the principles of democratic schooling, participatory action research that focuses on working with and through people, and problem posing that seeks to name and act on school community concerns. The goal is for the school community to examine conditions working against democratic schooling and understand the relationship between knowledge and power that hinders social justice. Connecting knowledge and power occurs when the community is informed and issues and concerns are addressed in open public spaces. This calls for educators to engage in dialogue and activism that works for democratic schooling policies and practices—seeking equal opportunity, access, and social justice for all.

In closing, we are reminded of the words of Cesar Chavez (Thinkexist, 2009), who stated,

> Once social change begins, it cannot be reversed. You cannot uneducate the person who has learned to read. You cannot humiliate the person who feels pride. You cannot oppress the people who are not afraid anymore. We have seen the future, and the future is ours.

Discussion Questions

1. Why is it important to recognize the social and cultural politics of parental engagement?
2. What role can critical theory and critical pedagogy play in understanding how our educational system produces social and educational inequality?
3. What is the role of democratic principles, participatory action research, and a problem-posing pedagogy in making parent and school community engagement a transformative process?
4. What are the five levels of transformative parent engagement that are proposed to enhance democratic schooling? How are the five levels interconnected?
5. How can school community participatory action research be used to understand race, gender, and socioeconomic inequality and what is needed for the construction of democratic schooling and society?
6. How can transformative parent engagement contribute to all parents, and specifically bicultural parents, becoming sociopolitically active in their school communities in pursue of democratic schooling?

Suggested Readings

Anderson, K. J., & Minke, K. M. (2007). Parent involvement in education: Toward an understanding of parents' decision making. *Journal of Educational Research, 100*(5), 311–323.

Anyon, J. (2005). *Radical possibilities: Public policy, urban education, and a new social movement.* New York: Routledge.

Apple, M. (2000). *Cultural politics and education.* New York: Teachers College Press.

Auerbach, S. (2007). From moral supporters to struggling advocates: Reconceptualizing parent roles in education through the experiences of working-class families of color. *Urban Education, 42*(3), 250–283.

Cummins, J. (2009). Transformative multiliteracies pedagogy: School-based strategies for closing the achievement gap. *Multiple Voices for Ethnically Diverse Exceptional Learners, 11*(2), 38–56.

Donato, R. (1997). *The other struggle for equal schools: Mexican Americans during the civil rights era.* Albany: State University of New York Press.

Ferguson, C. (2008). *The school-family connection: Looking at the larger picture: A review of current literature.* Austin, TX: National Center for Family and Community Connections with Schools.

hooks, b. (2003). *Teaching community: A pedagogy of hope.* New York: Routledge.

Ladson-Billings, G. (2009). Race still matters: Critical race theory in education. In M. W. Apple, M. Au, & L. A. Gandin (Eds.), *The Routledge international handbook of critical education* (pp. 110–122). New York: Routledge.

Lee, C. D. (2009). Historical evolution of risk and equity: Interdisciplinary issues and critiques. *Review of Research in Education, 33*(1), 63–100.

Portes, A., & Rumbaut, R. (2001). *Legacies: The story of the immigrant second generation.* New York: Russell Sage Foundation.

Smith, L. T. (199). *Decolonizing methodologies.* New York: Zen Books.

Spring, J. (2005). *Political agendas for education: From the Right to the Green Party.* Mahwah, NJ : Lawrence Erlbaum.

Valenzuela, A. (Ed.). (2004). *Leaving children behind: How "Texas-style" accountability fails Latino youth.* Albany: State University of New York Press.

References

ACORN (Association of Community Organizations for Reform Now). (2009). *ACORN.* Retrieved from http://www.acorn.org/index.php?id=12340

Bigelow, B., Christensen, L., Karp, S., Miner, B., & Peterson, B. (Eds.). (1994). *Rethinking our classrooms: Teaching for equity and justice.* Milwaukee, WI: Rethinking Schools.

Campbell, A., McNamara, O., & Gilroy, P. (2004). *Practitioner research and professional development education.* London: Paul Chapman.

Center for Lobbying in the Public Interest. (2009). *Make a difference for your cause: Strategies for nonprofit engagement in legislative advocacy.* Retrieved from http://www.clpi.org/publications

Cutler, W. W. (2000). *Parents and schools: The 150 year struggle for control of American education.* Chicago: University of Chicago Press.

Cutri, R. M. (2000). Exploring the spiritual moral dimensions of teachers' classroom language policies. In J. K. Hall & W. G. Eggington (Eds.), *The sociopolitics of English language teaching* (pp. 165–177). Clevedon, UK: Multilingual Matters.

Forhan, L. E., & Scheraga, M. (2000). Becoming sociopolitically active. In J. K. Hall & W. G. Eggington, *The sociopolitics of English language teaching* (pp. 195–221). Clevedon, UK: Multilingual Matters.

Freire, P. (2000). *Pedagogy of the oppressed.* New York: Continuum.

Freire, P. (2005). *Teachers as cultural workers: Letters to those who dare teach.* Boulder, CO: Westview Press.

Hinchey, P. (1998). *Finding freedom in the classroom: A practical introduction to critical theory.* New York: Peter Lang.

hooks, b. (1994). *Teaching to transgress: Education as a practice of freedom.* Boston: South End.

Kemmis, S., & McTaggart, R. (1988). *The action research planner.* Geelong, Victoria: Deakin University Press.

Kincheloe, J. L. (2008). *Critical pedagogy* (2nd ed). New York: Peter Lang.

Lareau, A., & Weininger, E. B. (2003). Cultural capital in educational research: A critical assessment. *Theory and Society, 32*(5–6), 567–606.

Lewin, K. (1948) *Resolving social conflicts: Selected papers on group dynamics.* New York: Harper & Row.

Macedo, D. (1991). *The politics of power: What Americans are not allowed to know.* San Francisco: Westview Press.

Macedo, D., & Batolome, L. (2001). *Dancing with bigotry: Beyond the politics of tolerance.* New York: Palgrave.

McLaren, P. (1998). *Life in schools: An introduction to critical pedagogy in the foundations of education* (3rd ed.). New York: Longman.

National Youth Leadership Council. (2003, Summer). The diversity yes! Learning circle. *The Generator* [Special section: An update on the service-learning diversity/equity project], 26. Retrieved from http://www.nylc.org/sites/nylc.org/files/files/211GenDiv.pdf

Olivos, E. M. (2006). *The power of parents: A critical perspective of bicultural parents in the public schools.* New York: Peter Lang.

Olivos, E. M., & Ochoa, A. M. (2006a). Operationalizing a transformational paradigm of parent involvement: Parent voice and participation. In K. Cadiero-Kaplan, A. M. Ochoa, N. Kuhlman, E. M. Olivos, & J. Rodriguez (Eds.), *The living work of teachers:*

Ideology and practice (pp. 199–217). Covina, CA: California Association for Bilingual Education.

Olivos, E. M., & Ochoa, A. M. (2006b). Toward a transformational paradigm of parent involvement in urban education. In J. Kincheloe, P. Anderson, K. Rose, D. Griffith, and K. Hayes (Eds.), *Urban education: An encyclopedia* (pp. 196–217). Westport, CT: Greenwood.

Olivos, E. M., & Quintana de Valladolid, C. E. (2005). *Entre la espada y la pared*: Critical educators, bilingual education, and education reform. *Journal of Latinos and Education, 4*(4), 281–291.

Pearl, A., & Knight T. (1999). *The democratic classroom: Theory to inform practice.* Cresskill, NJ: Hampton Press.

Pennycook, A. (1994), The social politics and the cultural politics of language classrooms. In J. K. Hall & W. G. Eggington (Eds.), *The sociopolitics of English language teaching.* Clevedon, UK: Multilingual Matters.

PIQE (Parent Institute for Quality Education). (2009). *Parent institute annual report.* Retrieved from http://piqe.org/Assets/Corporate/AnnualReports.htm

PICO (People Improving Communities through Organizing). (2009). *PICO.* Retrieved from http://www.piconetwork.org

Shor, I. (1980). *Critical teaching and everyday life.* Chicago: University of Chicago Press.

Shor, I. (1992). *Empowering education: Critical teaching for social change.* Chicago: University of Chicago Press.

Smith, L. (1999). *Decolonizing methodologies: Research and indigenous peoples.* New York: Zed.

Stringer, E. T. (2007). *Action research.* [Applied Social Research Method Series (3rd ed.)]. London: Sage Publications.

Thinkexist. (2009). *Cesar Chavez quotes.* Retrieved from http://thinkexist.com/quotes/cesar_chavez/

Wink, J. (2004). Critical pedagogy: Notes from the real world. Boston: Allyn & Bacon.

Yankelovich, D. (1998). *Eighteen propositions for citizen engagement.* Address to W. K. Kellogg Foundation Devolution Initiative, Ann Arbor, MI. Retrieved from http://www.danyankelovich.com

About the Editors and Contributors

Jim Cummins is a professor at the Ontario Institute for Studies in Education of the University of Toronto. He has published extensively in the areas of bilingual language, language proficiency, parent involvement, and language policy.

Carl A. Grant is a Hoefs-Bascom Professor in the Department of Curriculum and Instruction at the University of Wisconsin–Madison. His recent publications include *Intercultural and Multicultural Education: Enhancing Global Interconnectedness* (2011, edited with Agostino Portera); the six-volume *History of Multicultural Education* (2008, edited with Thandeka K. Chapman); and *Doing Education for Achievement and Equity* (2007, with Christine E. Sleeter). He is a past president of the National Association of Multicultural Education.

Oscar Jiménez-Castellanos is an assistant professor at Arizona State University in the Mary Lou Fulton Teachers College. His research focuses on school improvement in diverse communities, including critical bicultural parent engagement as an area of emphasis.

Mary Johnson is co-instructor of the Urban Parent Teacher Education Collaborative at Pepperdine University. Johnson has been profiled in several book publications and has conducted multiple workshops and seminars for teachers, parents, and administrators at all levels to improve teaching and learning in multicultural settings. Johnson is ex-oficio for the Parent Collaborative at the Los Angeles Unified School District and president of the advocacy organization Parent-U-Turn.

Kristal Lewis Menchaca earned her MS from Texas Tech University and continues to engage in research focused on the normative development of Latino children and families. Other research interests include the ethnic identity development of biethnic individuals.

Delores B. Lindsey, associate professor at California State University, San Marcos (CSUSM), earned her PhD in educational leadership from Claremont Graduate University in Claremont, California. She earned her MEd from Southern University in Scotlandville, Louisiana. She is the coordinator for the MA and Credential

229

Program in Educational Administration at CSUSM. Dr. Lindsey has served K–12 education as a middle grades and high school teacher, assistant principal, principal, and county office of education administrator. Her focus for research and teaching is developing culturally proficient leadership practices. She is co-author of *Culturally Proficient Instruction: A Guide for People Who Teach,* 3rd ed. (2011); *Culturally Proficient Coaching: Supporting Educators to Create Equitable Schools* (2007); and *Culturally Proficient Learning Communities: Confronting Inequities Through Collaborative Curiosity* (2009).

Randall B. Lindsey, professor emeritus, California State University, Los Angeles, earned his PhD in Educational Leadership from Georgia State University. He has served as a teacher, administrator, executive director of a nonprofit corporation, and interim dean at California Lutheran University. All of Randy's experiences have been in working with diverse populations and his area of study is the behavior of White people in multicultural settings. It is his belief and experience that too often White people are observers of multicultural issues rather than personally involved with them. With co-authors Kikanza Nuri Robins and Raymond Terrell, he published the initial book on cultural proficiency, *Cultural Proficiency: A Manual for School Leaders,* now in its third edition (2003). Since that time he has co-authored eight additional books on the application of cultural proficiency to educational practice.

Martha Montero-Sieburth is emerita professor at the University of Massachusetts–Boston, in the Leadership in Urban Schools Doctoral Program in the Educational Administration Masters Program, and is currently a research fellow at the Institute for Migration and Ethnic Studies at the University of Amsterdam. Her research interests include studies of Latino adolescents, communities, and parents; Latin Americans in Spain; and second-generation immigrants in the Netherlands. Dr. Montero-Sieburth has been the director of educational research at the Mauricio Gaston Institute at the University of Massachusetts, Boston; program manager for multicultural education at the Harvard Medical School; visiting scholar at the Stone Center for Research on Women at Wellesley College; associate professor at Simmons College and Harvard Graduate School of Education; and visiting scholar at Lesley College and Harvard Graduate School of Education. Among her recent publications are *Latinos in a Changing Society* (co-edited with Edwin Melendez, 2007); *Making Invisible Latino Adolescents Visible: A Critical Approach Building upon Latino Diversity* (with Francisco Villarruel, 2000); *The Struggle for a New Paradigm: Qualitative Research in Latin America* (co-edited with Gary Anderson, 1998); and over 75 journal, monograph, and review articles written in Spanish and English.

Robert P. Moreno is an associate professor in the Department of Child and Family at Syracuse University. His research focuses on familial influences on children's learning and academic achievement among Latino and immigrant families. He is particularly interested in how cultural variations in early parental teaching styles impacts children's learning. His most recent publications include *On New Shores: Understanding Immigrant Fathers in North America* (2008) and *Immigrant Children: Change, Adaptation, and Cultural transformation* (2011, co-edited with Susan S. Chuang.)

Edward M. Olivos is an associate professor in the Department of Education Studies at the University of Oregon. He is the author of *The Power of Parents: A Critical Perspective of Bicultural Parent Involvement in Public Schools* (2006). He has published work in the areas of policy studies, school reform, parent participation, critical pedagogy, and biliteracy issues in K–12 classrooms. He is a former San Diego elementary school teacher, where he taught for over 10 years.

Alberto M. Ochoa is professor emeritus in the Department of Policy Studies in Language and Cross-Cultural Education in the College of Education at San Diego State University. Since 1975, he has worked with over 60 school districts in providing technical assistance in the areas of language policy and assessment, bilingual instructional programs, curriculum programming, staff development, community development, organizational development and school climate, program management, monitoring, and evaluation. His research interests include public equity, school desegregation, language policy, critical pedagogy, student achievement, and parental leadership.

Art Pearl has been on the faculty at Howard University; the University of Oregon; and the University of California, Santa Cruz; and currently is adjunct professor at the University of Oregon. He was an invited speaker at the only White House Conference on Teaching of the Disadvantaged, in 1966, and a member and chair of the National Institute for Teaching of the Disadvantaged, 1967–1969. He is the author of dozens of articles and books, including *New Careers for the Poor* (1965, with Frank Riessman); *The Atrocity of Education* (1972); *The Value of Youth* (1978, with Doug Grant and Ernst Wenk); *The Democratic Classroom* (1999, with Tony Knight); "Systematic and Institutional Factors in Chicano School Failure," (2002, in Richard Valencia (Ed.), *Chicano School Failure: Research and Public Policy Agendas*, co-edited with Carolyn Pryor); and *Democratic Practice* (2006).

Aubree Potter currently works as an education consultant for the Wisconsin Department of Public Instruction. A former elementary bilingual teacher, Aubree worked hard to redefine traditional parent involvement approaches in order to more actively connect and unite parents and school staff. Aubree is currently pursuing a PhD in multicultural education at the University of Wisconsin–Madison.

James L. Rodriguez is associate professor in the Department of Child and Adolescent Studies at California State University, Fullerton. His research is focused on the intersection of language, culture, and learning within dynamic contexts, particularly among Latino children, adolescents, and families.

John Rogers is an associate professor in the Graduate School of Education and Information Studies at the University of California, Los Angeles and the director of UCLA's Institute for Democracy, Education and Access (IDEA). He also serves as the faculty co-director of UCLA's Principal Leadership Institute. Rogers studies public engagement and community organizing as strategies for equity-focused school reform and democratic renewal.

Sheila Shannon has taught at the University of Colorado, Denver, for over 20 years. In that time she has dedicated herself to call for social justice for Mexican immigrant families in the United States. She has accomplished this by teaching teachers to identify racism, including the hegemony of English, and reject it when it is practiced in the schools where they teach. She has explored dual language education and the challenge of bringing minority and majority communities together. Currently she is involved in bilingual teacher literacy projects and investigating the bilingualism of children who we have traditionally viewed as English language learners.

Veronica Terriquez is an assistant professor of sociology at the University of Southern California. She received her PhD in sociology from the University of California, Los Angeles; an MEd from the University of California, Berkeley; and a BA in sociology from Harvard University. Her research focuses on educational inequality, immigrant integration, and organized labor.

Maria Lombos Wlazlinski is currently a research and evaluation specialist and Title III monitor in the Georgia Department of Education. She has been involved in the education of English language learners in the United States and overseas for more than 30 years as an ESL teacher and a teacher educator at both undergraduate and graduate levels. She earned her PhD in curriculum and instruction in first and second language and literacy development in multicultural and multilingual settings from the Ontario Institute for Studies in Education of the University of Toronto. She serves on the ESOL State Advisory Board, and on the NCATE/TESOL Board of Program Reviewers (BoPR).

Index

Note: An "f" or "t" following a page number refers to a figure or table, respectively